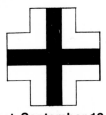

Sunset, September 12, 1943.
An overloaded Fieseler-Storch falls
through thin mountain air.
"It was a moment of real terror for me."
—Benito Mussolini
Painting by Gunter Scherrer

HITLER'S FAVORITE COMMANDO

Otto Skorzeny's kidnapping of Mussolini brought him into intimate contact with the most powerful Nazi leaders. A hard-boiled soldier, he watched them from close up. Again and again they came to him with impossible tasks—and with many of these he succeeded.

With such dangerous men as Skorzeny at large, a future enemy's superiority could be neutralized, no opposing leader could rest easy in his stronghold, no army could be free from penetration and disruption, and no vital stores or stockpile of atomic weapons would be secure from marauders.

"Future commanders of special forces can learn much from Skorzeny's experience."
—*Army Magazine*

THE BANTAM WAR BOOK SERIES

This is a series of books about a world on fire.

These carefully chosen volumes cover the full dramatic sweep of World War II. Many are eyewitness accounts by the men who fought in this global conflict in which the future of the civilized world hung in balance. Fighter pilots, tank commanders and infantry commanders, among others, recount exploits of individual courage in the midst of the large-scale terrors of war. They present portraits of brave men and true stories of gallantry and cowardice in action, moving sagas of survival and tragedies of untimely death. Some of the stories are told from the enemy viewpoint to give the reader an immediate sense of the incredible life and death struggle of both sides of the battle.

Through these books we begin to discover what it was like to be there, a participant in an epic war for freedom.

Each of the books in the Bantam War Book series contains a dramatic color painting and illustrations specially commissioned for each title to give the reader a deeper understanding of the roles played by the men and machines of World War II.

COMMANDO EXTRAORDINARY

BY CHARLES FOLEY

BANTAM BOOKS · TORONTO · NEW YORK · LONDON

COMMANDO EXTRAORDINARY

A Bantam Book / published by arrangement with
G. P. Putnam's Sons

PRINTING HISTORY
First Putnam edition published September 1955
Bantam edition / May 1979

Drawings by Greg Beecham.
Maps by Benjamin F. Klassig.

ISBN 0-553-12580-X

Published simultaneously in the United States and Canada

PRINTED IN THE UNITED STATES OF AMERICA

Author's Note

While stories of individual daring and success in the last world war already abound, no account that I have read so far attempts to go beyond the incidents portrayed with the object of discovering the method in the madness of the adventurous few. Such is the task of this book—a task in which the author's inadequacies must be made good by friends who have a better claim on public attention.

Our main witness to the revival of this personal element in warfare is Otto Skorzeny, and the choice is one which his Allied opposite numbers greeted with interest and pleasure. One of the first whom I consulted, Lieut.-Colonel M. J. Calvert, D.S.O. and Bar, M.C., of Burma fame, declared that Skorzeny was the ideal example to show what an individual commander, given his head, could achieve in modern war. Special Air Service officers who had explored similar techniques agreed; their depot adjutant, Major Anthony Greville-Bell, D.S.O., was tireless in his search for comparisons in the brief but illustrious records of this regiment. The closing chapter could not have been written without the co-operation of Colonel David Stirling, D.S.O.

Many others, in England and abroad, were generous with help and criticism. On one question all agreed, that although ideas may have no frontiers one cannot dissociate them from the preconceptions of the minds from which they spring. Skorzeny fought for Germany: he saw the war through German eyes. I have refrained from "correcting" his viewpoint where it differed from my own and I have avoided all moral issues as being outside the area of survey.

While filling in the wide gaps in my knowledge I incurred further obligation. In particular I must acknowledge the kindness I received from Mr. Allen Welsh Dulles, who lent me his most valuable report on the German "underground," from Major Karl Radl in allowing me to call on his record of the Gran Sasso expedition, and from Major Hummel for his clear exposition of the activities of the frogmen led by him. Much tedious research was curtailed by the Chatham House librarians and the archivists of the Imperial War Museum and the Pentagon Building. Lieut.-Colonel Donald McClure, late of the U.S. Army's War Crimes Group, was good enough to read through a manuscript of the chapter dealing with the trial; Wing-Commander Yeo-Thomas, G.C., M.C., contributed his impressions as a witness at the court.

I must, in conclusion, pay tribute to Colonel Skorzeny for his robust spirit under questioning.

C. F.

COMMANDO EXTRAORDINARY

Otto Skorzeny

I

> *Nothing is so impudent as success—unless it be those she favours.*
>
> JAMES ROBINSON PLANCHÉ

For a week during a grand crisis of the war in Europe, General Eisenhower, the Supreme Commander, was imprisoned in his own headquarters. He was confined as stringently as any erring ranker is to barracks.

He fretted, he pleaded, he stormed; but his Security chiefs were adamant. Even in his own offices there could be no guarantee against attack. Outside the closely guarded buildings assassins were waiting to kill or kidnap him. They wore American uniform. Above all, there was a man, they said, a German . . .

Unknown to Eisenhower, one of his staff who looked like the general took on the task of acting as his double. In this role he drove daily to and fro between Paris and Versailles in the famous five-star automobile.

Paris itself was under curfew. Tanks patrolled near the Café de la Paix: "the man" was expected hourly to drop in for an aperitif. People in the streets were stopped to prove their identity. Senior American officers were as sharply questioned as enlisted men or civilians. Even the white-helmeted military police who led this inquisition did not escape suspicion.

And away in the Ardennes during the Battle of the Bulge half a million Americans were looking over their shoulders for an unrecognizable enemy, asking each other who was friend and who foe.

All this because of one man. A man with a name so

1

charged with menace that the mere rumor of his presence behind the lines was enough to dismay an army and incarcerate its C.-in-C.

Two years earlier Otto Skorzeny had been an obscure soldier among the millions who fought. A few months later on he was to be swept up with the broken remnants of Hitler's armies. But within this time he had rein unprecedented for one so new to command. He raised, behind every battlement of beleaguered Germany, a legion imbued with the spirit of attack—and attack by any means, so long as it was unexpected. In the last twenty months of the Reich that was to last a thousand years he planned, directed and himself led a series of missions which were unparalleled in scope because they aimed at influencing the course not merely of a single battle but of the war.

By the time Skorzeny had become chief of Hitler's special troops, defeat stared every German in the face. Yet again and again the gathering darkness was lit by a flash which revealed the mark of Skorzeny's handiwork—improbability. And when the end came, this strange individual whom no one seemed to know was hunted down and solemnly accused by his interrogators of being the German soldier "most responsible for prolonging the war."

That much I remembered, but little more. Several years went by: then quite suddenly, the man and some of his works came into my life.

We were talking, a friend and I, one autumn morning in London. Mist was falling on Pall Mall; across the street an outline in bomb-gothic recalled the day the Germans hit the Carlton Club. From that we must have turned to other shocks to the established order; hence to the singular figure of Skorzeny.

My friend took up the theme. "Skorzeny," he said. "There was a soldier, if you like. Nowadays we are all so painfully respectable, but seldom were we given the glorious chances Skorzeny saw—and took. He mixed high politics with dynamite. He turned the battle routine inside out. After the war the Allies tried to hang him. I like to think we helped to get him acquitted."

The speaker was one of our brilliant younger commanders, who surprised his friends by staying on in the Army after the war. A vigorous critic of tradition, his assurance in the field is matched by a contempt for danger at staff meetings and in discussion with General Officers in the Mess. And as the incident he had mentioned was related I recognized that he saw in Skorzeny a fellow-spirit.

"I never met him," he began, "and our intervention in the proceedings was irregular . . . a chivalrous uprising in the first days of victory. You will remember there were quite a few of us at Versailles from various fronts: colonels in the twenties, 'colorful' brigadiers, sailors and airmen of temporary high rank who had managed to find a reason for visiting Supreme Headquarters, and Paris.

"One day some of us heard Otto Skorzeny had been arrested by the Allies in Germany and was being accused of all sorts of villainies; trying to kill Eisenhower was one of them. We saw nothing wrong in that: the more we thought about it the more indignant we became. After all, commandos had tried to raid Rommel's headquarters in the Western Desert—among other such affrays. Most of us had done things they didn't put in Army orders; and we were decorated when we got away with them.

"We all knew quite a bit about Skorzeny's activities: Intelligence had put out a special dossier on him. It seemed to us his only crime was being active in a line of country the regulars dislike.

"So we wrote a letter to the Secretary of State for War. A copy went to General Eisenhower . . . to make sure. The letter said that if Colonel Skorzeny, as leader of the German commandos, was to be punished for doing his duty, then we, too, begged to be placed under arrest. We were willing to plead guilty to similar charges and submit to the same treatment."

He went on: "Well, they didn't arrest us, but we heard later that some of the charges had been dropped and that finally Skorzeny was acquitted. Good luck to him; you can't make war with rose water, but in spite of his unusual ideas I believe he fought it clean."

This episode stirred my curiosity, and my interest was further roused by this remark which my friend threw in as if it were some kind of commonplace: "Skorzeny fought the last war by the methods we shall have to use for the next—if we wake up in time."

I began then to wonder about Skorzeny and his "unusual ideas." What had become of him? What was he doing now—was he still alive? I had come across puzzling rumors from time to time . . . a visit to a newspaper library reaped a harvest of clippings from the Press: reports which, beginning with what seemed fact, soared into an empyrean of fantasy.

First, there were messages from Paris on the alleged attempt to kill General Eisenhower, though "murder" was the term preferred. There had been a man-hunt by all the police and military of Europe for Skorzeny, at large and in disguise behind the Allied lines. Then, as chief of the werewolves sworn to carry on the war after the Armistice, Skorzeny had slipped into Denmark—a dozen Danish resistance leaders had vanished; it was "supposed" that the werewolves had disposed of them.

SKORZENY CAPTURED! the newspapers rejoiced. Photographs of the arrest showed Skorzeny in manacles; and then, in spite of repeated reports that he had broken out, we had him brought to trial.

The War Crimes hearings dragged on and were lost sight of; there was an inexplicable acquittal, but Skorzeny was still detained—being "too dangerous" to set free. The prisoner decided otherwise and headlines sounded the alarm: SKORZENY GETS AWAY.

A French newspaper identified the fugitive—or someone like him—on a Channel service to London. A Welsh hospital was guarded; Skorzeny might not know that its most celebrated patient, Hitler's errant Rudolf Hess, was no longer there.

And so it went on, with Skorzeny seen now in Buenos Aires, where General Perón charged him with an expedition to seize the Falkland Islands; now in Austria, searching the Alps for Hitler's buried loot; and now again conducting a secret conclave of a "Nazi-Fascist International" in Rome. A full year of this sort of thing; then an American magazine said that an espionage ring working under the code name of "Spider" had sent out tentacles to the United States; Chief Spider, Skorzeny.

Such energetic malignity in the wings by a villain who never took the stage! And then, at last, a French newspaper caught him in the spotlight and produced the most formidable of scoops: a picture, head-on and full length, of the "most dangerous man" in a setting that was unmistakable. The monster was in Paris; he was walking down the sunlit Champs-Élysées.

Uproar in the French Chamber; a solar-plexus punch for a Government which—or so the Communist leaders roared—had been harboring a Nazi murderer. Ministers were assailed; obedient to the Party call, a mob poured down the boulevards. At the fashionable Rond Point they fell on the offices of the newspaper *Figaro*. Riot police were belabored with chairs and tables snatched up from pavement cafés.

When order was restored to the capital Otto Skorzeny had vanished again.

A newspaper flew two special investigators out to take up the chase. They dashed through several countries and even across to Africa, but drew a blank.

There, some months ago, the trail of clippings ended; my paper chase came to a stop.

Where could the fellow be? I inquired through friends in South America; the German colony there knew nothing of him. The Quai d'Orsay assured me he was no longer in France. In Italy and Germany he would have met too many wartime acquaintances to pass unseen; in the smaller countries a stranger was quickly noticed; the likeliest place left was Spain.

Thousands of Germans had sought refuge and a livelihood behind the Pyrenees. Once the Spanish police were satisfied with a foreigner's credentials he could even work under an assumed name. Inquiries from abroad were not encouraged: General Franco had been ostracized since the war; now let other countries mind their own business and leave him to his.

While I was negotiating for a Spanish entry visa, another newspaper photograph settled it. The picture showed Skorzeny at a dinner table and it had been taken, the caption writer said, by a cameraman who had poked his lens through a window in Madrid. That alone was good enough for the front pages, but the photographer's agility was doubly rewarded, for beside Skorzeny, fork in hand, was Dr. Hjalmar Schacht.

Schacht, Hitler's Finance Minister and "economic wizard"! The inference of the headline, WHAT ARE THEY PLOTTING? did not, perhaps, take into account Schacht's break with the Nazis which nearly cost him his life, but such nuances were unimportant. The Spanish visa was stamped into my passport and next day I was on my way.

The conviction had been growing on me that unless Skorzeny were indeed a sort of superman out of the comic papers there might be a simple and sufficient reason for keeping out of sight. I did not take "neo-Nazi" conspiracies too seriously: the war was too recently over, the destruction too complete. Nor had I seen anything in the record, admittedly a slender one, of Skorzeny's wartime activities to justify an assumption that he was a political fanatic ready to pit himself against the reality of Germany's utter defeat. Above all, no German I had met had heard the man's name mentioned before the war; so, far from being politically important, he appeared to have risen from complete obscurity—and now, quite likely, wanted nothing better than to return to it. Why not accept this natural supposition—and advance from there? Granting that Skorzeny was normal enough to wish to live his life in peace, it would have to be pointed out to him that he was going the wrong way about it: very much better to give the world an explanation which would satisfy its curiosity than to keep open the gates of speculation by silence and evasion.

By the time my plane had touched down at Bordeaux for refueling, I had plumped for a policy of bold persuasion—and where could one find a better ally in pressing the virtues of public enlightenment on Skorzeny than in that irrepressible publicist Dr. Schacht? I had run into Schacht soon after his acquittal of war crimes at Nuremberg: since then he had been flitting from one capital to another prescribing cures for other people's economic ills. If he knew Skorzeny, he would arrange an introduction.

But, already, Schacht had gone. Landing at Madrid I found he had flown on to Paris the same morning. However, friends had seen the doctor: they led me to others who at length conceded that Skorzeny was still in Spain, living "not far from Madrid." He could be asked to see me, though they held out little hope. To end equivocation I said with obtuse heartiness that I had come a long way to meet their man and I would like him to lunch with me —next day. A few hours later, to the evident astonishment of our intermediaries, the invitation had been accepted, and in a way which suggested that my quarry wanted me to know he could come out into the open if he chose. So, far from urging some furtive rendezvous, he agreed to Horcher's, one of the three best-known restaurants in Madrid, and named the hour of two-thirty, when all Madrid begins to think of food.

Even in Spain, Germans cannot learn to be unpunctual. So it was in some disquiet that I waited alone over my sherry as the room filled with the chattering marquesas, the hand-kissing Ministers of Franco's Cabinet and the visiting Ruhr barons and Americans-from-the-Ritz who make up Horcher's following. It was nearly three o'clock when a shadow darkened the tiled alcove where I sat. A huge figure stood over my table. "How are you?" the stranger said. "I am sorry; my car was held up. Otto Skorzeny, at your service."

The voice was a fine, untroubled bass, but it was fit for larger spaces, and as I got to my feet I was aware of a drop in the conversational hum. People looked around; then they looked upward—and so, from my six feet, did I.

I am not sure what I had expected Skorzeny to look like. Newspapers insisted on a "giant"; nostalgic for Chicago's gangster days they had also dubbed him "Scarface." I suppose I had made the usual allowances, but here, with my hand in his grasp, was a man of towering proportions. "Scarface Skorzeny"—the term fell pat: from the left temple a chalk line scribbled its way to the corner of his mouth and across a massive chin. Life so far was living up to the legend.

As if to make amends, Skorzeny wore a subdued gray flannel suit, and his dark, springing hair was brushed firmly into place. His faintly apologetic air was all that could be asked; only a glint in his slate-gray eyes betrayed amusement. Later I heard a woman, of the sort that can be counted on for that kind of remark, say that Skorzeny was "a splendid animal" putting her in mind, she added, of a man-eating tiger on parole.

We sat down at a white-covered table while Herr Horcher himself pressed through a cloud of acolytes to pay the homage of his art. He had been Marshal Göring's pet restaurateur before moving from Berlin to Madrid; now he conjured up hearts of artichoke, lobsters' claws cooked in cream especially for the *Herr Oberst*.

"You are well known," I ventured. That brought a wide grin.

"Unfortunately," he said; "it seems I need no passport." We drank some wine and deployed our small talk. My guest used English as a workaday implement without

subtlety or sophistication. It was enough; behind the pleas-
antries and alongside a ready sense of humor, his mind
was sudden as a club.

I had rather feared to discover in Skorzeny what de
Madariaga has called "the German state of fizz and fuzzle,"
that steamy, psychological morass of the Teutonic soul
with its habit of boiling over. It was to be expected. Here,
after all, was a German demigod, whose name was used
as if he were an international gangster and a thug. But I
found Skorzeny lacked the vapor of self-pity; his outlook
was commendably dry.

Shortly, I launched into the argument I had prepared: encouraged both by his immediate admission that
he wanted to be left alone by the newspapers and by finding that his common sense met reasoning halfway. He
agreed that lying low had failed to shake off pursuit; he
admitted that as a result of all the mystification there was
nothing too ludicrous to be said or printed about him.
Well then, I urged, it was time for a change of policy;
let him end this cat-and-mouse game and the pursuit
would soon fall away. The appeal, I admitted, was an interested one, for I myself had many questions to put to
him, but after all, he would have to give the world an
account of himself some day—why not speak out now and
be done with it?

Skorzeny had listened patiently. When I paused, he
smiled. "All this rests on the supposition I have nothing
to hide. How do you know that is so?" And he leaned
forward with an air of quizzical enjoyment.

Luckily Herr Horcher intervened to advocate roast
suckling pig. This having been agreed, Skorzeny laughed
and said: "Don't worry; there is no one I cannot look in
the face, but I hoped that if I kept out of the way the
rumormongers would have less to go on. I underrated my
adversaries—a capital mistake in strategy."

The room was close, the wine refreshing. Course succeeded course in the steady Spanish tempo which is said
to open the pores of the soul and the windows of the
mind.

Then, Skorzeny brought out his final objection. He
felt it unbecoming for a defeated soldier to thrust himself
forward; and especially one who was, let's say, a shade
conspicuous already.

I acknowledged that his scruples did him honor; they

might well have been shared by some others who had changed sword for pen, perhaps as "a continuation of war by other means," the moment they were out of uniform. But the worst bitterness of war was past and what he had to tell was of widest interest.

As he still hesitated, I tipped the scales with the story of the hushed-up protest in Paris when British officers jumped to Skorzeny's defense after his arrest. His eyes lit up: he, too, had felt this spirit of freemasonry between "front-line soldiers" on either side.

By now it was five o'clock—no time to sit over the glasses in any country, even Spain. Skorzeny said: "I am not ashamed of what the men under my command did in the war or what I have been doing since: I will tell you anything you want to know. But first I should like to clear your mind on one question. I am not interested in politics. I don't believe in any Nazi revival; history never turns back, and for my part I don't want it to. It has taken years to resume my life and my career where they were broken off by the war. I have no appetite for glory; I want to live it down. It is true that we tried out some techniques for the future: if you want to hear about them, well, why not? You shall listen to what happened; then you can judge."

On that we parted until, in the evening, I drove out to an address he had given me. A pleasant little villa, white-painted, with a grilled peephole in the door through which, in Spanish fashion, a servant scrutinized the visitor.

The room in which Skorzeny greeted me was still shuttered; cool and dim after the sunlight of the street, it might have been in Chelsea. We sat under a chandelier in chairs covered with cretonne. The frames on the wall held flower pictures.

"So this," I mused aloud, "is the parlor of the Chief Spider. Where are the trap doors and the dictaphones; when do the plotters gather?"

As if to make up for the prosaic setting Skorzeny took off his wrist watch and put it in my hand. "Mussolini time!" he said.

I looked at it, a fine, gold timepiece, and on its back a Napoleonic initial M, with the date of the rescue: 12/9/ 1943. Skorzeny poured a drink as he told me how Mussolini had it inscribed for him and it was the one possession he had recovered from souvenir-hunters after his arrest. "But now," he said, "to work. What do you want to know?"

That is how this narrative began. I asked first about his early memories and his apprenticeship in arms: matters of which he spoke with simplicity and with some surprise that they should be thought worthy of attention. Next day, in the siesta hour, he came out to the balcony of my sky-scraper hotel room. We talked, while Spain slept, of the war years. He showed a grasp of facts, figures, dates and names which marks the disciplined mind, but what pleased me was his sensitivity in matters less material: remembered conversations and the tone of voice, the moods and inflections of men under stress. Some of these recollections arranged themselves in a pattern; others were strung together on a chain of reasoning which had begun before the opening of each episode he described and did not end when the episode had closed. My first inquisitiveness appeased, we worked together through his career, retracing its beginnings, considering not only what he had done but the thought behind each action. This procedure took time; Skorzeny had a hundred other things to do. So after a few days we fell into a routine of spending together intervals between his business appointments: each time he went off I would turn back on my notes to record, while it was still fresh, every new detail he had given me.

I knew before our meeting that Skorzeny's experiences must elucidate many mysteries, and I hoped to hear more of those "unusual ideas." What I did not anticipate was that his history would take on the spellbinding qualities of a novel by Dumas.

Who could resist a recital which puts kidnaping into the political armory, so that the first stage in resolving a crisis is to ravish a dictator's heir from a meeting in a rolled-up carpet? That is typical of Skorzeny's "direct diplomacy."

I learned of his design to deal with the Italian Crown Prince Umberto—this was dovetailed into a plan for carrying King Victor Emmanuel and his whole court off from Rome; and again of how, disguised, he went to France and laid an invisible noose about the Government—one tug would have wrenched Marshal Pétain, with his Ministers, into captivity.

Skorzeny's pace grew hotter as the end grew nearer; it was neck or nothing all the time. New York, it was laid down, must be bombarded by U-boats. London should have a rain of human bombs—the deadly flight to be led by Hitler's favorite pilot, a woman who had learned to ride a V1, Fraulein Hanna Reitsch.

So it went on, until my notebooks were peopled with a host of disputants, sketched in against a backcloth that extended from the English Channel to Kiev and from the gates of Moscow to Budapest.

And now, a warning to the chronologically inclined. Skorzeny clapped spurs to his career after being made Chief of Special Troops. From Mussolini's rescue onward it was a breakneck gallop in which promotion from captaincy to command of a division seems incidental; he felt himself to be leading several lives at the same time. The salient events on this helter-skelter rush are taken in order; lesser events may suffer.

Through most episodes the personal rôle of Skorzeny is pronounced. I was put in mind of this before leaving Madrid. An Allied liaison officer had been asked by his Embassy to inquire into yet another rumor—this time Otto Skorzeny had sent a group of German ex-officers to train the Egyptian Army in guerrilla warfare against the Suez canal area which the British then still occupied.

"No doubt," said the First Secretary, "this is a story like the rest, but is there any simple way of proving it's not true?"

"Why, yes," was the reply. "You can remind them that it is not Skorzeny's habit to send his officers ahead of him. He always goes in first."

Skorzeny claimed the right to go with his men and lead them himself. He knew that when you have laid out your plan in detail, when you have thought of every conceivable contingency, there still remain, as the best briefing of all, the two words, "Follow me!"

II

Had he been here, he would have thought of something else.

CASTELNAU, on Napoleon

In war the heroes always outnumber the soldiers ten to one.

H. L. MENCKEN

If Otto Skorzeny was no ordinary soldier, that may well be because he never wanted to be a soldier at all. For this Nazi paladin was neither the Prussian Junker nor the storm trooper prejudice entitles us to expect. He had hardly set foot in Germany before the war. He had never handled a rifle, except for hunting purposes, until he was called up.

The fall of France came without his having fired a shot. So far from maligning his luck in being cheated out of action, his relief was unaffected. The war, he thought, was over; he had done his duty. Now everyone could go home.

Skorzeny's youth offers few clues to the man he later became: an upbringing almost exasperatingly normal; no discontent, divine or diabolic, to kindle the fires of nonconformity. He had a belief in the reasonableness of the universe that is still unabashed today.

The home in which he grew up was typical of the solid, once comfortable Vienna bourgeoisie. Men of his mother's family had all gone into the army as a matter of course. They were old-style officers of the Hapsburg monarchy; in frogged jackets and shakos they went the round

12

of garrison duty or spurred their chargers against Turk and Tartar. During the three centuries through which his family's course can be traced from the East Pomeranian village of Scorzencin (from which its name was taken) there is no suggestion of any member having displayed an unseemly brilliance or originality.

Otto's boyhood ran through the worst years of Austrian inflation, when the need for keeping up appearances imposed a stoic discipline on gentility. He can still remember his first taste of real butter: "It was when I was fifteen," he says. "My father told me there was no harm in doing without things; it might even be a good thing not to get used to a soft life. And he was right!"

This last exclamation reveals what Skorzeny has never ceased to be, a puritan. There is a Cromwellian streak in his character which makes him accept hardship, and even pain, as salutary. While enjoying good things in fair measure—"Have a cup of brandy!" he will cry, in a startling idiom of his own, when you call on him—he avoids excess; above all he is irritated by the stories of debauchery which, in books and films, are inseparable from dueling at the universities, because they are a slur on the Spartan ritual he knew.

Student dueling, of course, is unlike what we mean by fencing. It was not so much a matter of warding off the opponent's blows as of accepting them without flinching. One did not think, as the hot blood trickled down one's face, "That hurt!" One thought: "Did I move my head? Did I blink?"

It was during the tenth of the fifteen duels he fought that Skorzeny's left cheek was opened by a sweeping stroke; stitched up on the spot without the use of anaesthetic, it produced the famous scar which links him in popular imagination with the underworld. The odor of carbolic in which the swords were freshly disinfected clings to his remembered anxiety lest the umpires should stop the fight if he lost too much blood and give the victory to his rival. He managed to last out the bout.

Skorzeny believes such minor bloodletting taught boys to be men. "Often later I was to be grateful for the self-discipline we learned in our student club," he says. "I never felt so bad under fire as I did at eighteen when I had to fight my first duel, under the sharp eyes of my fellow students. My knowledge of pain, learned with the saber,

taught me not to be afraid of fear. And just as in dueling you must fix your mind on striking at the enemy's head, so, too, in war. You cannot waste time feinting and sidestepping. You must decide on your target and go in."

Most of his duels arose from sporting challenges, but one, at least, was an affair of the heart; a week or two after the encounter, the Viennese dancer concerned became engaged to marry someone of whom neither principal had heard.

In his austere childhood, imposed both by parental authority and by economic rigor, in an earnest devotion to manly pursuits, he was simply one of his generation. Most of our captains of war have been born into leadership and their whole schooling trained them to command. In Skorzeny we can descry no special intellectual ability; his cramped youth did not encourage the independence which leadership demands. There is no "boyhood of Raleigh" to raise our expectations, no visions and no time to daydream.

Even at school he chose "practical" subjects: maths, physics, chemistry. His diploma thesis at the university was written on "The Calculation and Construction of a Diesel Engine." He had little love of reading for its own sake, unlike some allied commandos who, it is said, were apt to go into action carrying volumes of verse with flowers pressed between the leaves.

High-flown romanticism left him merely puzzled. He lacked the capacity for hero-worship and thought politics time-wasting. Drawn in almost casually during his early twenties to applying for a Nazi Party card because he thought it would relieve Austria's chronic economic distress if she were joined to Germany, he never made a speech or stood for office. Indeed, when one of the first acts of the triumphant Nazis was to ban dueling he protested to the point of imprudence. Were not these new men ready to stand up for their beliefs with a weapon in the hand? Seemingly they were not; in disgust he took up road-racing with cars provided by the Party's sporting section and won three gold medals. That was the sum of his "political activity"—there were always more interesting things to do.

No Lothario by disposition, he still liked pretty girls. His early marriage began with a meeting at a swimming pool; the honeymoon in Italy over, a more lasting passion resumed its rule. "Work, work, work!"—Skorzeny has always been driven by the urge to do things when the need is seen, at once.

Fate gave this most un-Austrian proclivity an early trial, and a dramatic one: failure would have led to serious trouble—at the least to some bloodshed, at the worst to a clash of nations.

The setting was Vienna in the spring of 1938, during one of those crises which sent the storm signals flying across Europe. The Government had fallen; Hitler's nominee as the new Chancellor was speaking on his balcony;

before him, in the great square below, a frenzied multitude was spread. The air was full of hysteria and threats. It was a day when anything might happen.

Among the overflow of the vast crowd in a street alongside the Chancellery was young Otto Skorzeny. He had driven there on a summons from the Vienna Gymnastic Club, one of many societies which, in times of factional tumult, tried to assist the police in keeping order. While he was listening to the boom of loudspeakers he saw the side gate of the building open and a limousine drive out: in the back seat was President Miklas of Austria. A moment later the chief of his Gymnastic Club was at his elbow.

"Skorzeny, you're a sensible fellow," was his greeting, and he hurried on to say that Miklas was on his way to the Presidential Palace, where there was every chance of a battle between the regular guards and a group of Nazi defense squads who were on their way to take over. What Skorzeny must do was to get to the Palace before Miklas, so as to smooth things over between the rival troops. He could say he had come in the name of the new Chancellor, who would be told of his errand at once.

Skorzeny got into his car and set off at top speed, but by the time the limousine came into sight it had been joined by two or three other cars he could not pass: the Nazi defense squads had tagged on behind Miklas already and a clash with the guards seemed inevitable.

When Skorzeny drew up before the Palace the President was already disappearing inside; Nazis with brassards and pistols were tumbling out of their cars. Skorzeny pushed past them into the lobby, where he saw Miklas mounting a staircase: the President was halfway to the top when he caught him up. Just then, from a landing above, a Guards lieutenant with several soldiers at his heels started to run down the stairs, shouting, "Halt there, or I fire!"

The lobby had filled up with defense-squad men, pistols at the ready. Skorzeny and the President were caught between two fires. Safety catches clicked; the next moment bullets would have been flying. Skorzeny shouted the first words that came into his head: "Nonsense! Quiet, I say."

A sudden silence was broken by President Miklas. "What does all this mean?" he demanded. Then, to Skorzeny, "And who the devil are you?"

Skorzeny's answer, loudly spoken, was that he came from the Chancellor, who would vouch for him if telephoned—and he told the lieutenant, facing him on the next step up, that he would be held personally responsible for any shooting.

The lieutenant's courage ebbed at the thought of "personal responsibility" in some political imbroglio. A truce was called while they went to the telephone. The Chancellor spoke in turn to the President and to Skorzeny, whom he thanked for his presence of mind. And now, the crowning irony: the rival forces in the Palace dispute both looked to the young intruder for "orders." He decided that the lieutenant should insure security inside the building, while the defense squads mounted guard outside. Honor was satisfied: the men went their ways. Again, Vienna was at peace.

These few minutes were enough to hint at qualities which were to make Skorzeny an easy choice for tasks out of the common run. When the chief of his Gymnastic Club sought him out it was as "a sensible fellow" who would prick the swelling bubble of a crisis. While yet untrained in arms or in the habit of command he showed an aplomb which quelled the itch to fire—and a sure sense of his opponent's weakest point.

"Scarface Skorzeny": this label of the licensed killer hardly fits the picture. His very success as a soldier is made interesting by an inborn aversion to violence; by a knack of seeing the funny side of unpleasant happenings and by a friendly interest in *people* even, as his observations on the Russian campaign show, in people who should be distasteful to a Nazi officer: "squalid" peasants and "dumb" Red soldiers. On the outbreak of war his first regret was for the English and French friends he and his wife had made on their holidays in Italy; jogging through France in the wake of the *blitzkrieg* armies he was relieved to see his soldiers giving drinks and cigarettes to British prisoners: the young men of Europe had not yet learned to hate each other.

What spark transformed this rather stereotyped conscript into a man who caught his soldiers' loyalty and trust? It might have been ambition; he enjoyed promotion and medals as well as anyone, but for a climber he sadly lacked pliancy and pace when a main chance offered itself.

For instance, toward the end Skorzeny commanded a

division on the river Oder before Berlin, and should have claimed major-general's rank but he remained a lieutenant-colonel because he could not find time to fill out the required forms. Nor was he a respecter of persons or powers if they sought to override his notions of duty. He was rash enough to snub the Nazi Party and later to treat even the mighty Himmler with scant courtesy when he interfered with the job in hand. Three times, at least, while on the Oder he flouted such authority, once inviting a fate which brave men fear more than battle wounds: court-martial.

He was aided by a tolerance which usually enabled him to look down with humor on the stupidities and exasperations of life. It upheld his spirit and that of men around him; even in captivity he could sometimes impose his will, by some strange magic, on those who held him at their disposal.

When war came Skorzeny was putting all his efforts into a Vienna building firm in which he had bought a share, but as he had to go, his first thought was to avoid the boredom of army life. Having done some flying, he offered himself to the air force as a pilot. "Much too old," was the reply. He was thirty-one.

Instead, he had five months' desultory training in an Air Force communications depot in Vienna; from there he was posted as an officer-cadet to the artillery of the Armed S.S.—a military force which fought alongside the army and was distinct from Himmler's political phalanx. His transfer came on February 21, 1940: a few hours later that day his daughter Waltraut was born. She was a big, strapping girl, and Skorzeny went off in fair spirits to join the Adolf Hitler S.S. Regiment in Berlin. "Win a medal if you like," was his father's farewell, "but it doesn't have to be the Knight's Cross."

He went to Berlin, and infuriated the Prussians he met by describing their capital as a hideous brick-pile compared with his beautiful Vienna. He also got to know the drill sergeant on his own ground. It was a reserve battalion which was being built up by time-honored methods. If, as Skorzeny willingly avows, he learned much on the barrack square, not all of it was what his instructors hoped.

"I saw how some of the 'regulars' sinned against the fine human material that is brought to them, how stubbornly they bent the individual will and crushed personality. It seemed to me .the reverse of what was needed for the tasks which a soldier in modern war can carry out." From this seed sprang his doctrine of turning the training of the well-drilled enemy against them; a precept that never failed to work.

Officers, like their men, were cast in rigid mold. Versatility was not expected, nor welcomed as a rule. Shortly after the French Armistice (and a picnic trip across France as an officer cadet with the rank of sergeant), Skorzeny found himself in Holland in the midst of what were obvious exercises for invading England, and here he astonished his superiors with what, to his civilian mind, seemed a modest show of resource. Heavy tanks were lined up to go aboard the ships, but the army had no ramps strong enough; Skorzeny was asked if he could design one to take their weight. This quickly done, he found a local factory where the ramps could be made. Warned that Dutchmen would work only at pistol point, he cozened them instead with schnapps and chocolate. They kept going all night: next morning he awoke his commanding officer to see the first tank driven aboard.

Not long after, a sharp brush with bureaucracy nearly cut short his career. He needed tires for his lorries on the road; the N.C.O. at a depot where he stopped refused to part with any unless he could show written authority from above. Skorzeny promised jocularly to bring his guns and blow up the dump if the man did not see reason. He got his tires, but three weeks later he was recalled from leave to explain his conduct to a full general and suffer a reprimand.

In April, Yugoslavia. Skorzeny heard only that the Belgrade Government had been overthrown and the new rulers had torn up their pact with Hitler. The Germans went in. It was Skorzeny's baptism by fire. That night he saw his first corpses, neatly laid out for burial, and he could not help the melancholy thought that it was a soldier's fate to do everything in rows: he had to fall in in a row, he marched in a row, ate in a row. And when he was dead he lay in a row.

A few days later Skorzeny went out with a platoon to patrol the hills; he let a much larger body of the enemy walk right into him before jumping up and calling for their surrender. The bluff won; the hands went up. Returning with sixty-three prisoners, three of them officers, he was promoted to First Lieutenant and cited "for bravery in the face of the foe." And that without pressing a trigger; the lesson was not lost on him.

Ten days and Yugoslavia was over—another nation subdued; another army, this time of thirty divisions, destroyed. It was a textbook invasion that upheld Hitler's invincibility. That summer he turned on Russia.

Skorzeny had traveled east, Lawrence's *Seven Pillars* in his kit. In the troop trains rattling through Poland the men sang "Marching against England": they believed they had been given leave to pass through Turkey and Russia— to reach the Middle East. With Rommel's Afrika Korps attacking from the other side the German jaws would meet on the British Eighth Army.

But, then, a day or two before reaching the Soviet frontier they stopped. Skorzeny's unit went on, by road, traveling at night. Behind the fields of corn, the barns and haystacks, they saw guns dug in and tanks ready to attack.

From outposts near a wide and muddy torrent—the river Bug—sentries on wooden towers could be seen on the farther shore. That night of June the general who briefed them said: "The enemy is Russia. We go over at five A.M. Gentlemen, the fate of Germany, nay, of Europe, depends on us. We shall not fail. Within a few weeks we will parade in Moscow."

So it might have been, but for elements outside the calculations of the General Staff, and one factor in particular, the Russian character.

Skorzeny, who harbored no illusions of racial superiority, saw his comrades' contempt for Russia turn to respect, then to something close to dread. After eighteen months he was taken out of the line, so he was not tried too far—just far enough. The Russians, he objectively concluded, are the only people who know what they are talking about when they speak of "total war."

Skorzeny explains: "It is like this. You go into Russia, win tremendous victories, advance hundreds of miles. Prisoners flow back, an endless river of humanity with one guard to five hundred of them. The fields and forests are a graveyard of captured tanks and vehicles left to rust.

"When you retreat . . . they all rise up to meet you. This is how it happens. Thousands of prisoners slip away into the forests. New leaders cross the lines to them by night. Abandoned guns and tanks are secretly patched up. A host of special troops are dropped from planes skimming the snow; careless of broken limbs, they jump by moonlight without parachutes. And so there is a striking force where none was before."

The Russians, he found, could march incredible distances, sleep in wet rags, live on roots from the fields. They had stomachs that would digest anything: he saw prisoners tear raw chunks from a long-dead horse and march on, refreshed.

Such insensibility is a high military asset. It meant that they could drink from marshes and shell holes while the Germans had to send ten or twenty miles through hostile territory for water. They could even exist without supply columns. Before one big attack Skorzeny was assured the troops opposite had no transport left at all; yet they never ran short of munitions. Prisoners explained that villages behind the front had been emptied of women, children and old men; in a human chain the people had to pass munitions from hand to hand up to the fighting line. Gasoline was rolled along in casks. Lacking food or shelter, thousands of these people died. But the Red Army carried on.

The Soviet soldier, Skorzeny found, was not only tough, cunning and instinctive, but he also showed high qualities of improvisation and technical ingenuity. He was never at a loss: one spare part would be made to replace another, tires would be stuffed with straw to keep lorries going. He was a master of camouflage and deception, and of devices such as the "invisible" bridge: built below the surface of a muddy river, it was used only at night and could not be spotted by day. Russian planes and tanks, lacking many gadgets, were all the sturdier for that.

In the last year of the war the Red Army forced down the throat of the invader a full dose of his own medicine. They subjected the Germans to the same *blitzkrieg* and pincer-movement technique which they themselves had suffered earlier on. It was obvious that the West had nothing now to tell them about war, while what the Russians could still teach the West was not so easily learned.

Skorzeny is not among those who believe Russia to be invincible. While agreeing that Hitler paid the forfeit for his overconfidence, he sees no need for a rebound in the

Russian T-34

direction of exaggerated fear: the "Russian neurosis" in its cold-war form. Even after that first winter of retreat from Moscow the German armies swept on again and might have brought down the edifice of Soviet power had it not been buttressed by supplies and promises of help from America and Britain.

In the last days of December, 1942, while all Germany held its breath for the fate of Field-Marshal von Paulus' army at Stalingrad, Skorzeny was invalided home. He returned to Vienna with a wound, an Iron Cross and the illness that was to pursue him for years. In Russia he left his copy of *Seven Pillars* with the last of his illusions. The fires of the Eastern front steeled his character and also armored it against shams.

III

How did he get the job? Why did destiny pick Otto Skorzeny for the Mussolini adventure and lift him from the
regimental rut to become a military prodigy overnight?

Chance, in the shape of a chronic illness, had brought
him back from the Russian front and dumped him in a
Berlin office classified as "fit for home service only."
Chance thus saw to it that he should be on the spot when
Hitler, jolted by the daring of British sea and desert commandos, ordered the High Command to try the same game.
And chance placed a university acquaintance of Skorzeny's
in the department which was charged with the selection
of an officer to train these new "special troops."

If Skorzeny had not been a victim of his gall bladder,
the opportunity to wage new kinds of warfare might never
have occurred. The passionate energy with which he seized
this opportunity was of no chance origin. It was generated
by the Allied call from North Africa for Germany's unconditional surrender.

Meeting in the glow of the Casablanca Conference,
Roosevelt and Churchill may well have intended their
declaration as a pious pledge to Stalin that they would not

treat with Hitler on any terms. However soothing its influence in Moscow, the declaration rang in other ears like a tribal challenge. Berlin called heaven to witness. The Allies were bent on destroying the nation and war-weary millions were stiffened to win or perish. Until that day in February, 1943, Skorzeny had taken things as they came. Casablanca hit him fair and square; it was a goad as effective as that with which Frederick the Great rallied the Prussian Guard: "Dogs, would you live forever!"

There was nothing subtle in the way Skorzeny made his decision, as he explained it to me. "For anyone with blood in his veins there is, at certain turning points, only one way to go. A man who can still see a choice of two roads then may be a clever fellow—I could not say much more for him."

He argued his way into an active unit, the 3rd S.S. Armored Division, only to be let down by dysentery. He was returned to his repair depot. Then fate played one of its tricks with the offer of a "secret" job which would make him practically his own master and allow him to work up a school of warfare on "commando" lines. The term was adopted to cover the whole range of surprise attack by comparatively small bodies of picked men.

So unworldly was Skorzeny, so untutored in the arts of circumvention, that he never stopped to wonder why such an enviable appointment should be conferred on a junior officer with no strings to pull. The reason is not far to seek. Hitler had asked for "commandos" and would have them, and at once. The High Command were even willing to adopt the Allied term as an evidence of zeal. And someone must be found to launch the new formation: not a career officer, because he might become puffed up with ambition and try to elevate it to real importance. What was needed in such cases was someone "suitable," presentable, and unaspiring. One can visualize the selectors, when Skorzeny's friend put forward his name with the remark that he was kicking his heels in Berlin, going through those confidential reports that hover in the background of every young officer's life: "Good war record, temporary commission, a head for technical detail, soberminded . . ." He would do very well!

So they settled on a safe nonentity and turned with relief to more serious problems. After all, they could not complain. The High Command had arrived at the fourth year of the war before the distasteful question of having independent "commandos" was pressed on them by the Leader. (In England, too, "special troops" were fathered on the War Office by adversity. Only after Dunkirk was Churchill able to send forth raiders with blackened faces and Fair bairn fighting knives to restore British self-respect.)

The war was going badly for Germany: Stalingrad lost, Rommel in flight, and the blow was poised which would split Italy from the Axis. The High Command and its Leader had lost their infallibility. Enemies with land, sea and air superiority on every front were mustering for the siege of Fortress Europe. No help, no hope in sight. Manifestly the moment was ripe for the raising of commandos: conditions were desperate.

On April 20, 1943, Lieut. Skorzeny was breveted Chief of Germany's Special Troops, Existing or to be Created in the Future, and given a rank that indicated the modest expectations attached to that grandiloquent appointment—he was promoted to captain. A mixed company led by a Dutchman was found, renamed a battalion, and put under him; a second such battalion was to be built up by degrees. Among the impedimenta wished on to the new command were three "training schools" of spying and sabotage: mysteries into which their new chief had yet to be formally initiated.

Shortly after his advancement Skorzeny was ushered into the presence of the famous Admiral Canaris, Hitler's Intelligence Chief. It was a painful interview. Instead of testing the newcomer's qualifications for the secret-service part of his job, Canaris spent a full three hours wrangling over the transfer of some junior officers who sought employment with Skorzeny—and then put off deciding.

Skorzeny was dazed by the encounter. In later months, when the sensation was repeated and became familiar, he came to recognize that Canaris had given him his baptism to the war of the "higher echelons." How lucky for him that he seldom met, in the early days of his first command, so exalted a master of obstruction! Canaris sat with the military caliphate, in the quiet heart of a cyclone: where all was still. Outside, the storm raged. Dapper figures in the red-striped trousers of the General Staff directed a whirl-

wind of forms, orders and applications. Too often Skorzeny
was lost in this blizzard of paper as he battled to set up
and equip his outfit.

Radl saved him from despair; Karl Radl, a gay comrade of student days whom he met providentially in Berlin
and made his adjutant. Skorzeny alone could never have
matched his bureaucratic adversaries with their single-
minded devotion to preserving the order of things and
their place within that order. Officials were irked by his
enthusiasm and objected to having their thinking hours
stretched by his troublesome requests. When he pressed for
action beyond a point where his demands could be ignored,
well, they knew many a snare which could be set for young
men in a hurry and could enjoy many a crow of retributive
triumph when he punctually fell into them.

But Radl had read for the Bar and was marked as a
future judge when the war began. He found military regulations a fascinating child's game compared with the Central European jurisprudence he had studied. With Austrian
irreverence he indulged the "beautiful nonsense" of bum-
bledom: instead of arguing with officials he capered
alongside them on the road which led to total absurdity.
Bureaucrats skilled in the art of evasion found themselves tripped up by their own red tape and badgered by
Radl for more and more forms until they cried for mer-
cy. In the demonology of the new unit their opponents at
G.H.Q. became "The Generals," a slightly comic term
evoking brassbound complacency and the flash of a
rebuking monocle in the Senior Officers' Mess. Later on
Skorzeny was to meet German officers of high rank and
brilliant gifts who did their best against the creeping
malaise of bureaucracy. Then it was too late to make
amends. Letters signed on behalf of General This or
General. That had given Radl his warrant, and to the end
the generals were the scapegoats when anything went
wrong.

With his bubbling good humor and a genius for
squeezing out of dilemmas, Karl Radl was seldom at a
loss. Soon he was mapping the whole field of bureau
strategy and advancing on many sectors of this vital front.
Before Radl joined him, all Skorzeny's effort was being
spent on this campaign of attrition; now he was able to
devote quite half his time to considering the forgotten war
against the Allies.

A later entrant in the commando field, Skorzeny made a start by asking Intelligence what his contemporaries had already done. He was sent over a vast dossier which had been painstakingly compiled and briskly put aside. The story began with the raids the Allies had launched on St. Nazaire, Dunkirk, Lofoten, and went on to describe the work of sea and desert raiders in the Mediterranean; it was documented with field reports and prisoners' statements.

The High Command had dismissed these operations as "pinprick attacks" and "the work of amateurs," but the confidential reports made up a very different picture. As he read them Skorzeny felt his whole horizon change: this was what he had been waiting for—here was a touch of the sublime. A wider space for military imagination seemed to open before him. Projects of a kind he hardly dreamed of had been pioneered; and every step already taken offered new vistas. If Casablanca topped the charge of his explosive energies, the study of British methods lent them meaning and direction.

Skorzeny had established his commando school in a hunting lodge at Friedenthal (the Valley of Peace) not far from Berlin. It stood in a vast park amid wide acres of woodland and heath. Soon, barracks and hangars arose and there, while he worked on training programs and the evolution of new methods, his mind kept constantly abreast of the successes—and failures—of the British.

One of the most fruitful reports to come into his hands told of the attempt to kidnap General Rommel in the Western Desert by commandos who appeared two hundred and fifty miles behind the lines by submarine. This mission evoked Skorzeny's theory that battles may be half-won before they are fought by "carving out the brains" of the enemy. The raid failed because it was based on faulty intelligence. Rommel was on a trip to Rome at the time and in any case the wrong building was chosen for the attack. Skorzeny was convinced that the only way of finding out what was happening was to go out and look.

In the meantime he came upon a profitable game to play—and engaged the Allies as his unwitting partners. Now in Intelligence, he knew that British planes which scurried night after night across the Continent were parachuting agents, radio sets, explosives and dangerous gadgets into the occupied countries. On a visit to Holland he found

that most of the equipment and nearly half the agents
had fallen into German hands. From the captives—some
were double agents who did not mind which side paid
their wages—he learned the British techniques of spying
and wrecking which had been brought to a high pitch of
excellence. He also used the codes of captured spies for
radio messages in English ordering any piece of equipment
that interested him; often it was dropped by the British
next night. A silenced pistol, for example—they had no
such thing in Germany—was ordered by Skorzeny's Dutch
"bureau" and punctually dropped; to test it he opened a
window and shot a duck on the canal below—no one in
the street turned his head.

Skorzeny was enchanted with the weapons which came
in from England, and the ease with which he was able to
steal the enemy's inventions. But when it came to copying
them for his men, he ran into malevolently pigheaded
objections.

For instance, a Sten gun fitted with a silencer; to convince the experts he invited them to Friedenthal and took them walking while one of his men following ten or twelve yards behind fired off a clip. The experts heard nothing; when he showed them the shell cases scattered on the ground, Skorzeny expected them to share his delight. On the contrary, the visitors were ruffled by the surprise he had arranged and could only pick holes in his proposal.

Ah well, thought Skorzeny, at least we can have the Sten without the silencer. He took the gun to the generals, full of its merits. Of course, he explained, it was not meant to be accurate at more than short range—it was a close-combat weapon; but it was foolproof; you could drop it in the mud, jump on it and then go on firing. The German tommy guns were much more expensive to make—and much more delicate.

No, said the generals. They could not copy it. Hitler had ordered that the German soldier must be equipped with weapons "of the finest quality in all respects." And all respects, they pointed out, included range.

This was the kind of answer Skorzeny came up against. With one hand the High Command bade him create special forces for unprecedented tasks and with the other it withheld the means to do so. While Mountbatten seemed to conjure up for his commandos superb weapons and fleets of planes and ships, the staff at Friedenthal had to fight for every single cartridge. Supplies were tight all around: that was the pretext, but the huge appetite of regular formations was met with an unsparing largesse compared with the pinch-fist which doled out cheese parings and candle ends to their poor relations at Friedenthal.

One of the first missions Skorzeny took over planned to cut the Middle East supply route to Russia. A German officer had been smuggled into Teheran, where he was intriguing with the Persians under British and Russian noses. The plot was thriving. Persian-speaking Germans had been parachuted to subvert the mountain tribes. More were following with the needful arms. Then up would go the country, like a powder barrel—so they hoped.

A grandiose project: it was delayed at the start while Berlin's antique shops were ransacked for silver-handled pistols and inlaid fowling pieces (even Radl's buoyancy was not equal to indenting for gifts to tribal leaders), and it ended when the loan of a single long-range plane to drop reinforcements was refused.

The Persian fiasco was one of many ideas tossed into his lap without means to nurse them to fruition. Frostbitten from the start, these frail seedlings must still be tended as if they would blossom in the end. And then Skorzeny found that he had not merely one set of masters to please; he had two. Besides the High Command, the politicians had a hand to play.

Magnitogorsk was an example. While still campaigning in Russia his interest had been caught by stories of new Soviet war plants beyond the Urals. With new Intelligence reports available he began to work on a plan for crippling this industrial complex in what is still today the most secret area on the globe. Thousands of Soviet prisoners were questioned; masses of air pictures were pieced together. At last two power plants were chosen as nerve centers for the commando attack. Then someone told Heinrich Himmler, Hitler's Minister of Interior, that the real place to go for in Russia was Magnitogorsk.

Magnitogorsk?—that was in the Urals too. Next day Skorzeny had a message from Berlin: orders to destroy the Magnitogorsk blast furnaces (on which he had no information at all). As soon as could be, he would let Himmler know when the attack would be launched.

Impossible. That was the reply Skorzeny sat down to write; no one would let him send it. Karl Radl objected with cheerful guile that it would be fatal to anger Himmler, if only because his help might be useful one day on the main front against the General Staff. Finally, sleek young Lt.-Colonel Walther Schellenberg took over Skorzeny's education.

Schellenberg was a Himmler creation; in no time he had shot up to be Chief of Political Information in Berlin; now he imparted a secret of success:

"The more absurd the idea put up to you by a really important person, the more rapturously you should welcome it. Showy preparations should be started forthwith; assurances must be incessantly given that plans are advancing apace. Then gradually, drop by drop, the notion that certain outside factors may defer the glorious consummation may be allowed to seep through; until the author of the project finds himself wondering at his own earlier enthusiasm and begins discreetly to shelve the whole thing—if he hasn't forgotten all about it already."

It took eighteen months, applying the drop-by-drop technique, before Himmler's order was shelved. Nothing could be done about the perfectly practicable plan for blowing up the power plants until Magnitogorsk had been forgotten—and then the chance had gone.

Skorzeny had to contend against the popular belief that a commando attack was a glorified Red Indian raid, whooped up on the spur of the moment by a rabble of homicidal delinquents. In practice, success called for just the opposite approach—one of patient, tireless premeditation. He had to create a staff able to judge every tiny fact dug up by Intelligence. He had to create a supply section which could be trusted to anticipate all needs, from uniforms to driving licenses, from explosives to matches, from food to special weapons. And he had to live at the center of this intricate machine while being able to detach his mind from its problems—for his was the leader's task of spotting the simple beyond the difficult.

Above everything else, as Skorzeny saw it, came the job of welding his fighting men into small, compact units; volunteers though they all were, each man had to be chosen singly for each mission and watched up to the moment he went into battle. He must know how to act entirely on his own, yet never forgetting his comrades' interests and the main purpose of their operation. If the smallest wheel of all this machinery slipped everything was imperiled, and even if they brought off the action it might be at a higher cost. "One for all and all for one" was no copybook maxim in Skorzeny's command, but a rule of life and a condition of survival.

He spent four months at Friedenthal, nursing the cold headquarters into life, bringing his troops to fighting pitch, making his own mistakes in his own way. Only four months, but in that time he had attained imaginative heights and breathed the mountain air. Nothing had happened that the world could see and nothing had warned him of the coming phase: that as the days of July ran out he would be one of six chosen from all the armed forces of his country to be scrutinized and appraised by Hitler himself.

IV

*The Führer . . . kept Dönitz and Student back
to discuss the liberation of Mussolini. I hope this
job won't be put on my plate. I can see no good
in it.*

GENERAL ROMMEL, The Rommel Papers

Until that Sunday in July when Mussolini's arrest became
known, Skorzeny had never set eyes on Hitler—nor did he
expect to, unless perhaps as one of thousands in a parade.
The summons, when it came, seemed as absurdly unreal
as an order from Olympus. Not only could he scarcely believe it possible; he almost missed it altogether.

He had lunched with a don from Vienna whom he
had met in the Eden Hotel in Berlin. Free from uniform
for a few hours, they were gossiping over ersatz coffee;
the day was theirs, yet Skorzeny unaccountably felt uneasy. He telephoned Friedenthal to ask if anything was
happening.

Anything happening? For nearly two hours they had
been searching all Berlin for him. He was wanted at Hitler's headquarters. A special plane was waiting at Templehof airport. It must take off at five—with Skorzeny in it.
No, they had no idea what it was all about.

Hitler's headquarters? Skorzeny said: "Tell Radl to
meet me at the airport with my uniform." When the taxi
reached Templehof, Karl Radl was there. He gave Skorzeny the warfront bulletins and said there had been some
change in the Government of Italy; he could not say what
it amounted to. The plane's engines were ticking over.
While Skorzeny changed, he hurriedly promised Radl he

32

would telephone as soon as he could. Meanwhile, he said, stand the men to; they might be wanted.

In a deep armchair in the plane, Skorzeny settled down, the solitary passenger. The whole affair was mad—some brass-hat extravaganza, some ludicrous mix-up. He saw in front of him as they took off a built-in rack of liquers: French brandy, too—he poured a glass. Otto Skorzeny, with a V.I.P. plane all to himself.

He found a map in his brief case—Radl, who thought of everything, had put it in—and decided to follow their route. Here was a chance to pinpoint Hitler's fabled headquarters: he had often wondered where they were hidden. For the world, the Wolf's Lair, as the headquarters were called, lay "somewhere on the Eastern Front"—a romantic public was permitted to suppose that the Leader shared the hazards and discomfort of his troops. The plane's route took them to East Prussia; over plain and stream they flew to Rastenburg, then in the gathering dusk touched down on an airstrip. A Mercedes was waiting. The headquarters turned out to be no front-line dugout but a sizable village in a forest; hidden from the air by camouflage nets and trees; protected by antiaircraft guns, bunker defenses, masses of barbed wire and hundreds of guards.

Skorzeny was greeted by an aide-de-camp who led him at once to a comfortable anteroom. There he was introduced to five officers, all senior to him; they too had been summoned without explanation from all parts of Europe. It was a long wait; Skorzeny grew impatient—what could it all be about? When one of the other officers mispronounced his name he found himself snapping, "It's not so very difficult. All you have to do is break it up: Skor-zay- ny—it's quite simple!" At that moment, when he was feeling foolish and on edge, the aide-de-camp returned. "Gentlemen, you will now enter the Leader's presence."

Hitler himself would see them! No one had bargained for that. They filed like schoolboys into another building; after a moment's delay the Headmaster walked briskly in. Hitler wore a tunic without badges, and an Iron Cross. Skorzeny, lined up with his companions, saw that they saluted their Commander-in-Chief with Prussian empressment; all that he could manage for his supreme moment was an awkward bow.

Hitler stopped before each of the six men he had sent for; he looked into their eyes in turn as each man briefly recited an outline of his career. Then he stepped back to put a question. "Which of you knows Italy—and what do you think of the Italians?"

One by one, the other five offered hopeful replies: the Italians were their gallant allies, Rome was Germany's Axis partner, and so on. Skorzeny, last in the line, thought hard.

He knew that Hitler, like himself, must resent the loss of the Alto Adige, Austria's loveliest Alpine region, and yet for policy reasons had been obliged to let Italy have it. How could he touch this hidden spring without presumption? It was his turn: he said: "Leader, I am an Austrian."

Hitler stared at him with an unblinking gaze, but Skorzeny added nothing. Then he said shortly, "Captain Skorzeny, you will stay behind. The rest may go."

They were alone, and he heard Hitler say, "I have a mission of the highest importance for you"—but what this mission was did not immediately appear. Instead, there was a long preamble: Hitler, in tones of rising anger, said his partner Mussolini had just been betrayed and arrested. Italy lay wide open to invasion and at any moment Rome might fall to the Allies. The King of Italy had plotted this treason with the King's friend, Marshal Badoglio; now they meant to go over to the Allies and take Mussolini with them as a prisoner.

"I cannot and will not leave Mussolini to this fate," exclaimed Hitler loudly at this point. "He has got to be rescued before these traitors can surrender him to the enemy."

While Skorzeny was flattered at receiving the confidence of his Commander-in-Chief, he could not help wondering what all this had to do with him. In these quietly spoken words the answer came: "You, Skorzeny, are going to save my friend."

He listened in a daze as Hitler went on to warn him of the need for utmost secrecy. Only five or six other men should know of his decision that Mussolini must be rescued—no matter whose feelings might be hurt. One already informed was General Student, chief of Airborne troops, under whose command Skorzeny would act. Neither the General Staff in Italy nor the Rome Embassy must be told anything about it; they could not be trusted to keep quiet. No one knew where the prisoner had been taken, so that Skorzeny would not only have to rescue him; he would first have to find out where he was.

Fixed in the hypnotic stare, Skorzeny was not asked for an opinion. "You will avoid no risk," Hitler concluded. "You will succeed—and your success will have a tremendous effect on the course of the war. This is a mission for which you will be answerable to me personally!"

With this equivocal farewell, and a double handclasp, Hitler sent him off. He turned at the door; the eyes were still on him.

Back in the anteroom, Skorzeny had just taken out a badly needed cigarette, when the aide-de-camp came to lead him to his new chief, Student. He found the general, jovial, potbellied, scarred across the brow by a bullet at Rotterdam. Hardly had they met when in walked the S.S. Grand-Master Heinrich Himmler. Skorzeny cast about for yet another pretext to delay the Magnitogorsk raid, but

Himmler had not come to talk of blast furnaces; instead he wanted to brief them on the immediate task.

He began by repeating that nobody in Germany—or in Rome either—had any idea where the "turncoat" Italian Government had hidden Mussolini, but they suspected secret talks were already going on for transferring him to an Allied prison—where he would serve as a scapegoat for Italy.

Now for people who might help in the search—and he began to rattle off names: scores of Italian politicians and noblemen still said to favor Germany; some were trustworthy, some not. Skorzeny started to make notes, but Himmler stopped him with a shout and glared through his prim, silver pince-nez. "Put that pen away at once. Can't you use your memory? All this is absolutely secret!"

After half an hour of this "briefing" Skorzeny excused himself and went to a telephone box to call Radl. As he waited for his line to Friedenthal he lit the long-awaited cigarette. At once Himmler's thin face was peering through the glass door. "So you can't live without smoking," he snapped. "A fine choice for an important job, I must say!" The suspicion that Skorzeny had escaped for a cigarette in the midst of his formal discussion was too much for the chief of all Hitler's secret police.

Radl's excited voice came through. Skorzeny told him to be ready to take off first thing next day, with fifty of his best men, including those who spoke Italian. They would fly to the south of France and from there to another destination which they would be told of on the way.

"Equipment? Bring everything," he said. "I'll send you a teleprinted list of extras when I have a moment. You will need tropical uniforms and mufti for a start."

Midnight found Skorzeny sending over the ticker to Friedenthal list after list of items—portable radios, grenades, tracer bullets, first-aid sets, machine guns . . . He asked for coffee and continued. Everything might hang on a detail: Italian currency; priests' robes as a possible disguise—and then they would need black hair dye and false papers.

At three A.M., his head spinning with names and half-formed plans, he found a bed and tried to sleep. He had no idea what he would do with the paraphernalia he had ordered, even supposing that Radl could raise half of it in the time; he did not know how he could find and res-

German Paratrooper

cue Hitler's friend. All he knew was that something was happening which would lift him right out of the trough of mediocrity—if he succeeded.

After breakfast he set off for Italy with General Student in a plane flown by the ace flier Capt. Gerlach, whom Student had made his personal pilot. They took a new route over the Alps to avoid Allied planes—an unpleasant reminder of the enemy's air ascendancy—and on the way they looked down on Skorzeny's native city of Vienna. Since he was passing as an A.D.C. to the General, he wore a fur-lined air-force suit and arriving in the heat of Rome, he sweltered, yet had to keep it on until he could find some suitable change. This was a foretaste of what he must often suffer in the future, when to avoid attention he had to borrow uniforms which were either too thick or too thin for the climate and always too small, because nothing could be found to match his bulk.

Rome looked peaceful enough; and by evening he had been crammed into a paratroop officer's tropical mess kit to pay a social call. He drove with Student up the cool heights of Frascati; here, at the German headquarters of the Alban hills, they dined with Field-Marshal Kesselring. It appeared absurd that the Commander-in-Chief in Italy should have been kept in the dark about the Mussolini rescue project, but presently Skorzeny guessed why. Kesselring's upbringing in an outmoded school of chivalry made him seem out of place in an arena filled with Machiavellian factions. He believed that every officer must naturally be a man of honor; when Skorzeny ventured to doubt the Italian generals' protestations that they had no idea where Mussolini was, his host brusquely corrected him.

Three days later the Friedenthal party arrived; eager for action, they were told there was nothing yet to do. Only Radl was let into the secret: his alert mind and quick eye were badly needed, for the whole enterprise was already enmeshed in a web of false clues and tangled theories.

Field-Marshal Kesselring still believed that in spite of Mussolini's overthrow and the Allies' successful landing in Sicily, he could keep Italy fighting on Germany's side. Hitler was skeptical, but wished to avoid an armed clash which would drive Italy into the Allied camp at a time when German forces in the peninsula were heavily out-numbered; he also hoped that an apparent acceptance of Italian assurances might help him to trace Mussolini. The façade of friendship likewise suited the King of Italy and the new Government of Marshal Badoglio; having Musso-lini safely in the bag they could secretly bargain for peace while pretending to the Germans that despite the change of government they meant to fight on beside them.

It was touch and go who would move first—the Ital-ians to change partners or the Germans to occupy all the strong points in Italy and imprison the Government as traitors to the Axis cause. Skorzeny saw that in this game of bluff and counterbluff the fallen dictator was the vital piece.

For Hitler, the salvage of Mussolini promised a re-vival of Fascist military energy on his side, a second wind for his deflated prestige, and reassurance to all the other little Mussolinis of the satellite countries.

For the King and Badoglio, Mussolini's removal meant the final collapse of the Fascist power, and possession of his person was a trump card in their deal with the Allies; his guards were not to let him get away alive. Until the Allies plunged into Italy to protect them, Badoglio's Gov-ernment were bent on temporizing.

Temporizing suited the Germans, too. They could quietly draft in troops on the pretext of bolstering Italy's defense; simultaneously they worked on a plan to carry off the entire Italian Royal Family and Badoglio's Govern-ment when the showdown came. Skorzeny's part in this was to capture the Crown Prince Umberto from the Quiri-nal Palace. Much time was spent on such scheming, while both sides pretended they were still devoted friends.

For Skorzeny the political charade was an infuriating distraction from his first objective. Every day the scent was growing colder. Mussolini had been arrested on leaving the Palace, bustled into an ambulance and whisked away. After that—well, there were a hundred sequels, all dif-ferent, since the Italians are profligate in their use of ru-mor.

It was not long before Skorzeny saw that Badoglio's Government were shrouding their secret in a cloud of plausibility. All kinds of inspired reports were going the rounds, freely attributed to generals, ambassadors and Vatican statesmen. Mussolini was in hospital; he had been flown to Portugal; he was still hidden away in Rome. Small wonder that, in Berlin, Himmler sent for astrologers and clairvoyants.

After three weeks of maddening talk, a love letter appeared: that it was to a servant girl made it seem the more credible. A gendarme on the island of Ponza—where politicians who offended Mussolini used to be confined—had written to his girl on the mainland to say that Mussolini himself was imprisoned there. Careless chatter by an Italian lieutenant led the trail on from Ponza to the naval base of Spezia—his cruiser had taken the prisoner there.

"Board the warship and remove its captive!" Such were the baffling orders which came that night from Hitler's headquarters. Just how a modern cruiser on a war footing could be taken by assault was not indicated. Luckily a liaison officer still in touch with the Italians established that Mussolini had been moved again: first to a village in Sardinia and thence to the fortified port of La Maddalena on a tiny island three miles off. He was held there in a house called the Villa Weber.

With a subaltern who spoke excellent Italian Skorzeny crossed over to Sardinia. To pass unnoticed, they had rigged themselves up as German sailors—for there was still a German liaison officer with three or four ratings in La Maddalena. Skorzeny asked his companion, Lt. Warger, to do the round of the waterside bars; if Warger insisted, in his cups, that Mussolini had escaped or was dying—no matter which—some Italian would surely bet that he was not.

Somebody did. A market gardener who, as luck would have it, supplied the Villa Weber. Taking the now unsteady Warger by the arm, he led him to a spot from which the terrace of the Villa Weber could be reviewed: on that very terrace the gardener had seen Mussolini walking that morning between his jailers.

Next day, by astute questioning, Warger made sure of Mussolini's presence—and of the number of troops who guarded both town and villa as if against a siege. Skorzeny saw that the defenses would have to be attacked in strength. How were the Italian guns placed? He got a plane from Rome and the two flew over, taking pictures. A group of British fighters joined them—and before they had time to wonder whether the R.A.F. were in the secret too, their plane was forced into the sea. There Skorzeny's quest almost ended: he broke three ribs and was knocked out. Hauled aboard a rubber raft, he came around in time to dive back into the plane just before it sank and to recover the camera with its films.

Half an hour later the Germans were picked off a cluster of rocks by an Italian antiaircraft ship. Skorzeny had qualms when he faced the commander, since clearly the ship was protecting Mussolini's hiding place. Luckily, the castaways were not too closely questioned and soon, wearing a pair of white shoes and shorts lent him by the crew, Skorzeny was ashore in Sardinia again.

So back to Frascati. Radl, having had word that Skorzeny's plane was lost in the sea, received him as if he were a ghost. And here another set of orders waited.

Mussolini was not, as they had supposed, on La Maddalena; he was on a tiny island off Elba and "Captain Skorzeny will indicate the earliest possible day on which an attack can be made."

This astonishing information had come from Admiral Canaris, and who could hope to argue down the head of the secret service? Skorzeny had clashed with him already; yet even if Canaris's version had been swallowed by Hitler himself he felt that he must challenge it, for he knew that he was right and Canaris wrong. He won over General Student and with him flew to Hitler's headquarters to put his case against the orders of the High Command.

It was a forbidding audience which had gathered in the Wolf's Lair to pass judgment on this upstart captain. By now the leading Nazis had been let into the secret of the search for Mussolini. They were grouped around a monumental fireplace. Ribbentrop was on Hitler's right; the two military top men Marshal Keitel and General Jodl, Chiefs of the High Command and Operations Staff, were beyond. Himmler was there, poker-faced as ever. Then Grand Admiral Dönitz and the impassive bulk of Marshal Göring. They sat brooding in leather armchairs.

Presented by Student, Skorzeny said what he had to say. After a stumbling start, he talked, as Austrians will, "from the heart." The notes he had compiled were forgotten as he told of his stubborn search. He was sure Mussolini was still in La Maddalena, he said; he showed facts to prove he could be nowhere else. When he came to the story of Warger's impersonation of a drunken sailor, and let out that the young man had never touched drink until in Sardinia he was ordered to do so, Göring broke the tension with a roar of laughter.

Skorzeny ended his story; it had taken more than half an hour. Everyone looked at Hitler. Presently he got up and shook hands with Skorzeny. "You are right," he exclaimed. "I withdraw my orders. As you propose, we will attack La Maddalena. How would you set about it?"

The others gathered around, murmuring agreement. With a penciled map, Skorzeny found himself showing the heads of the armed forces the plan which Student had already passed.

It was to be an affair of momentous dash and energy. On the eve of the attack there would be a naval courtesy visit to La Maddalena: under cover of this a speedboat flotilla would enter the harbor; its commander would even exchange protocol calls with the Italians. Next morning, while the speedboats were still in harbor, a flotilla of mine sweepers would briefly call at a neighboring island; and as they sailed away from it they would veer sharply and run straight into La Maddalena with Skorzeny's commandos and the men of the Armed S.S. German antiaircraft guns from the main island of Sardinia, and the ship's guns, would give unostentatious cover for a polite march through the streets, led by Skorzeny, which would bring them right up to the Villa Weber. The plan was based on Skorzeny's belief that if you march your men peaceably through a place, and show by your demeanor that trouble is the last thing you expect, or are thinking of, ten to one you will get away with it.

Hitler approved; everybody approved: it was agreed that all the units should come under Skorzeny's command. The young soldier's dream had come true; the great men of the land were benignly studying his own plan; the marshals and the admirals taking their cue.

But Hitler, as ever, had a last warning. "You must understand, Captain Skorzeny, that if you fail I may have to disown you, since Italy is still nominally our ally. I should have to say, for reasons of state, that you acted without orders—you misled the units supporting you by turning the commanders' heads; your foolhardy action was prompted by excessive zeal, by ambition, even. And if you fail, you must not defend yourself against public repudiation."

Skorzeny nodded; there was nothing he could say.

But a gaunt image crossed his mind; Rudolf Hess too, it had been whispered, was warned that he would be disowned as a madman if his flight to England failed to secure a separate peace.

But Hitler believed in speeding his soldiers into battle with *élan*. He lifted a hand to Skorzeny's shoulder. "You will succeed," he said.

Back in Rome, Radl heard of Hitler's threat and pulled a face: "Oh well, we can always share a padded cell in one of Himmler's special sanatoria."

The eve of D-day came. Skorzeny was in one of the six speedboats which entered the harbor. Radl would lead the mine-sweeper party. Everything was ready for tomorrow. Skorzeny was assured that it would go like clockwork. Even the telephones to the mainland were all marked out to be cut.

He was still not happy. With Lieut. Warger, both in ratings' uniform, he went for a last prowl near the Villa Weber and fell in with a guard who was taking a parcel to a laundry. As a tried opening gambit, they asked whether Mussolini was not dead. The guard denied the rumor, the more warmly when they insisted it was true. "I have it from a doctor who witnessed the Duce's last moments," cried Warger in a wicked flash of inspiration. This was too much for the guard. "Dead?" he cried. "Of course Mussolini is not dead! Why, I saw him myself this morning. I was one of his escort down to that white ambulance seaplane which took him off the island."

It was so: there had been an ambulance plane in the harbor and now it was gone. And suddenly Skorzeny realized that although the guards around the villa were as numerous as ever, the stiffening had gone out of them; they were lolling about. There was just time before zero hour to cancel everything; he had narrowly escaped the humiliation of storming a prison without a prisoner—and the penalty that went with failure.

Back once more in Rome, to find the game of let's-pretend still going on. The Italians, bland and charming exponents of hanky-panky, were cleverest at it. Already an Armistice had secretly been signed in Sicily and now Badoglio had to spin out the time until the Allies landed in Italy.

The suspense was hard on the Italians, who held the

capital. But the Germans, too, were playing with a caution worthy of the stakes: Mussolini, Rome, perhaps all Italy. Their troops were disposed on the hills outside the city. Who would move first?

Keeping doggedly to his search for Mussolini, Skorzeny was rewarded with a series of false trails and assignations, in this villa and that café, each requiring minute investigation. He longed for Friedenthal as the days went on. Suddenly he was galvanized by an intercepted code message to the Italian Ministry of Interior. It said: "Security measures around Gran Sasso completed." That was all, but it was signed "Cueli"—and Skorzeny's spies had told him that a General Cueli was the Ministry's official responsible for Mussolini's safety.

The Gran Sasso, if Mussolini were really there, would present a problem. It was the loftiest peak in the Apennines, and in this area, a hundred miles from Rome as the crow flies, the mountain groups and ranges towered up to ten thousand feet.

Where in this cloudland could you house a prisoner of state with a regiment to guard him? According to their prewar maps, nowhere; but a winter-sports center called the Hotel Campo Imperatore had recently been built on a crag six thousand feet up. A gaudy tourist leaflet was produced. While maddeningly vague about the site and building it did say that the hotel could be reached only by funicular—and such a mountain railway was an easily broken link with the outer world: ideal for achieving quick isolation.

Agents soon found that roads to the Gran Sasso through the pine forests were blocked. Nobody knew what was happening in a wide area all around. Skorzeny decided that he and Radl would have to fly over and find out.

In a plane fitted with an automatic camera, they took off on September 8. Nothing went right; as they flew over the Gran Sasso they found the camera had jammed. So Skorzeny had to struggle with a hand camera, hanging head-first out of the rear gunner's turret in the freezing air while Radl, laughing uproariously, held his legs. In a second run over the spot Skorzeny insisted on reversing the rôles; he pulled Radl back into the plane with the laughter frozen on his lips.

They got their pictures: the hotel, square and massive

as a blockhouse set on a spur, and beside it, a triangle of ground and the little upper station of the funicular.

More trouble on the way back; they had to skim the ground to avoid a swarm of American bombers and fighters which were dropping an avalanche of explosives on the German headquarters and barracks at Frascati. As luck would have it they landed just in time to dash over to their own quarters, which were in flames, and salvage a few things, but the photographic studio which would have made stereoscopic enlargements of the Gran Sasso pictures had been blown to bits.

Rome was in uproar; the air raid was in celebration of an Allied radio announcement that Italy had surrendered. That night the Allies landed at Salerno. The game of make-believe was over. Italy had changed sides—officially. Scattered fighting between Germans and Italians had already begun. Now that pretenses were at an end, Mussolini could hardly be rescued without a battle; but at least, as Radl pointed out, the threat of Himmler's padded cell was removed. The showdown had come, and any brusque action against the Italians would not be fraught with diplomatic perils. They could go ahead.

Skorzeny had seen the Campo Imperatore from the air; independent checking now seemed to clinch the issue of Mussolini's presence there. A day or two earlier, Skorzeny had suggested to a Grman Army doctor that if he wanted to requisition an Alpine hotel for a convalescent home he knew just the place—it was on the Gran Sasso mountain. The doctor had set off right away; now he returned dejected. The Armistice, he supposed, had nullified the idea anyway, but Skorzeny might as well know that he had sent him on a fool's errand. He had not been able to get within miles of the hotel; the whole area was sealed up. He must have run into at least a battalion of carabinieri, and another two hundred and fifty were said to be billeted in the hotel itself. He had telephoned from a village and asked for the manager: a short-tempered Italian officer had sent him to the devil.

This looked really hopeful; and then Skorzeny got a report that trade unionists were complaining about the injustice of expelling the hotel's civilian staff at a moment's notice, "simply to accommodate that Fascist Mussolini." That was it, then: the Gran Sasso was the place.

Looking at it all from the Italians' point of view, Skorzeny conceded they could be proud of themselves. Even if Mussolini's whereabouts became known his prison was obviously impregnable. Merely to surround the mountain and insure that Mussolini was not moved out would need a full German division; huge losses would have to be taken among those jagged peaks: long before the Germans reached the prisoner—if they ever did—he could be hidden in some rocky cave or killed.

The Italians could sit back; their defenses were impassable. They had overlooked nothing; nothing, that is, except an individual's determination to get through.

Skorzeny had his facts, such as they were, and his photographs, such as *they* were—holiday snaps four inches square—on which to base a plan of attack. If an orthodox land assault were ruled out, there was only the sky left, and the altitude had even ruled that out: paratroops plummeting through the thin air would be dashed to pieces; planes had nowhere to land; gliders——

Glider Model DFS230C-1

He looked again at his pictures, at that triangular patch by the hotel. If it were really flat and smooth, a few gliders might land there. In that event shock troops might just reach Mussolini before his guards put a bullet in him; they could rush him to the funicular—the lower end having

been seized by paratroops at exactly the same moment—
and away. Skorzeny calculated that with everything going
perfectly they should reach Mussolini within three minutes
of the shock attack. Time to get away? That must be left
to luck.

Student raised a scarred eyebrow when Skorzeny put
the scheme to him; both men were weary after three almost sleepless nights of crisis and the general was in no
mood for hare-brained escapades. He sent for two technical officers of the Airborne staff, and Skorzeny had to ex-
pound the scheme again in detail as plausibly as he could.

The staff officers were not to be beguiled; experts
never are. A glance at his snapshots told them that the
proposed landing space was ridiculously small; nor had
gliders ever come down in such rarefied air. They estimated
that of a hundred men who made the trip twenty might
survive—twenty men to storm a fortress defended by two
hundred and fifty!

Skorzeny argued; the experts would not budge. At
last he offered to drop the plan if they could put forward a
better one. Student looked anxious; unless they were to
abandon the mission given them by Hitler, there was no alternative in sight—and no time to look for one. Finally
he yielded: but it would need three days, he said, to get
the gliders from the south of France. Ninety of the men
must be drawn from his trained airborne battalion; the
rest Skorzeny could supply. D-day would be on September
12, with a seven A.M. take-off.

That night Skorzeny called his men together and told
them that he was going to lead a group of them on a
dangerous and difficult operation ordered personally by
Hitler.

"Candidly," he said, "the experts don't give much for
our chances. They expect us to lose most of our strength
even before the fighting starts. I hope it won't be as bad
as all that, but losses are bound to be high. No one is ordered to take part. Anybody who wants to think twice
about coming, or who has a family to worry about, can
drop out now. He will have nothing to fear. His refusal
will not be known outside our ranks nor put into any
record, and we shall respect him no less."

Skorzeny might have spared his pains. Every man
stepped forward and he had trouble persuading them that
only eighteen could be picked. The remaining hours before

D-day hurried by as they tried to catch up with a thousand details: direction of approach, position of gliders en route and in landing, distances, altitudes, timing.

Skorzeny and Radl spent the last evening together with their soldiers. They drank a bottle of champagne to their chances and agreed on the principle that life was diverting and it was a shame to leave it.

Skorzeny summed up. "There are some things you can't work out with a slide rule. That's just where our experts may be wrong; and the Italians too. The safer the enemy feel, the better our chances of catching them unawares. Well, we'll soon know."

Just after the paratroops left that night for the drop into the valley, Allied radio put out an announcement: Mussolini had been handed over by the Italians; an Italian battleship had brought him to North Africa.

For a moment Skorzeny could not get his breath. Then he remembered where the Italian capital ships had been stationed; it could not have been done in time. The broadcast must be a hoax to throw the Germans off Mussolini's trail. Italian brains were still at work.

from the Chancellor, who would vouch for h...
phoned—and he told the lieutenant, facing him ...
step up, that he would be held personally resp...

V

Tales of escape and rescue—dramatic, romantic,
sometimes fantastic—are to be found in the history of every epoch and of every people; but my
escape from the Gran Sasso prison appears even
today as the boldest, the most romantic of all,
and at the same time the most modern in method
and style.

BENITO MUSSOLINI, Storia di un Anno

It was bright and windless, that September morning which
the knot of men waiting at the airfield knew must be the
last for quite a few of them. Great banks of white cloud
lying athwart their northeasterly course might help to get
them on their way unhindered; and the still, transparent
morning would have softened the trials of their landing—if
only they could have taken off as planned.

The start had been set for dawn—when they might
hope to float down unperceived by a sleepy enemy—but
the gliders were held up on their journey from the Riviera;
they could not arrive before eleven A.M. at the earliest.

That meant, by Student's reckoning, twenty-four
hours' delay—but there were not twenty-four hours to
spare. They would simply have to accept the further risk
of approaching in daylight and, moreover, at an hour
when they would be the sport of warm air currents which
might whisk the gliders from their path like so many paper
darts.

Certainly, Skorzeny thought, since nobody in his
senses would expect a glider operation at high noon, an
added measure of surprise, if they lived to exploit it, might

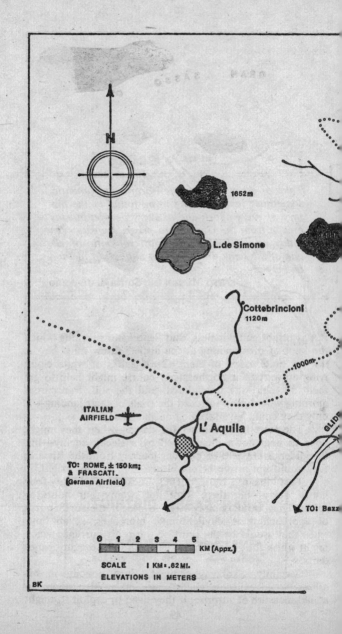

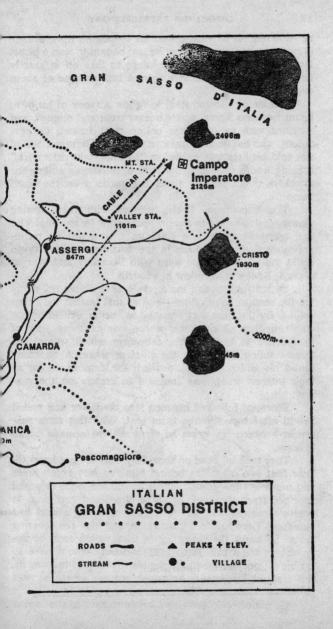

GRAN   SASSO   D' ITALIA

2498m

MT. STA. ⊠ Campo
              Imperatore
              2126m

VALLEY STA.
1161m

CABLE CAR

ASSERGI
847m

M. CRISTO
1930m

CAMARDA

·2000m·

·45m·

ANICA
·0m·

Pescomaggiore

ITALIAN
GRAN SASSO DISTRICT
• • • • • • • • • •

ROADS ━━   ▲ PEAKS + ELEV.

STREAM ━   ● • VILLAGE

be achieved. So he went cheerfully among his men, distributing boxes of fresh fruit that he had bought to lend a picnic touch to the expedition. They were to take off at exactly one P.M., which would give them a landing time of about two o'clock.

The delay allowed Radl to follow a fancy of his own; he hurried into Rome, where uneasy truce still reigned, and returned with an otherwise unimportant Italian, General Soletti, who had shown much favor to the Germans. Soletti was told his help was needed in "an important enterprise," it being Radl's hope that the sight of an Italian among the attackers might help to upset the garrison on the Gran Sasso.

The expedition, twelve gliders with their towing planes, was to be led to the dropping zone by the pilot who had taken Skorzeny and Radl on their numbing reconnaissance flight. Ten men in the first two gliders would cover the landing of the third with Skorzeny and Warger aboard; Radl was to follow in a fourth.

By half-past twelve the aircraft were drawn up, ready for the men to board them—and at that instant the sirens wailed. By the time they were all in shelter, Allied bombs were bursting all over the place—one of those jests of Providence as cruel as the rainstorm which wrecks the family outing. Yet when the all-clear sounded, Skorzeny found his gliders were untouched; the damage, as far as their interest went, was confined to craters on the runway.

Skorzeny followed his men into his glider and pulled Soletti after him into the front seat. With this extra passenger between his knees he signaled: the armada began to leave.

They took off dead on time. Skorzeny did not know till later that two machines behind him ran into bomb holes and never left the ground. What he did see, once they had emerged from the bank of white cloud and had risen to twelve thousand feet, was that his two leading gliders had vanished. They had lost their guide, and also the covering party. So much the worse; since they would soon be approaching the Gran Sasso area Skorzeny would have to tax his memory of the photographic trip to lead the way in. But wedged in his seat he could not see where he was going.

He pulled out a knife and began to hack at the canvas

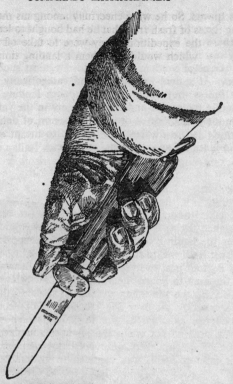

German Paratrooper Knife

deck and bulkheads. As they gave way, he blessed the flimsy fabric. Cool air rushed into the overheated shell, crammed as it was with men and weapons, and, peering through the rents, he could see the granite mountains below.

The Gran Sasso came into view. Soon they were on top of it: there was the hotel again, and on that dizzy perch alongside, the triangular ledge on which they would alight.

"Let go!" he told the pilot. The tow rope parted and they were swooping freely, with no sound but the gush of the wind on their wings. Then the pilot was jabbing with his finger at the triangle below while he turned his goggled face toward Skorzeny. By no flight of hyperbole could the space be called a landing field: it was a sloping shelf, for all the world like a ski jump; and as they lost more height they saw it to be studded with outcrop rock.

General Student had provided against such a contingency. At a final briefing he had categorically laid down that unless they could make a smooth landing they must abandon the attack and glide to safety in the valley. Those were his unquestioned orders; in a spasm of defiance Skorzeny elected to disobey. He shouted to the pilot: "Dive—crash-land! As near the hotel as you can."

Gran Sasso

They hurtled toward the mountain, the parachute brake whipping from their tail. In another instant the glider was jolting and pitching over the boulders like a dinghy flung upon a reef. A shuddering crash, then it was still.

He was alive, was Skorzeny's first thought; his second: *three minutes.*

He burst out of the wrecked glider; before him, like a cliff face twenty yards ahead, was the wall of the hotel. An Italian carabinier was standing there, rooted to the spot; he was stupefied by this apparition which had fallen almost at his feet out of the silent sky.

Skorzeny plunged past him to the first doorway: inside was a signalman tapping at a transmitter. A kick sent the chair from under him; Skorzeny's gun smashed the radio. But the room led nowhere.

Out again and full-tilt around a corner; he heard his men pounding behind him. A ten-foot terrace—they hoisted him up to it. From there, at an upper window, he spotted an unmistakable shorn head. "Get back!" he yelled to Mussolini. "Get back from the window." And dashed off around the terrace.

At last: the main entrance, flanked by two sentry posts. The guards wore a look of wild amazement; before they could get their breath, Skorzeny's men had booted their machine guns off the supports and scrambled through the door. A voice far behind was shouting in Italian; Soletti was adding to the confusion.

Skorzeny butted his way through a press of soldiers in the lobby; they were at too close quarters to shoot, even had they known what had come on them. He took a flight of stairs, turned a corner and flung open a door. The first thing he saw—Mussolini, with two Italian officers.

One of Skorzeny's brawniest subalterns, Lieut. Schwerdt, panted into the room after him. And just then two shining faces bobbed through the window: a couple of his men had swarmed up the lightning conductor to be with him. They overcame the Italian officers and dragged them from the room. Schwerdt took over as Mussolini's bodyguard.

From the window Skorzeny saw how other friends were faring. Radl was in sight, bounding toward the hotel; his glider had made a tolerable landing. Skorzeny hailed him with a shout: "We've got him here. All well so far. You look after the ground floor for me."

Three more gliders crash-landed, and men poured out. A fourth, landing some distance away, was smashed to pieces—no one moved from the wreckage. He could not hope for much more strength, so he turned back across the room, threw open the door and shouted in his bad Italian: "I want the commander. He must come at once." Some bewildered shouting—an Italian colonel appeared.

"I ask your immediate surrender," Skorzeny said in French. "Mussolini is already in our hands. We hold the building. If you want to avert senseless bloodshed you have sixty seconds to go and reflect."

Before the anxious minute was up the colonel came back. This time he carried a goblet brimming with red wine. "To a gallant victor," he bowed. Skorzeny thanked him and drained the beaker—he was thirsty. Cheers arose from the Germans below as a white sheet was flung from the window.

And now Skorzeny could spare time for Mussolini, who had been put into a corner of the room and there shielded by the bulk of Lieut. Schwerdt. He came forward: a stocky man looking older than his portraits showed him, in a blue suit that was too large. He wore a stubble of beard; his pate sprouted gray bristle. But his eyes were black, ardent and excited.

It was a moment for history—the thought crossed Skorzeny's mind. He spoke in German: "Duce, I have been sent by the Leader to set you free." And Mussolini, who always considered his public, replied for posterity: "I knew my friend Adolf Hitler would not abandon me. I embrace my liberator."

Skorzeny went to see to the disarming of the Italian garrison and discovered he had captured an important personage from Rome—none other than the General Cueli who was responsible for keeping Mussolini sealed up and shut away. Having, through his intercepted code message, unwittingly put Skorzeny on the scent leading to the Gran Sasso, he was further unfortunate in choosing this day for a visit to his charge. Skorzeny was delighted to see him.

But now for a more urgent matter: the getaway. Both ends of the funicular were in German hands; a telephone call from the valley station said the paratroops had carried out their part. Since Mussolini could never hope to reach Rome by road once the alarm was given, it had been arranged that paratroopers should capture the nearby airfield at Aquila and hold it briefly while Mussolini was taken off by three Heinkel planes. But now Skorzeny's luckless radio operator could not get through to signal the rescue planes to set out from Rome. The alternative plan worked out in advance called for a single light aircraft to land in the valley: this had been done, but in coming down its landing gear was damaged. There remained a third, desperate choice: Captain Gerlach, Student's personal pilot, might try to land a tiny Storch spotter plane alongside the hotel itself and pick up Mussolini from the mountain ledge—an operation so hair-raising that Skorzeny and Radl had put it to General Student as the most theoretical of possibilities.

Now it was their only hope.

Skorzeny glanced heavenward, and there, sure enough, the Storch was circling. Well, there was nothing for it. It had been said that Gerlach could do miracles in the air—let him perform one now.

Skorzeny got his troops, helped by some prisoners, to move the biggest boulders from a strip of the landing ledge and at a signal Gerlach came delicately down on it. Gerlach was ready for anything until he heard what was actually wanted. Then he recoiled. To weigh down his frail craft with the united loads, each in its own right substantial, of Mussolini and Skorzeny! It was mad: he refused point-blank to consider it.

Skorzeny took him aside. He told how Hitler had personally commanded him, Skorzeny, to deliver Mussolini: now Gerlach had in his hands the only means through which that mission could be fulfilled; if he should stand aloof he would be defying Hitler's wishes. And what would there be left to them to do if they failed the Leader? Blow their brains out; that was all.

Mussolini and Skorzeny

At last Gerlach gave in: "Have it your own way. If it's neck or nothing anyway we had better be on the move."

Squads hurriedly set to work again on the strip; even Mussolini lent a hand in rolling one or two boulders.

They squashed into the plane; Mussolini behind the pilot, Skorzeny behind Mussolini. With the engine turning, twelve men clung to the Storch, digging their heels in for a tug-of-war. Gerlach held a hand aloft until the engine's pitch rose in a crescendo; as he dropped his hand the men let go and the plane catapulted across the scree.

Skorzeny grasped the steel spars on either side of him, throwing his weight from side to side against the swaying motion as one wheel or the other was lifted by a rock. Suddenly a crevasse yawned before them; the plane shot over it and continued its career beyond, with the port wheel buckled. Then it went hurtling over the edge of the ravine.

In the group of Germans standing on the Gran Sasso, there was suddenly a gap. Radl had collapsed; he had fainted.

Gerlach brought off his miracle. With consummate skill he lifted the Storch gently from its nose dive to flatten out a few hundred feet above the valley floor.

The rest seemed smooth sailing; even the side-slip landing on starboard and rear wheels. And there, immaculate on the dusty airfield, forewarned by that instinct for an Occasion that animates aides-de-camp and diplomatic vice-marshals, there waited General Student's A.D.C., standing stiffly at the salute while the three crumpled figures stepped onto friendly soil.

It might not be friendly very long. There was fighting nearby and no time for ceremony. So Skorzeny helped Mussolini into a transport plane and soon they were flying through bumpy weather in the Alps.

Few are privileged, at ten thousand feet in a wind-tossed plane, to be the confidants of a Man of Destiny; Skorzeny would gladly have foregone the honor as he strained to follow his companion's account of betrayals, imprisonments, and wanderings from jail to jail. Mussolini went on shouting in German over the roar of engines and the storm that beat upon them; he was still intoxicated by the melodrama.

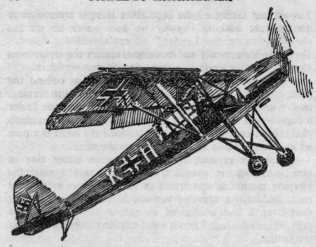

Fieseler Fl-67 Storch (Stork)

They put down in Vienna. Even in wartime the Imperial Hotel does not welcome with open arms visitors who arrive unshaven, unkempt and without luggage. However, the rooms had been booked by the Government and as the two guests, shabby as they looked, arrived in an important flurry of "security" toward midnight, the management had to put the best face on their displeasure. Then the telephone calls began.

Mussolini had gone straight upstairs. "I don't need anything at all," he said. "Not even pajamas. I'm going to bed." But there was to be no sleep for his deliverer.

Skorzeny had scarcely gained his room when the first call came—from Berlin. It was Himmler! He reached for an ash tray.

The Grand Master conveyed his stilted felicitations. Then, with an effort at solicitude, he suggested that since Skorzeny was in Vienna, he should have his gracious lady at the hotel with him until he went with Mussolini to be presented.

Presented? Why, of course, to Hitler.

While Skorzeny was calling his wife a full colonel was ushered in. He wore the regalia of the Knight's Cross, and now in the center of the carpet he clicked his heels, bowed, and taking off the decoration hung it around Skorzeny's neck.

"Orders of the Leader," he explained: for the first time this high award had been conferred on the very day that it was earned. It was the colonel's own Cross that he was giving him.

Skorzeny's wife entered. Hardly had they met when the telephone jangled once more. This time the hotel operator was beside himself: Adolf Hitler on the line from the Wolf's Lair.

Hitler was in a transport of delight. "Major Skorzeny," he burst out, thus festively announcing his protégé's instant preferment. "Major Skorzeny, you are a man after my own heart. You have gained the day and crowned our mission with success. Your Leader thanks you!"

Marshal Göring took the telephone from Hitler. Keitel and others of the great were also clamoring to speak to him. Vienna radio had spread the news; the capital was in a ferment—all Europe was roused from sleep.

VI

*Let us rejoice with all our hearts. . . . I now have
the feeling that our lucky streak has set in again.
. . . The liberation of the Duce has caused a great
sensation at home and abroad. . . . Even upon
the enemy the effect of this melodramatic deliverance is enormous. Friend and foe alike are full
of admiration. . . . There has hardly been a military event during the entire war that has so
deeply stirred the emotions. . . . We are able to
celebrate a first-class moral victory.*

GOEBBELS' DIARIES, September, 1943

It must not be allowed to happen too often. That seems
to have been the unspoken agreement of the High Command when their world of prudent calculation was rocked
by a storm of triumph which almost blew them off their
feet.

The Gran Sasso exploit shone out, a *coup de théâtre*,
against the dark backcloth of Germany's misfortunes. That
the stroke should have been carried through by an outsider in brazen defiance of the rules was bad enough; but
what was almost too much to be borne was the opportunity it gave to that other outsider, the Stage Director,
to step into the limelight and regild his own prestige.

One cannot but feel for the High Command. Long
had they suffered Hitler's caprices; now, just when his
famous intuition had become a byword, so that there
might at last be some chance of sound judgment—*their*
judgment—taking over again, the wildest chance of all had
outrageously succeeded.

The Leader was in his seventh heaven—quite insupportable. He danced at the news as he had danced only after the fall of France. The romantic had always drawn him; he respected the bizarre: to his incurable Wagnerianism the whole affair was pure intoxication. What other tyrant, he must have asked, would risk the mockery of the world to save a bankrupt friend—or send forth an unknown champion on so crucial an errand?

So when Skorzeny arrived at the Wolf's Lair, which a few weeks before he had approached with such trepidation, he was received like a conquering hero. Pictures show a delighted Hitler clasping Skorzeny's hand while the generals dutifully applaud. Medals rained down on him.

Mussolini—shaved, refreshed and full of plans for a comeback—bestowed on his rescuer the Order of the Hundred Musketeers, of which there might be only as many members. Marshal Göring made an adroitly timed entrance, by special train, to present the Gold Medal of the Air Force. At the Sports Palace in Berlin a few days later Skorzeny was starred in a patriotic rally and there, in his turn, he pinned awards for gallantry on other soldiers.

Invitations poured in. Lunch with Martin Bormann, Hitler's deputy. Tea with Foreign Minister Ribbentrop. Dinner with Dr. Goebbels—he was becoming a drawing-room lion. But when the Propaganda Minister told him venomous anecdotes about other Cabinet Ministers there could be no vestigial doubt—he had arrived.

At midnight he was privileged to join the intimate circle of those to whom Hitler opened his heart at each day's end. The Leader sipped an amber fluid from a glass balanced on a silver saucer. A servant whispered in Skorzeny's ear: "If you don't really like tea at this hour—I can always get you coffee." But although Hitler made much of him, discoursing on his plans to embellish the Austrian city of Linz when the war was won and saying that he must return often for such talks, Skorzeny went to no more tea parties at the Wolf's Lair.

A more ambitious man might have turned this season of delirium to any account he liked. But Skorzeny quickly tired of the dash and glitter of Hitler's court and the heavily curtained atmosphere of sycophancy which surrounded him. Above all, he was sickened by vainglorious accounts of the Gran Sasso action; Allied reports were just and generous enough. If anything made up for all the fuss it was the thousands of letters from men on every front saying that his success had put new heart into them.

One task which Hitler imposed before letting him leave headquarters was delicate. He had to give an audience of tight-lipped generals a lecture on the techniques of commando attack as exemplified by Mussolini's rescue. It seems their peace of mind was disturbed by what he said, because next morning the Chief of Security took him on an inspection tour: he wanted to be sure that in case the enemy thought of making a similar attempt to reach Hitler there would be no gaps in their defenses. Skorzeny pointed out two or three weak points: the officer went blue when cheerfully assured that, whatever he did, a determined and ingenious enemy would always find a way in.

It was obvious by now that the generals were willing to accept Skorzeny on their own terms, just as they accepted the "Commandos," with nothing of the commando spirit. But if there could be no common ground between them, at least his hour of glory put him on easy terms with people he had known only through the enlarging lens of propaganda. If on approach their stature shrank; if public men turned out to have but little interest in the public weal, while senior officers showed a blank incomprehension of realities—he would know better how to deal with them in the future.

There was an unexpected sequel in the British Parliament to Mussolini's rescue. It came in a speech from Winston Churchill, to whom this evidence of a new force at work in the Axis camp was no less challenging than the flight of a captive Caesar. When he had given the House of Commons a full account of the rescue, as far as it was then known, the Prime Minister declared:

"The stroke was one of great daring and conducted with a heavy force. It certainly shows there are many possibilities of this kind open in modern war."

Hitler had reached the same conclusion, and he was always quick to act on a heterodox idea. Every step in the Leader's rise to power had been taken by outwitting the complacent. Now, with the tide against him, he had found the one man he could trust to go ahead on his own —an up-to-date d'Artagnan with a dazzling technique.

On the wings of his first, incredible success, Skorzeny soared over the heads of his contemporaries into Hitler's favor. And although their future meetings were few and formal, the aura which this favor lent Skorzeny helped him to get at least token sanction for enterprises which, in another pilot's hands, must have splintered on the reefs of bureaucratic obduracy.

Before allowing Skorzeny to leave the Wolf's Lair on this second visit, Hitler gave his new favorite the one prize that he wanted: a battalion of special troops for every front. Under the Leader's eye, General Jodl beamed agreement. Where would Skorzeny find the men? Why, said Jodl, he could straightaway enlist four thousand from the Brandenburg Division—wonderful material there, excellent stuff.

Skorzeny needed no second invitation: he had enjoyed a foretaste of the Brandenburgers' quality in the person of Adrian Freiheer von Foelkersam, who with some other officers from that division had asked for a transfer to the commandos. Born in Riga, he was the scion of a Baltic German house—his grandfather fought as an admiral in the Czar's navy against the Japanese. At twenty-nine he spoke fluent Russian, French and English; he had studied economics at Berlin and Vienna universities and was a tireless worker.

Like many others eager to take the craziest risks if they could use their heads in doing so, von Foelkersam had joined the Brandenburg unit when it was created in 1939 as a hush-hush battalion in which foreign-language speakers and specialist volunteers might enroll. In the first few months they were used on work of secrecy and danger; then as the battalion grew, first to a regiment and then to a division, the generals began to employ it on everyday front-line work. Thus Germany's young men of brains and background, the men who had traveled abroad and spoke Western languages, were being squandered in routine battles in the Balkans or on the Eastern front.

That was why von Foelkersam arrived at Friedenthal to join the commandos. The gifts which made him Skorzeny's chief-of-staff unhappily robbed him of many chances to be in the forefront of action. "Adrian was a Junker, but in the best sense of that discredited word—otherwise," Skorzeny baldly explains, "we should not have got on at all. He regarded duty and leadership as the privileges of a noble name."

By 1943 complaints about using the Brandenburg division as cannon fodder, and defections such as von Foelkersam's, had soured the temper of the High Command. What to do with all this unmilitary versatility in the mass? Then came Skorzeny, and they were doubtless glad of the chance to dump the problem into his lap.

Back at Friedenthal—a "valley of peace" indeed after the turbulence of Berlin and the Wolf's Lair—vigorous training began. Skorzeny wanted the moon: each of his commandos should be a parachutist, a swimmer, a linguist, a saboteur; he would be able to drive—and repair —anything from a steam roller to a locomotive; and so on. Soon enough, he realized that he would have to cut his coat according to his cloth, and there was precious little time for tailoring. Snapshots, hundreds of them, taken at Friedenthal, show Skorzeny in the happiest camaraderie with his men; the officers can be picked out by their careworn look. "Naturally!" said Skorzeny, when challenged with this. "I worked my poor young officers to death."

Armed S.S. had told him to put in for all the equipment he needed. An exhaustive list was sent; for weeks there was no response. When the letter came Skorzeny tore it open: all their requirements were approved! But, ran the last sentence, since Major Skorzeny now exercised the powers of a divisional commander, he could not look to the Armed S.S. for these supplies; he must become independent.

Radl roared at the mad logic of the headquarters mind: then quickly became practical. Why, this letter was a license to plunder every arsenal and supply depot in Europe! So, at least, they could use it; and desperate situations needed desperate measures.

Skorzeny grimly agreed. Such was the start of his career as a bandit. He abstracted weapons and left promissory notes. He borrowed stores with no intention of returning them; Radl joyfully involved himself in streams of applications for supplies he had already taken or quoted nonexistent permits for requisitioning more.

They started by stealing equipment, and went on to steal men. The Gran Sasso had lit a beacon at Friedenthal for the adventurous. Since Skorzeny's command included elements of all three Services he was besieged by volunteers not only from the Army, but from the Navy and Air Force too. They came thronging to his new flag: the fire-eaters, the knights-errant and the ne'er-do-wells, all ready to march up to the cannon's mouth instantly—if only they could wangle a transfer to Friedenthal. Skorzeny and Radl began to "rustle" men as border raiders lift cattle; once in sanctuary at Friedenthal, the toughest malcontents from other units became docile, trembling at a word lest it should rob them of their chance. Radl eluded the pursuit; his eager lip service to regulations bemused all who were not hobbled from the start by festoons of red tape.

This period of recruiting and training was further enlivened by two calls from the Wolf's Lair. Hitler's mind was still running on prestidigitation, for he asked Skorzeny to snatch him two more international figures—and everything was made ready to do so.

First victim was to be Marshal Pétain, the Vichy Head of State who had sat on the fence so long between Germany and the Allies that nobody was sure what he would do next. Hitler had been inflamed by alarming—if contradictory—reports from his spies. One group said the old man was preparing to spirit his Government off to North Africa, there to throw in his lot with the Allies. A second warned that Pétain's London rival, General de Gaulle, was about to do him some mischief because he meant to help Germany after all. Hitler ordered that whatever it was all about—and it is amusing to find that the Germans were just as badly stumped by the Vichy riddle as were the Allies—Skorzeny was to be ready to whip the chief actors from the stage.

He went with von Foelkersam to Paris; there he would get his orders. They called hopefully at the Hotel Continental in the Rue de Rivoli and found it swarming with German staff officers, who knew very little; then at the Champs-Élysées bureaus of the all-seeing S.S. Police, who knew still less. So with sanction from the Wolf's Lair they collected a few thousand troops and police for whatever lay ahead. The force was headed by a general—Skorzeny was a major. When they got word at last to go on to Vichy, the general solved the problem of precedence on the outskirts of Pétain's capital; he vanished into an *auberge* renowned for its cooking and did not emerge again.

Skorzeny had been told he must quietly surround the town so as to be able to block all highways in and out of it. On getting the signal "The wolf howls," he should move into the town and seize the Government.

He made his dispositions: a double cordon laid lightly around Vichy, but not close enough to put Pétain on his guard; and an assault force which would reach the Government offices in ten minutes. With von Foelkersam he strolled through the unsuspecting spa, enjoying the disguise of mufti and discussing over coffee and *croissants* how the troops would dash across the formal gardens and then, by seizing a covered bridge which linked two hotels, occupy the main buildings before French troops were alarmed.

The plan was based on first-hand observation—and particularly on the discovery that Vichy had the siesta habit. Skorzeny determined—when the wolf howled—that he would march peaceably into the town at two in the afternoon when everybody was asleep. He also impressed on his little assault force that there was to be no shooting without orders, even if the French garrison fired first. Then he waited. He waited a month: at midnight he was called to Paris and connected by telephone with Hitler's headquarters. Orders at last: "Return to Vichy and stand by." Finally, just in time for Christmas leave, he was told to pack up and send his men back to their units; the only dash they made was to board the Paris express. Pétain was left to pursue his enigmatic course, quite unaware of the travel plans that Skorzeny had prepared for him.

"Get Marshal Tito—alive or dead!" That was the next challenge tossed to Skorzeny. He snapped it up with relish. The guerrilla chief had beaten off repeated offensives and his ragged partisans were pinning down forces badly needed on other fronts. The High Command were willing to have this Yugoslav thorn pulled from their flesh by anyone—even Skorzeny.

He flew to Belgrade: where was Tito? Five different intelligence reports put the marshal in five different mountain areas. Days of head-splitting argument followed. It was clear only that a war of bloodthirsty reprisals was laced with Balkan politics which Skorzeny found more obscure than Vichy's, more entangled than anything in Rome. As well as Tito's communists, the Germans were still supposed to be fighting General Mihailovitch's royalists, while motley forces of Serb Chetniks and Croatian Ustachi changed sides and positions in a confused mêlée. Italian garrisons, marooned since Badoglio's surrender, had laid down arms, which were joyfully seized by their several enemies. What really mattered was the swelling threat of Tito with his one hundred thousand "full-time" guerrillas who held wide tracts already and could strike everywhere else. Tito was the key, and now that the British were arranging for massive air drops, the Germans must make an end of Tito—at once.

Skorzeny knew he would never make sure of anything in this hotbed of rumor, so with two N.C.O.'s he left the capital for Agram, in the heart of Tito's territory. Driving in his Mercedes through country which had seen no German car for months, he knew that half the workers in the fields were ready to put down the spade for the rifle at a moment's notice, and he had to gamble on passing before the moment was up. They reached an isolated outpost on the mountains at Fruska Gora; at lunch the German commander told spine-tingling tales of ambuscades ahead. Even their village doctor was honorary surgeon to the Partisans, he said, and honorary surgeon to the Germans as well. When at last they got to Agram no one there would believe they had motored from Belgrade.

It took four weeks to trace Tito. He was in Western Bosnia at Dvar with a British Military Mission. His secret headquarters were in a cliffside cave which overlooked the town—and all approaches.

Skorzeny intended to pounce with men disguised as Partisans and he sent von Foelkersam to inform the German general in nominal command of the Dvar area. The general was extremely chilly. The reason came out a day or two later; a Yugoslav agent of Skorzeny's said the general had his own plans for storming Tito's base—and in the next few days this was advertised by planes which reconnoitered Dvar.

Skorzeny radioed the general that as his own agents knew about the impending operation it was likely the Partisans had wind of it too; and if Tito got away this time, he would not be easy to approach again. Skorzeny was willing to put himself under the general's orders—they could work together.

But the general would not be stayed. He acted as if Skorzeny was a rival. To a task calling for the scalpel, he brought a sledge hammer—full-scale airborne invasions of the Dvar Valley with bombers, paratroops and gliders. The hammer missed, of course. All the Germans captured was an empty uniform stitched with gold stars. The marshal had moved on, but his Partisans stayed behind to give as good as they got: German infantry had to battle through the mountains to rescue the general's survivors.

When next heard of, Tito was away in the island of
Vis, off the Adriatic coast of Yugoslavia. Skorzeny wanted
to make a swoop across the straits, but by then he was up
to the ears in other enterprises.

"Secret Weapons," for instance, which sounded so
esoteric but were often simple improvisations, came into
his sphere. In the underwater world the individual was
still king: a solitary man could slip under the guard of
thousands in armor-plated ships, could pass through nets
and minefields and radar screens to make his kill. It called
for nerve that transcended anything Skorzeny had met in
land warfare.

Midget submarines were still in their teething stage in
Germany, so Skorzeny was glad to learn from Italian experience of underwater raids on Gibraltar and Alexandria,
where the battle line of the British Mediterranean fleet
had been put out of action at a critical time by attacks on
the *Queen Elizabeth* and *Valiant* in harbor. After Italy's
collapse her famous small-boat leader Prince Valerio Bor-
ghese joined Mussolini's new Government in the North
with his entire unit. He worked closely with Skorzeny on
developing new devices such as the explosives-packed
speedboat which ejects its pilot just before it strikes.

If the German Navy was penned into port by Allied
might as the war went on, many sailors were not. The
best of them tumbled into a force of sea commandos
headed by Admiral Heye who enjoyed studying "secret
weapons" with Skorzeny. The Neger was one of the most

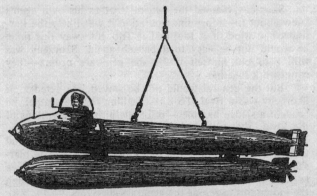

Neger

effective results of their collaboration. To construct a Neger you simply scooped the charge out of a torpedo, fitted controls with a glass cupola for a pilot, and slung a second (live) torpedo underneath it. The pilot would unleash the live torpedo as he swerved away from the target —and from the explosion which followed. Twenty Negers went out against the Allied bridgehead fleet at Anzio, south of Rome: fourteen pilots reported back to Skorzeny. For the loss of six men they had damaged a cruiser, sunk a second warship and crippled or sent to the bottom six thousand tons of merchant shipping.

Soon Negers were out in the Channel as well as in the Mediterranean. The enemy came to know them, so empty glass cupolas were floated out; then, when all the Allied guns were firing in one direction, the real Negers would attack from the other. These were essentially surprise weapons: crude, primitive, but the more effective in being the invention of a moment, since they could be replaced or adapted as soon as their secret was out.

D-day in France loomed near. Studying air pictures of English ports, Skorzeny racked his brains over unfamiliar shapes—and never guessed they were pieces of jigsaws which, assembled off Normandy, would become prefabricated harbors. He was shrewder in his estimate of the landing places: those the Allies chose were among the ten he had decided on after a scrutiny of naval charts. He planned his own "reception party" and moved heaven and earth for approval of the scheme. Sea commandos would greet the Allies with new devices, planes would set off, by radio, explosives buried under the beaches—there were all manner of ingenious ideas which might throw an invader off his balance at a critical moment. When the verdict arrived Skorzeny found that he had banged his head against the unchanging fortress of Headquarters.

His plan, on which everyone at Friedenthal had worked double hours, was commended in warmest terms: it redounded to their credit; it was deserving of all praise. "But," said the Western Front Command in Paris, *"since the Leader has said the Atlantic Wall is invulnerable, and since the preparations Major Skorzeny proposes might suggest to the troops witnessing them that there are some doubts about this question after all, the scheme cannot be approved, either in whole or part."*

The landings were met by regular forces in well-regulated array. Hard pounding followed; the Allies pounded the harder. In a few weeks the crust was broken: Paris was open—and at Friedenthal they tried to swallow their misgivings about the war. The German generals, they argued, might still have something up their sleeves, some special surprise. . . .

And so some of them had.

VII

In the dictionary of the soldier the terms "treason" and "Plot against the State" do not exist. This is the worst dilemma a soldier can be faced with.

GENERAL HALDER, before the Nuremberg Tribunal

Let dog eat dog.

WINSTON CHURCHILL

I agree that the Allies unfortunately discounted the German plots against Hitler. This was true both in your country and my own.

ALLEN W. DULLES,
Chief of the U. S. Central Intelligence Agency,
in a letter to the author, May, 1953

The events of July 20, 1944—that day of infamy in the Nazi calendar—are treasured in Skorzeny's mind as a classic of confusion. But for the fact of his own, accidental, rôle in it he might be inclined to fancy that the whole affair in all its chaotic detail had been staged by some master hand. He still feels, looking back on it, rather like a man who strayed into some Wild West film depicting a gambling den when the stakes are high—and the lights are suddenly shot out.

At noon on that day, which was six weeks after the Allies got ashore in Normandy, a group of high staff officers, utterly quiet, were waiting for news in the War Office—and it was not news from the front. They stood in the room of General Olbricht, Chief of Staff, Home Forces, like souls expecting Judgment. They had ears only for the telephone: its ring next minute, in an hour, in two hours, might be the signal for revolution.

Half-past twelve—the bomb must have been planted by now, surely. One o'clock: nothing mattered but that telephone. Two . . . two-thirty.

At half-past three it rang. "Who? What? He's dead!"

It had happened at last. It had come off. The men in the room knew just what to do. "Plan Valkyrie!" ordered General Olbricht. The others jumped to it—exultant in their relief. Within seconds the code name "Valkyrie" went flashing around Europe from Berlin. In Paris, Vienna, Munich, Brussels, at every H.Q. in every country, envelopes were being slit, sealed orders to be opened only when the signal came were being read.

"Valkyrie" ordained the round-up by the Army of all the Party chiefs, starting with Dr. Goebbels, Berlin's boss; and the seizure of the capital by Home Forces. It meant the transfer of power to a surrender Government and the ending of the war at once.

The men who had waited for the telephone call set about their work with triumphant confidence. There was much to be done—for was not Hitler dead?

"Hitler dead?" The frightened question was being whispered in the capital that afternoon. Skorzeny was there and heard it, but he set little store by Berlin rumors. He was busy getting off to Vienna, where there was an interesting new job; and he was looking forward to being home again, especially in midsummer when Austria would be at its best. With Karl Radl, he settled down in a reserved carriage; they were in high spirits as the train rattled into the suburbs.

"Major Skorzeny, Major Skorzeny!" They had pulled up at the last stop before leaving Berlin—and there his name was being called. A panting subaltern came up to the

window. Orders to come back at once. He was wanted at
Armed S.S. Headquarters. It was true—someone had tried
to kill Hitler.

Still incredulous, Skorzeny let Radl go on alone, promising to join him by the next train. As they drove back to
Berlin, the breathless messenger told him that Hitler had
been wounded by assassins. Armored units were moving
on the capital. Conflicting orders were coming from all
over the place. No one knew who was in charge. The
Army and the S.S. might come to blows. . . .

At S.S. Intelligence Headquarters they came upon the
first picture of panic. A group of uniformed clerks surged
around the entrance: someone had put machine pistols
into their hands and told them to bar the way. Skorzeny
herded the clerks down to a basement. They must learn to
handle weapons before they carried them, he said—and
locked them up.

Upstairs he found who had issued the guns: young
Walther Schellenberg, his mentor of the drop-by-drop technique. By clinging to Himmler's sleeve Schellenberg had
become Intelligence Chief, a post of dignity and power he
would gladly have relinquished until this crisis was over.
In the black-and-silver trappings of an S.S. brigadier, he
sat at his desk behind a loaded revolver. "If they come for
me I am ready," he burst out. "I shall defend myself; you
can be sure of that."

Skorzeny asked what he knew. It was little enough;
all they were sure of was that Hitler's death had been pro-
claimed—and then it had been denied. The announcement
came from the Home Forces Headquarters in the War
Office; the denial from the High Command at Hitler's
headquarters. There were rumors of clashes in Berlin; of
marches and countermarches. How could one know what
to believe?

Not, thought Skorzeny, by waiting behind a desk for
"them" to come. First he telephoned von Foelkersam to
alert all their units and to hurry over with a company of
troops to guard the S.S. Intelligence building. Then he
went out into the streets to see what he could discover.

He drove down the Wilhelmstrasse—it looked as life-
less as any other Government quarter, in peace or war,
after five P.M. Schellenberg had babbled something about
armor moving up against the Ministries; he decided to take
the bull by the horns and go up to Armored G.H.Q.; but

on turning in that direction he found the avenue leading to it was barred by tanks. Whose side were they on? Did they know themselves? Skorzeny drew himself up in the moving car to suggest that their side was his side and that his presence was expected. The tankmen saluted and let him pass: he was in.

Quickly he made his way to the office of General Bolbrinker, the commanding officer, but Bolbrinker, too, was completely at a loss. He had been told by the War Office to bring his armored units right into Berlin—right, he had done it; then he had been told to smoke out a mutiny at the barracks of the Armed S.S.—well, he was ready to do that too; but a signal from the High Command countermanded it. Really he supposed he should not take orders except through his own chief, General Guderian. But with Guderian away, what was he to do?

Skorzeny foresaw that even a reconnaissance group of tanks sent over to the S.S. barracks while all Berlin was on tenterhooks might be enough to start the shooting. And soon it would be dark; that would add to the confusion. He had better try to soothe the ruffled Bolbrinker.

"Do nothing for the moment," he advised. "I've just come from S.S. Intelligence; no trouble there. If you like, I'll go over to their barracks now and let you know if I scent mutiny."

Bolbrinker accepted this idea with relief. Arrived at the barracks of the Armed S.S., Skorzeny found that no one had mutinied and no one had orders to intervene anywhere; so on the colonel's promise not to do anything hasty, he telephoned General Bolbrinker that he could keep his tanks at home.

What other units might have received inflammatory orders? Skorzeny's mind jumped to the Airborne troops— they, too, were based in the capital. He drove out to see them at their lakeside center. All seemed quiet, yet if a call should come from the War Office, which seemed to be the origin of the mischief, there were enough paratrooping desperadoes under the hotheaded young officers to rush out and set all Berlin by the ears. Their commander must be warned—but he was not to be found.

It was nine-thirty before Skorzeny tracked down General Student. The victor of Rotterdam and Crete, whose orders not to crash-land on the Gran Sasso he had disobeyed, knew nothing of the hubbub in Berlin. Sitting in his dressing gown on the terrace of his house, he was tut-tutting over sheaves of office memoranda while his wife stitched at her embroidery: they made an idyll of sub-urban peace under a frilly reading lamp.

Midway through his visitor's recital Student threw himself back in his wicker chair. "Plots and mutinies?" he cried. "My dear Skorzeny, you must be dreaming." The leader of Germany's most modern arm refused to believe anything so irregular could happen. Nor would he be bus-tled into signaling his detachments all over Europe to take orders only from himself: that was much too unusual. Only after long argument did the general give ground—and then the telephone rang.

It was Göring. The marshal was calling from the Wolf's Lair. Skorzeny could hear his voice rasping with excitement: "Plot to murder Hitler . . . War Office gone crazy . . . They're all up to the neck in it."

No one should accept orders from the Home Forces, Göring said; they were traitors; only the High Command should be obeyed. The airborne troops everywhere must be kept in. Calm, the marshal bellowed, was all-important—unless they wanted civil war.

Leaving a subdued Student to warn his battalions one by one, Skorzeny drove back to S.S. Intelligence Head-quarters, where he found Schellenberg protected by the newly arrived company of troops from Friedenthal. The sleek and slim brigadier looked more than ever like a ghost —for Himmler had just telephoned him orders to arrest Canaris. Admiral Canaris, the former head of Military Intelligence, to be arrested! Well, he would have to do it, of course, but not single-handed; Skorzeny must give him a bodyguard: an officer, and at least ten men—on second thought, he would like a full platoon.

Since Canaris, however formidable his past, had fallen months ago from power and was now known to keep house guarded only by a swarm of dachshunds, Skorzeny suggested a single officer might be help enough to appre-hend him; and Schellenberg, seeking strength in the feel of his revolver, went out into the night to bring Canaris back.

Now that was over, Skorzeny decided he could go on and join Karl Radl in Vienna. But no; Hitler's headquarters were on the telephone for him. He was to hurry over all the troops he had "to help Major Remer outside the War

Office." It was the first order Skorzeny had been given since his recall to Berlin—and it would be the last.

Major Remer, it seemed, commanded the Greater Berlin Guard Battalion. He introduced himself at the entrance to the War Office when Skorzeny arrived, explaining that he had already cut off the whole group of buildings with his men.

Here was another topsy-turvy situation. A few hours earlier the major had been suddenly ordered by the War Office to occupy Hitler's Chancellery, as well as the chief Ministries, and to arrest the Party leaders. At the Propaganda Ministry, however, Goebbels persuaded him to speak on a private line to the Wolf's Lair. Hitler himself came to the telephone—and then the fat was in the fire. Where had Remer got those orders from? Was his battalion ready to march? Then let him march it at once to the War Office and seal off that nest of traitors. So there he was.

While Skorzeny was standing outside the War Office there was a sudden flurry of salutes. No one to leave: then what of this dignitary who emerged from the gateway and got into his car? Skorzeny was told it was General Fromm, Home Army Commander-in-Chief; and he heard Fromm's parting words: "I shall be going home now; you can get me at my flat." With a crunch of tires he was away. Skorzeny and Remer agreed that from now on no one, however exalted in rank, should be allowed to pass out.

Posting his troops inside the courtyard of the War Office, Skorzeny then marched upstairs with von Foelkersam and another of his officers. Their boots echoed from silent stone walls; all at once, on the second floor, they fell into an ambush. A group of staff officers sprang out on them, waving machine pistols and demanding their business. Much relieved to know the intruders had come in peace, they burst into high-pitched explanation.

It seemed the curtain had just come down upon a scene of military fratricide that had left them shaking in their shoes. There had been murders, suicides and executions. The paroxysm was over now, they hoped; never had they known the like.

Skorzeny went from one room to another; in each his arrival startled a group with pistols in their unaccustomed hands. These were the disheveled remnants of what Karl Radl had called "the main enemy": the dapper tribe in red-striped trousers who booby-trapped provincials like himself; the haughty clerks who refused supplies; the desk-bound feudatories no soldier dared offend. White-faced, they stared as if he were some dangerous djini from Arabia who would not be conjured back into his jar.

From room to room he went, from floor to floor. Telephones were ringing; no one picked them up. Message machines were ticking out their unread screeds. This had been going on for the most part of a day, and Skorzeny was shocked to see it. So often had he chafed because some order had not come through from the War Office: now that the whole monstrous honeycomb was hushed, the flow of supplies and reinforcements all over Europe must be coming to a standstill. Paralysis would begin to set in unless someone awoke the hive to life.

He went up to some officers he had met before; they admitted something should be done—but what, and by whom? The Commander-in-Chief had gone off. Other senior officers had been victims of—well, of what had just happened. Nobody had been able to get Hitler's headquarters for hours; telephone lines to the High Command were jammed with calls.

Skorzeny broke into this flow of pretexts for nothing being done; he knew it could go on forever. He suggested to the officers around him that they should set an example by going back to their desks—nothing so reassuring, after all, as doing the usual thing. They yielded to this appeal. Other officers, seeing them at work, joined in the march back to normality; soon they were sharply recalling their own subordinates to a sense of duty. With a rising hum, the hive began to buzz again.

And now Skorzeny could begin to piece together an outline of "what had just happened." Staff officers told him how they had been unwitting witnesses, if not accessories, of a day of historic betrayals—and of the months that had led up to it; they "simply had no idea" what was going on in their midst. Now, of course, the details hung together. It started in the War Office with that fellow von Stauffenberg. . . .

Count von Stauffenberg was a new broom; to the chagrin of the career men he had been brought in a few months ago and at once made General Olbricht's right-hand man in the office of the Chief-of-Staff. Von Stauffenberg had risen to colonel in Rommel's desert campaigns; he had lost his right arm, two fingers of the left hand and the sight of one eye. Yet this was the agent—the one disabled man among them—whom the plotters had chosen to kill Hitler: he could not even fire a pistol; it had to be a bomb. Von Stauffenberg was made liaison man with the Wolf's Lair.

Just before Skorzeny had arrived at the War Office, they went on, Hitler himself had spoken on the radio to prove that he was not dead. Those who heard him said he fastened the plot onto "a small clique of traitors"; it had nothing to do with the Armed Forces. His listeners in the War Office knew better, for already it was clear to them that young von Stauffenberg had been maneuvered into his new post by Army confederates who knew it would give him the opportunity of taking his bomb to the Wolf's Lair.

All sorts of people, as it later appeared, were mixed up in the July 20 plot, but its prime sponsors were a group of active and compulsorily retired officers. In corners of the Mess, in castles and country houses with their civilian accomplices, they discussed endlessly what they should do. How they talked, these generals. Some wanted to make sure the war could not be won before casting out the Nazi leaders; others would have welcomed defeat so as to be rid of them. Some would kill; others imprison the dictator. Some were for friendship with Moscow—most of them detested Russia more than they hated Hitler. If it had been left to the generals, then very likely nothing would have been done. It was purely by chance that they found in Colonel von Stauffenberg the one man who knew his own mind and would lose no time.

Once von Stauffenberg had been wangled into the War Office it was simply a matter of going on an official mission to the Wolf's Lair. On the morning of July 20 his chance came. . . . He left the dispatch case with a time bomb under Hitler's conference table and walked out of the meeting under pretext of a telephone call. A few minutes later he saw the building blown sky high; it was his jubilant voice from the airport on his way back to the War Office that had set "Valkyrie" into effect.

Skorzeny got an officer to show him von Stauffenberg's room. His desk had already been broken open and the drawers ransacked, but one or two things had been overlooked. The first was a copy of Plan "Valkyrie"—its trumpet sound mocking Hitler's Wagnerian passion—which had been thrust into a file labeled "Scheme for defending Berlin from air attack"; von Stauffenberg had been rightly confident that it would gather dust under this camouflage until he wanted it. The second find was a parlor game in which pawns representing armies moved across the map of Europe according to the throw of the dice—so this was how they killed time in the "higher echelons" of the War Office!

Skorzeny turned back to the "Valkyrie" file and was freshly amazed to read its instructions for seizing nerve-centers and rounding up Hitler's followers. For weeks copies of this candid document had been docketed in offices all over Europe in the form of orders which were not to be read until the code word "Valkyrie" was received. Had a single copy been opened anywhere before the proper time the whole conspiracy would have blown; but the plotters had counted—and not in vain—on strict compliance with the rules.

So then, it seemed, von Stauffenberg's telephone call had set the wheels of chaos moving. The "Valkyrie" signal flashed out from the War Office; revolution by rule at once began in Paris, Brussels and many German cities which were told Hitler was dead and an anti-Nazi Government had taken over. The key posts had been allocated in advance: General Ludwig Beck would head the new State; Field-Marshal von Witzleben would be Commander-in-Chief of the Armed Forces; and General Olbricht, who had sent out Hitler's executioner from the War Office, would be Minister for War.

In the War Office center of the plot the one enigma for the conspirators was their Commander-in-Chief, General Fromm. Here was a cat that might jump either way. So after they had sent out the "Valkyrie" signal the conspirators, led by Beck and Olbricht, marched into Fromm's office. Hitler was dead, they told him; he could come out now into the open as one of the nation's saviors. But Fromm wanted to be sure. He picked up the telephone and asked for the Wolf's Lair. To the horror of the plotters he got through.

Once again a general had bungled. The communications chief at Hitler's headquarters, who was in the plot, had failed in his undertaking to blow up the signals center, so that in a few minutes on the line to Göring, Fromm knew the truth. Hitler's luck had held: scarred, deafened, and scorched by the bomb which had killed or wounded twenty-four others, he was still capable of collecting his senses—and of getting his revenge.

Just as Fromm put down the telephone, von Stauffenberg burst into the War Office: "Hitler is dead—I killed him!" he shouted. "Hitler is alive—you are all under arrest," was General Fromm's retort. Then and there—since there was no going back now—the conspirators should have made an end of Fromm; instead, they locked him in an office while they tried to get one of their number, General Hoeppner, to take over as Commander-in-Chief. Hoeppner objected that he must have his instructions in writing. Written orders for a mutiny! Small wonder General Fromm was soon able, with the help of some of his cronies, to turn the tables on the plotters: his jailers had overlooked that the room in which he had been put contained a telephone. Then the Commander-in-Chief started a counterrevolution of his own. He began a series of drumhead court-martials—and executions—to kill off the plotters before they implicated him. Thus he began the shootings which had so unnerved the War Office.

Fallschirmjäger Gewehr (F.G. 42)

Terrified onlookers told Skorzeny how von Stauffenberg, with General Olbricht and another officer, had been taken out into the courtyard and held in the headlights of an armored car before a shooting squad. Then there had been a volley of shots from the Commander-in-Chief's

room: it was explained that General Beck had been offered
the privilege of the pistol; failing twice to kill himself he
had been given the *coup de grâce* on Fromm's orders. General Hoeppner was also offered a revolver; juridical to the
last, he refused to act as his own judge and executioner.

During this private purge, Europe had been thrown
into chaos for the second time in the day. Unending calls
from the Wolf's Lair put Plan "Valkyrie" violently into
reverse. Berlin received a torrent of signals; as the night
drew on the War Office became more and more the target
of Hitler's suspicions: it must be isolated, it must be cut
off. General Fromm did not wait. Having polished off the
men who might have blabbed, he washed his hands,
locked his desk and went on his ambiguous way just in
time for Skorzeny to see the last of him.

So now, the hive lacked its queen bee. This brought
hiatus: a staff colonel told Skorzeny that a call for reinforcements to the Eastern front had just come in: they
had the order ready, but there was no Commander-in-
Chief to approve it. What could be done? "I'll sign for
him," Skorzeny found himself replying: he was thinking of
his comrades at the front. The colonel accepted the stranger's usurpation of authority. Presently there was a dispatch
needing the initials of von Stauffenberg—his body lay under a tarpaulin in the courtyard below; then an erroneous
message which only General Olbricht, who also was no
more, could countermand.

There was still no way of getting through to the High
Command. Who would answer for it if there were mistakes? Shutting his eyes to the chances of retribution,
Skorzeny said he would. Since no one else was willing to
shoulder responsibility in this labyrinth of proper channels
or to close the links in the chain of command, he would
have to do so himself, and since there was nobody he
could ask for emergency powers—well, he would have to
take them. At least men and munitions would be kept
moving; and for once, with expedition.

When, some hours later, he got through to the Wolf's
Lair he was simply told to carry on; someone would eventually take over. All next day it was the same: whenever
he spoke to the High Command they fobbed him off with
promises. Orders still went out to the armies with no more
weighty authority than his own.

Not until July 22 was Skorzeny relieved. Then in

walked Heinrich Himmler. The trouble was all over, he said, but unfortunately General Fromm would not be returning to duty. He himself would take over as Commander-in-Chief, Home Forces. Hitler trusted nobody else.

When Skorzeny walked stiffly down the staircase of the War Office thirty-six hours after he had entered it, he felt a question moving somewhere at the back of his mind, but he was too tired to put a finger on it. He drove directly to Friedenthal and tumbled into bed. Ten hours later he awoke, and fell to pondering.

First, the unbelievable: for nearly two days a temporary soldier, and an interloper at that, had been in absolute control of the vast and complicated apparatus of the War Office. Nobody appointed him; he showed no credentials: it was just that a void had opened and he let himself be drawn into it. All the mummery of "Security" did not stop him from taking over the chair of the Commander-in-Chief, that uneasy chair which had already changed occupants twice in a day.

Now supposing, Skorzeny's thoughts ran on, that he had been secretly in league with the conspirators; or, for that matter, with an external power? What an occasion to play the devil with the machinery so that it would take weeks or months to put the pieces back again—always granting that such a breathing space had been allowed by a remorseless, swiftly acting, *efficient* enemy.

And here Skorzeny marveled over the inactivity of the Allies on July 20. It needed only an airborne landing to turn confusion into civil war. All the troops Hitler could count on were a garrison of three thousand, Bolbrinker's armored training school, Skorzeny's own two battalions at Friedenthal and a few dribs and drabs, apart from headquarters staffs whom he did not take into account.

But if the Allies were slow in reaching for their prize, and if the plotters threw up the sponge as soon as they were faced with a fight, July proved to Skorzeny's satisfaction how, in times of real disorder, almost anyone can get away with anything.

Nor was the effect on Hitler as skin-deep as his injuries. When next Skorzeny met him he had aged; he had to clasp his hands together to stop their trembling. More than ever he was given to jealous outbursts; had he not been assured up to the very moment the bomb exploded that no German general could ever betray his oath? Skorzeny was warned that the Leader would accept no advice that did not exalt his own prejudices; no reports that conflicted with his beliefs. Disproof was contumacy; argument was treason. Once the unity of the German officers' corps had been split, Hitler saw traitors everywhere—at night he dreamed of them.

The attempt of July 20, to all appearances a failure, had sown unbearable suspicion in the victim's brain. And there can be no germ warfare more terrible than the disease of doubt.

VIII

At last we are eye to eye with death. We must renounce all hope of freaks of fortune. Sacrifice to the last drop of blood is demanded of us. Surrender would paralyze and sap our race for generations.

German Army's radio spokesman
in a broadcast to troops in the battle for Hungary,
October, 1944

By the autumn of 1944 Europe was shaking under the march of Hitler's enemies; they had advanced to the Rhineland border and the threshold of East Prussia. Germany's cities lay in ruins; her industries were broken; to the horrors of the air by night were added new fleets of American bombers by day.

Which of the invaders would reach Berlin first? That was the only doubt; inevitably, all would be over before winter.

The turn of fortune that enabled Hitler to fight on

into yet another year presents a lesson in a neglected field of study: the art of holding on to shaky allies; and in this affair, too, Skorzeny played a most unusual part.

On September 10 he was torn away from his work by a summons to the Wolf's Lair. General Jodl said he wanted him to attend a series of discussions on grand strategy: it would enlarge his outlook for a job Hitler had in store for him.

In spite of Skorzeny's impatience at such inactivity, it was time well spent. Germany's real plight came home to him. The Western scene looked black enough; on the Russian front the position was catastrophic. In the North Finland was gone, the Baltic states had crumpled. In the Center the Russians had bounded four hundred miles in a month; the Wolf's Lair was an hour's drive now from guns. In the South the victors of Stalingrad had thrust the Germans back more than a thousand miles into the Balkans. Rumania, with her oil fields, was already lost; Bulgaria would go next; Tito's Partisans had joined hands with the Red Army in Yugoslavia.

This picture, which at close range struck awe into Skorzeny, did nothing to disturb High Command routine. Twice every day—no more, no less—an august assemblage stood at the long table in the map room. Hitler alone had a stool, which he seldom used, and an array of colored pencils, all freshly sharpened. Weary as he looked and sounded, his mind card-indexed every unit on the front: as each fresh gap appeared he would call on reserves or switch forces from one front to another. Since one reverse now followed on the next, disaster itself had become banal and must conform to rule. The generals' talk was all in terms of divisions and army corps, and hearing the names of some units he knew, Skorzeny's heart fell. He had seen them coming out of the line: infantry divisions wasted to battalion strength; armored divisions with a dozen tanks left, and he knew they had not been repaired. But here at headquarters such matters were not spoken of. A division was a flag pinned into a situation map; so long as the flags were there all must be well—the Order of Battle was intact.

This, then, was the powerhouse of the greatest military machine the world had known. On July 20 he had seen it dislocated by a single jolt, and a short spell watching its workings explained why. Many of the master cogs did not engage at all: even the so-called High Command controlled only some areas of the battlefront; something called Army Operations Staff had usurped others. Air Force and Naval liaison chiefs made little connection with the military. No department was ever sure what another might be doing—and it would invite reprisals to inquire: enough that it had always been so.

When Hitler had gone off, leaving the situation map covered with angry whorls and arrows, the generals relaxed. Vermouth lit a companionable sparkle. There would be murmurs: "Not much to talk of, really!" "It's always much the same."

Nothing rippled the surface of this imbecile serenity except the Leader's frequent tantrums. Skorzeny remembers a day when his entrance was awaited with peculiar foreboding. He strode to his place and swept the colored pencils to the floor: no maps would be marked today. Forthwith Jodl and Keitel were accused of trying to pull the wool over his eyes: in Poland—what was going on? It came out that the underground army had risen and turned Warsaw into a battleground. None of the High Command had dared tell Hitler; all hoped the mess could be cleared up before he came upon it—now he had found them out! Skorzeny wished most heartily that he was back at Friedenthal.

At last, one evening, Hitler gave him a sign to stay on after briefing. With Keitel, Jodl, Ribbentrop and Himmler they settled in a group of armchairs. Ribbentrop had a hunted look—it was plain the Foreign Minister had been "sent for"; his cabal of puppet states and gimcrack kingdoms having collapsed, he was to serve as scapegoat for the impending scene.

Hitler started with a sarcastic curtain-lecture. He had news for them, he said: the generals' stupidity had at last been surpassed; his diplomats had gone one better. They had thrown his one remaining ally to the Russians; they had brought down his last bastion; they had probably lost him the war.

Ribbentrop sat pale and wordless through this philippic. Keitel and Jodl studied the ceiling. Only Himmler was unaffected. As others' fortunes waned, his star ascended: his features were arranged in a mask of woeful virtue.

Hitler rushed on. The last ally was Hungary. If Hungary went, Germany would fall—there were no two ways about it. Hungary was now almost his only source of oil, of grain, and of bauxite for the jet-plane program. But economics were not all: Hungary's collapse would cut off seventy divisions from the main battlefront. Italy, Greece, all that was left of Occupied Europe, would be overrun within a week. The Red Army would pour across the Danube plains into Austria.

Skorzeny knew there was no line to fall back on even when Vienna was reached: from his home the Russians would fan out into Germany; the war must end in weeks.

And yet—he could not understand Hitler's extreme pessimism. Hungary did not seem in such urgent danger. Her armies were fighting stoutly in the Carpathians, and had a million Germans to help them. Together they held a mountain chain which had shielded Southern Europe for centuries. Why should Hungary fall?

Germany was being betrayed, Hitler went on to explain, by someone outside his reach. Admiral Horthy, the Hungarian Regent, was a traitor to their cause. He had been trafficking with the enemy. First he went slyly to the British: they told him to try Moscow, since it was the Red Army his troops were facing. Now Hitler had learned that Horthy was about to throw open the road to Budapest—turntable of all German communications in the south—the road to Vienna and Berlin.

Skorzeny's eyes went to the map of Southern Europe: an arc of flags—sixteen of them, each standing for a Russian army—was pinned beside the horseshoe contours which formed Hungary's eastern border: that meant a total of a hundred and twenty enemy divisions along the Carpathians. If the dams which held them fell, a Russian tidal wave would burst over the Danubian plain: and the first to be engulfed would be the German troops, a million men for whom there could be no Dunkirk.

Hitler was addressing him directly: "You, Skorzeny, will deal with this Admiral Horthy."

The task he outlined was both formidable and delicate. Skorzeny must pluck Horthy's sting, but not so as to bring the hornets' nest about their ears. While the Hungarians at least acted friendship, Skorzeny would be able to go about the country and make his plans.

It began to sound like an echo of the Mussolini mission; except that this time, the climax would be reached not on some remote Alpine peak but in the heart of

Budapest: at one stroke, Hitler said, the Regent in his Castle and his Government must be overturned. Admiral Horthy was ready for the worst—and in particular Skorzeny should know that, since the Gran Sasso affair, he had taken precautions against being kidnaped. No half-measures would do—the Castle would have to be taken by storm.

Then it was Jodl's turn to speak. Hitler had already mentioned the General Staff's ideas for an airborne attack: for this they would furnish a squadron of gliders, two para-troop battalions and a crack battalion made up of officer-cadets. Also Skorzeny would have for his own use a special plane of the Leader's squadron—nothing was too good for him today.

Before hearing his master's steely adieu—"Mind, Skorzeny; I count on you!"—he was handed by Hitler a crackling sheet of notepaper. Surmounted by the German eagle and Iron Cross in gilt, it read:

> FROM THE LEADER AND CHANCELLOR OF THE STATE
>   Major Skorzeny has been directly charged by myself with secret and personal orders of ut-most importance. All personnel, military and civ-il, will assist Major Skorzeny by every means and will forward all his wishes.
>   (*Signed*) ADOLF HITLER

Here was trustingness itself: Hitler had put into his hands a lever which could be used to turn Germany upside down. Who dare question its authority or deny its bearer anything? Creators of wartime forgeries never produced anything so simple.

Skorzeny put the paper away. He did not enjoy exact-ing blind obedience; a nice use of friendly connections, he decided, would take him further than this power to dra-goon everyone and mobilize all the power of the State.

And then, he was humbled by the enormity of the task that had been thrust on him. Since Skorzeny's boy-hood in Austria Admiral Horthy had ruled the eastern marches of the former Austro-Hungarian Empire as an heir to a revered tradition and a link with the Emperor Franz Joseph, whose reign had opened nearly a century before. Though the Regent did not yet wear the Iron

Crown of Hungary, he was said to covet it. Already he could declare, like Louis XIV, *"L'état c'est moi."* How to pull down the man and leave the State entire?

And then, again, how could Horthy be reached? The Regent lived like some feudal monarch: attended by Ministers and guards, fenced in by troops, he had his being on the heights of Castle Hill which dominated all Budapest. Skorzeny, in his student days, and often later on, had toured those time-honored ramparts. Now, without warning, he was asked to burst through them.

It was no swashbuckling commando who landed in Budapest a few days later. Instead, there stepped from the airliner a Dr. Wolf from Cologne, who drove past the hotels used by German officers on their way to the front, and took up his quarters in a private house.

Presently, guidebook in hand, he was enjoying the air on the summit of Castle Hill—and confirming his memories of its granite strength. The walls enclosed a township of patrician houses, Embassies, Ministries and quarters for a garrison of thousands. The streets were full of troops; sentries and guns were well sited; and crowning all, from the magnificent palace which overhung the Danube, there flew the standard of the Hungarian Hapsburgs—the Regent was at home.

To make this personal tour of Castle Hill was convenient, but it led to the gloomiest conclusions. An assault force would be butchered before it got halfway up. The use of siege artillery would only enrage the Hungarian armies at the front and turn them against the Germans—then the Russians would be through. At the Wolf's Lair they had suggested airborne troops—he found the only landing space anywhere near was ringed by buildings: a broadside would be poured on them before they could cut free their parachutes. Skorzeny noted the name that Baedeker gave this space: "The Field of Blood."

Looking down toward the city which lay spread out below, Skorzeny decided his assault must be based on a clearer idea of Hungarian intentions: the first fortress to be entered was the Regent's mind.

Admiral Horthy was behaving strangely. This autocrat who had seized power from a Communist régime in 1919 and kept a tight hand on the country ever since—how could he think of selling out to Stalin? Hungary

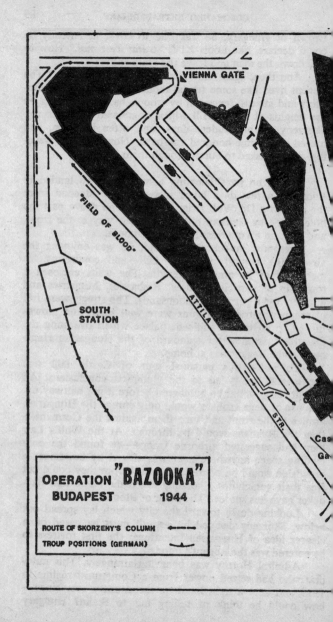

VIENNA GATE

"FIELD OF BLOOD"

SOUTH STATION

ATTILA

STR.

Cas
Ga

OPERATION "BAZOOKA"
BUDAPEST   1944

ROUTE OF SKORZENY'S COLUMN ← ← ← ←
TROUP POSITIONS (GERMAN) ⌐⌐

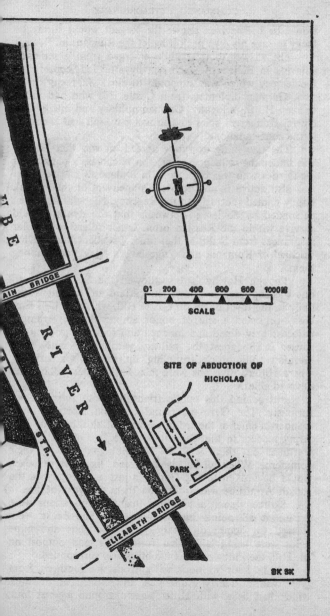

DANUBE

AIN BRIDGE

RIVER

STR.

0' 200 400 600 800 1000M

SCALE

SITE OF ABDUCTION OF
NICHOLAS

PARK

ELIZABETH BRIDGE

BK BK

would be bolshevized anew: the Regent would surely be lucky to save his own neck if he let the Russians in.

The answer to this riddle emerged from a series of palavers in Budapest—each heavily attended, considering the secrecy which was supposed to cloak Skorzeny's mission. German diplomats from Castle Hill who had failed to keep Horthy's loyalty, German military and intelligence chiefs, Hungarian spies in German pay—all had their say in the confabulations.

The one thing everyone agreed on was that Horthy was under the influence of his son Nicholas, a playboy in his thirties who was often seen in Budapest's cabarets, but was also active in the political maneuvers of the capital. Lately named successor to the Regency, Nicholas had been persuaded by Soviet go-betweens that the dynasty could survive within the Russian orbit. Other rulers got similar assurances from Stalin at that time: President Benes, King Michael of Rumania and Yugoslavia's King Peter among them.

Though Horthy had swallowed the Soviet bait, no one was supposed to know. Hungarians and Germans met daily in the town or up on Castle Hill, where Hitler's Embassy occupied a site of honor among the Government palaces: they dined and lunched and toasted the common cause. In Budapest the railway yards were noisy with German rollingstock trundling up to the Carpathians, where Hitler's divisions were mixed with their gallant and devoted allies.

But behind this public friendship both sides plotted furiously. The Germans found out that Horthy's commander-in-chief at the front, General Miklos, had met Red Army leaders in the Carpathians; the fate of the million Germans out there was the bargaining-counter of their commerce. When all had been agreed, the news of peace would be broken to the Germans just as abruptly as the Italian Armistice was sprung on them the year before.

Skorzeny soon ascertained that the Hungarians were armed at all points against surprises. The decks were cleared for action on Castle Hill; new guns and mine fields were being laid. That forlorn German outpost on the Hill, the Embassy, was unobtrusively surrounded.

From hour to hour news from the southern front grew worse. Thirty Rumanian and Bulgarian divisions which had been with Hitler turned around against him;

if now the Hungarian armies changed sides too, the front would surely collapse. Something, however risky, must be done soon.

It was at this point that an agent who had wormed his way into Nicholas Horthy's circle reported a second set of surrender parleys going on in Budapest itself. Here the Soviet brief was held by a group of Yugoslavs—Marshal Tito then being Stalin's trusty—and that very evening the two sides were to meet in a villa outside the capital. Nicholas Horthy himself would be there. This was a chance to catch the "crown prince" red-handed: and then, confronted with the proofs of guilt, Admiral Horthy would surely give up his double game.

Skorzeny laid a cordon around the house: Nicholas's car drew up at the appointed time. The Germans were about to swoop, when out of the car there stepped not only Nicholas but his father, too. Skorzeny had been told to avoid a head-on clash with the Regent: disgusted, he called off his men.

The meeting must have been fruitful, for at it a final conclave was fixed for the following Sunday, October 15, to initial the surrender pact. This time Nicholas would go alone, but with a large force of troops on call. And the rendezvous would be no isolated villa, but a second-floor office on a square near the Danube.

The Germans made counterplans. They found rooms to let on the top floor of the building; four agents moved in, with orders to break into the meeting five minutes after Nicholas arrived. At the same time other Germans from outside would dash upstairs to close the trap on the conspirators.

It was a sparkling autumn morning when the rival troupes prepared their entrances for a modern Hungarian *opéra bouffe,* and bullets instead of bouquets might come at the curtain's fall. Skorzeny drove up alone in his Dr. Wolf disguise. The square by the Danube wore an empty, Sunday look, but two Hungarian vehicles were parked outside the office building: a canvas-covered army lorry and a car Skorzeny recognized as Nicholas Horthy's. He drew up just ahead of them: then he got out, opened his car bonnet and began to fiddle with the engine. At that the canvas of the lorry was jerked back by an inquiring hand; Skorzeny saw three Hungarian officers inside, with a machine gun. And two other Hungarian officers were strolling with excessive unconcern in the gardens of the square. The conference had started; Nicholas's guard was set.

Skorzeny had his friends, too, ready for their cues. His chauffeur and one of his N.C.O.'s lounged on a park bench. And from the corner of the square two more of his confederates were coming on the scene: German military police who moved toward him with dawdling steps. They drew level with Skorzeny, exchanged a dramatic wink— and in a flash were darting up the stairs into the plotters' building.

The trap was sprung.

But the Hungarians had kept a sharp lookout. Before Skorzeny could move, fire came from the canvas-covered lorry; the second German policeman spun around on the threshold of the building and rolled down the stone stairs to the pavement. Skorzeny dragged the man behind his car; at once machine-gun bullets began to play a tattoo on it.

The loiterers in the gardens hastened to join in. Firing from the hip the Hungarians dashed forward to join their brother officers in the covered truck; the park-bench loungers sprinted over to help Skorzeny. His chauffeur was hit in the thigh as he tumbled down beside him; all three Germans tried to get in a shot or two at the covered truck from behind Skorzeny's car. But pistols against machine guns; a diversion was overdue. Skorzeny had hidden von Foelkersam with a company of men in a street not far away. While dodging bullets and trying to shoot back, he blew three blasts on a whistle and a minute later he heard the tread of his troops coming up at the run.

The Hungarians left the lorry and ran. But instead of seeking shelter in the plotters' house, they decamped into a neighboring building. Skorzeny raised a wary head over his car. The second doorway was full of Hungarian troops: Nicholas Horthy had secreted his reserves next door—now they were coming out in force.

To get his blow in first, Skorzeny led a dash for the conspirators' house. As the Germans ran they lobbed grenades at the neighboring portico: down came brickbats, blocks of concrete, shattered marble slabs, on the Hungarians in the doorway: the rest of them were penned up on the other side.

Crossing the threshold of the plotters' house, he ran into a group struggling downstairs: the German agents planted on the top floor had invaded the peace conclave and captured young Horthy with three others. Nicholas was flailing the air and shouting vengeance when Skorzeny saw him. A Persian rug lay across the hall; a curtain rope hung nearby—in no time the "crown prince" was rolled up, trussed and slung into a lorry.

"To the airport," Skorzeny shouted. "I'll follow." He paused to tell von Foelkersam to move off his men—"and no more shooting"—before jumping into another car.

As he tried to catch up to the lorry a hundred yards on, a company of Hungarian troops came toward them at the double; another company was behind and a third, all making for the square: the Regent's reinforcements—somehow they must be delayed. He accosted the leading officer: "Halt! You must not go that way."

The Hungarian pulled up; his men stopped short behind him. "What's the matter?" he demanded. Skorzeny argued for a few minutes; then, guessing the square would by now be clear of German troops, drove off unchallenged. At the airport he saw a protesting roll of carpet being heaved onto a plane. With a roar of engines, Nicholas Horthy was on his way to Germany, a prisoner.

So far so good: at the cost of a few pawns a rook had been swept from the board. It remained to see how Admiral Horthy would take this reverse.

Skorzeny went over to the hotel which served as German Army Headquarters to await events. A telephone call from the German Embassy said Castle Hill was in a state of siege with all approaches barricaded and mined. Their military attaché had tried to drive down to the town and been turned back. In diplomatic jargon this was an "unfriendly act." Feinting was almost at an end.

Then the radio warned listeners to stand by for a declaration by the Regent. At two P.M. it came: a tirade against his German allies, ending: "It is clear today that Germany has lost the war. . . . Hungary has accordingly concluded a preliminary Armistice with Russia, and will cease all hostilities against her."

The Regent had called "Check." Anger at his son's kidnaping had precipitated this Armistice announcement: that was all to the good if it meant the Russians were unready yet to move into the Hungarian positions.

A German general raced up to the Carpathians to head off Horthy's commander-in-chief before he could go over to the enemy—too late; General Miklos with a few of his staff officers had already crossed the lines. But the Germans were pleasantly surprised to find the Hungarian armies reluctant to lay down their arms before receiving an official cease-fire. Radio statements, even by the Regent, did not rank as "orders."

In their confusion the Hungarian War Office had not sent out the agreed signals—all the more reason, said Skorzeny, for striking now at Castle Hill: if they were quick the tables might be turned once more. But how could the attack be carried out? Brute force had advocates, chief of them an S.S. brigadier called Bach-Zelewski, renowned as a professional tough. Bach-Zelewski had carted to Hungary a twenty-five-inch mortar which had

"Karl" 60 cm. self-propelled Howitzer

been used to smash a way into the Black Sea citadel of Sebastopol; in the recent fighting it had razed much of Warsaw too. All Bach-Zelewski asked for was a free hand and he would reduce the Castle to powder. Skorzeny stood firm: Hitler wanted Hungary to be won back—not blasted into Stalin's arms.

The other Germans were undecided. Bach-Zelewski might wish to go too far, but what else could be done? If

Skorzeny ruled out the General Staff's airborne landing; if, as was obvious, an infantry assault must fail, what did he suggest? He knew the odds: against the three Hungarian divisions in the Budapest area, the Germans had less than one division. Even the élite troops Jodl had lent for the attack would be outmatched by Horthy's bodyguard of nearly two thousand on the Hill. What chance would the Germans have?

The chance, Skorzeny replied, of the side which is so much the weaker that others may drop their guard. He would employ all the forces available, but not in the expected way. The German division, or what there was of it, was gradually surrounding the Hill as if a leisurely siege was intended. At dawn the attack would start. Forays would be made on the perimeter by two battalions to distract and mislead Horthy. Meanwhile the real assault would be going through like a dagger slipped between the ribs: or, to be up-to-date, like a shell from that new rocket-firing gun which killed a tank with a single shot. "Bazooka"—that was it: an apt code name for this assault.

The staff officers were skeptical; Bach-Zelewski was impolite. Skorzeny's plan was at last accepted—as so often—only for lack of a better. And then, toward midnight, a senior Hungarian officer asked for a parley. Skorzeny's friends agreed that although the Castle was simply playing for time until the Armistice became effective, they should take the move at its face value.

The visitor began by complaining of all this German military activity: Horthy's anxiety for peace with the Russians did not, he hoped, exclude friendship with his old allies.

Why, then, the Germans asked, were their diplomats penned up on Castle Hill? Why should they not come down into the town? Surely the chivalrous Hungarians respected diplomatic privilege? An Ambassador and his staff isolated by force—it was unheard of: worse, it was discourteous.

The visitor flushed. Skorzeny thought this a hopeful sign that others on Castle Hill might be shamed into softening their betrayal with at least the forms of courtesy. So he asked that as a token of faith the road which the Ambassador usually took—that which brought him through the Vienna Gate—should be reopened. The demand would be made official: unless the mines and barricades were cleared from this one road by six A.M. Germany would "draw the necessary conclusions."

The Hungarian wavered; the Germans pressed their argument. It might be that the Regent—an old sailor—did not recognize the absurdity of blocking a road already protected by crossfire, every step of it under the guns of the garrison. But their visitor, a military man, could surely see this with half an eye. He should also understand the value of give-and-take in this tricky situation.

The Hungarian promised at least to try to have their wishes met. Nobody wanted to fall foul of the Germans, he protested, so long as they kept the peace. And then with a mannerly farewell he drove off into the night.

So far so good, but whatever the Hungarians chose to do, "Bazooka" must go on. Skorzeny called his officers to explain to them the plan. Then half an hour before daylight his units quietly moved into the approaches of Castle Hill. To every man was repeated: "Do not open fire. Safety catches on. Whatever happens you must not fire unless an officer tells you to."

In the dim light before an autumn dawn the column was drawn up—not for a battle, one would have said: rather for a march-past in battle array. Once more in uniform, Skorzeny took the lead in a command car with five N.C.O.'s: each carried a bazooka and a bunch of grenades on his belt.

Four Panther tanks followed; they had been borrowed on their way up to the Russian front, for there were only six German tanks in all Budapest. Then a group of radio-piloted land torpedoes: dwarf tanks, packed with explosives, which could be sent head-on at a barricade to blow it up.

Platoon by platoon, the assault troops crowded in their vehicles brought up the rear of the column. A last check to see all safety catches were on; this was made by Skorzeny's old hands, who no longer believed the army adage that the soldier's best friend is his rifle: they relied on their leader, his legend and his luck.

Luck now was surely wanted. Without benefit of patrols, scouts or covering fire, Skorzeny was going head-foremost into a hostile area, highly fortified. Once again he was backing his estimate of the soldier's mind. No garrison, he hoped, could fire on peaceable troops peaceably marching: men whose credentials were vouched for by

Goliath

their very lack of precautions. It simply was not in the book.

Of course, if he proved wrong, his tightly bunched columns would be ripped from end to end.

Five minutes to six: engines broke the tension with a roar. Upright in his command car, Skorzeny raised his hand and swept it forward. They were off.

The main hazard on the first lap—the long, steep road that led to the Vienna Gate—was the danger of land mines. When Skorzeny got under way he was braced every moment for an explosion under his wheels. Fifty yards, a hundred, he stood rigid as they gathered speed. Nothing happened: the mines had after all been moved. Now for the barricades.

Another minute and the dark bulk of the Vienna Gate came into view. There was a barrier across the road; but a gleam of light beyond proved a passage had been cut in it. So their midnight visitor had prevailed on Horthy to trust in his garrison's alertness.

Men moved out of the shadows of the gate—sentries. This was the testing moment. Skorzeny held his course with only a slight drop in speed. The sentries stared; no orders had reached them about a German column coming, but people who rode up with such noisy assurance surely had permission. The leading car rushed on them. Skorzeny waved cheerfully; the darkness of the gate enveloped him —he was through.

Behind came a tank and then three more tanks: each thundered up to the gate with its commander standing in the open turret, hand at the salute: the very acme of military politeness. Skorzeny heard the deep, unbroken roar gaining ground behind him. The road ahead was clear; already he was high above the roofs and treetops of the sleeping capital. A huge, square shape appeared as they reached the summit. It was the Castle barracks.

Sandbagged emplacements flanked the gates; machine-gunners stood ready; the first burst of fire would bring a thousand men tumbling out. But again Skorzeny's airy salute as he came up—and the certainty that this column had passed unhindered through the Vienna Gate— reassured the sentries. Skorzeny passed on without a backward glance. The column wheeled after him: row after row of backs presented to the enemy. Two kinds of discipline were matched: the mechanical reaction of the defenders, the self-control Skorzeny had taught his troops.

The machine-gunners did not fire. Instead, they accepted the vulnerability of the Germans as proof of title to be there. Away down the mile-long avenue which led past the German Embassy Skorzeny drove at top speed. Half the column followed; the rest had split off to take a second avenue which also led to Horthy's palace. The roar of trucks and tanks rose in crescendo as his convoy crashed past the Ministry of War, where lay another thousand men at arms. The Castle Square opened out before them. An immense mass rose up across the chasm of its courtyards: the Regent's palace.

Action! Three heavy tanks were facing them. When their Hungarian commanders saw the tornado approach-

Pzkw VI Tiger II

ing, their guns turned upward to the sky. A high brick wall shielded the palace gate. Skorzeny swerved aside and waved a Panther on: it crashed through the rampart. He jumped from his car. Eight men went after him through the gap, led by von Foelkersam, who would take over if he were hit.

And there, guarding the palace, were six antitank guns. How would the Panther fare? Skorzeny did not pause to see. He bolted through an archway into the building. Already the alarm had sounded. An agitated figure rushed toward him—the colonel of the guard; von Foelkersam leaped forward and a pistol went spinning from the colonel's hand.

Another Hungarian officer sprang out as they ran on. "Quick," shouted Skorzeny. "Come with me. I have to see the Commandant at once."

Politics are the soldier's curse: the Hungarian must have supposed the situation had somehow changed—someone else should sort this out. He headed up a marble staircase, with Skorzeny at his heels. Von Foelkersam and his corporal's guard followed to the second floor, there to be posted while Skorzeny went on with the Hungarian to the Commandant's office. In the anteroom a soldier was training a machine gun through the window at the Germans: it was struck out of his hand and dropped down into the courtyard. Then Skorzeny knocked on the Commandant's door.

One cannot enter into the feelings of the Hungarian general who was faced by a gigantic intruder demanding his surrender. Castle Hill, said this stranger, was already in German hands, but some shooting could still be heard: a cease-fire must at once be sounded. Further bloodshed would not do anyone any good—and the hint was given emphasis with a revolver.

Then one of Skorzeny's N.C.O.'s came in to report, with Major von Foelkersam's compliments, that the courtyard and main entrance had been secured; what orders next? Skorzeny looked at the general—and the general, after a brief internal struggle, gave in. Fire was still crackling from the gardens of the castle: officers went out to stop it.

Skorzeny was not yet content. Gentleness, "more powerful than Hercules," should lead the way to reconciliation; and for that, *amour propre* must be restored.

First, the Hungarian general. His hand enfolded in a consoling clasp, he heard himself congratulated on his humane decision to submit. Hungary, he was glowingly assured, would think well of him.

Next, the officers. Skorzeny found a hostile group in the anteroom; before they could protest he asked the names of two majors and appointed them his liaison officers. They were to see to the piling up of their soldiers' arms in the courtyard: chivalry dictated that the officers should keep their revolvers. Then Skorzeny called them all together in the Coronation Hall and addressed them in German, which is understood by educated Hungarians.

"Gentlemen," he began, "I am happy that we have now put an end to our misunderstanding. Germany and Hungary have never in history quarreled; always they have fought together against a common enemy. Now that once again the barbarian is at our gates we must close our ranks against him."

And so on; it was Skorzeny's first political speech, but it struck a soldierly note and he could see the Hungarians were softened by the cousinly Austrian accent to which he gave full play. When he had ended his appeal, they stepped forward one by one to salute and take his hand. Then they withdrew unescorted. Skorzeny was master of Castle Hill.

Famous victories, battles which make a noise in the world and leave their mark on history, are expected to pay a dignified fee in casualties. The battle of Budapest cost altogether seven lives, while twenty-six men were wounded. The departure from custom in adding together casualties on rival sides must also be excused, since Skorzeny insisted on a joint funeral. This ceremony was held next day with military pomp, which was balm to the feelings of the Hungarian Army.

The Regent, in the meantime, had flown. Skorzeny found his apartments empty. Later he heard that Admiral Horthy had left the palace to put himself under the protection of General Pfeffer-Wildenbruch, a relation of the ex-Kaiser. Within a few hours his abdication was announced and his rudderless Government had been replaced. Count Szalasi, who had the Germans' confidence, became Prime Minister; he at once canceled the Armistice proclamation.

Next morning the new War Minister, General Bereckzy, called to thank Skorzeny for driving Horthy out and capturing the Hill without harming the proud buildings. Skorzeny accepted this tribute to the German Army —saying nothing of Bach-Zelewski with his monstrous cannon.

Congratulations came from the Wolf's Lair, and orders to "take up residence" in the palace. Skorzeny moved into the Regent's wing, with its sumptuous furniture and tapestries, reminders of a vanished world. That evening he splashed about in the imperial bathtub carved with cupids for Franz Joseph. In the banqueting hall, his officers held festival. Skorzeny took the high chair: cobwebbed vintages were brought up for "His Excellency's" approval. There had always been a Constable of Castle Hill—now the office was Skorzeny's.

Three days later, Skorzeny met his antagonist for the first time. He was formally presented to Admiral Horthy in the house of General Pfeffer-Wildenbruch: with the end of his régime the Regent was to be conveyed to Germany in Horthy's own special train. Skorzeny explained that he would be lodged as a guest of honor in a Bavarian castle, a very secure castle indeed, to which he himself would have the privilege of escorting him. The conversation was constrained. On Horthy's last drive through the capital he had ruled for so long hardly a hand waved him farewell.

Operation "Bazooka" let Hitler out of a very tight corner. The million Germans on the Carpathians hardly knew the fate they had escaped; the Hungarian Army fought on beside them to the last day of the war.

IX

> *They are decided only to be undecided, resolved to be irresolute, adamant for drift, all-powerful for impotence.*
>
> WINSTON CHURCHILL
>
> *Pas trop de zèle.*
>
> TALLEYRAND

"A commando mission depends absolutely upon long and minute preparation." With this axiom from a captured enemy report Karl Radl often raised a smile in the early days of extemporization at Friedenthal; but as time went on with no easing of the breathless scramble it ceased to be a joke.

For each project Skorzeny carried out, a score of others were stillborn, or foredoomed by the slapdash assumptions of superiors whose eyes were shut to the first essential of strategic surprise: preparation.

"Immense ability" has been credited to the German General Staff, yet even their most generous professional critic, Captain Liddell Hart, has acknowledged that his Prussian paragons "frowned on all novel ideas, especially by amateurs." Skorzeny was an "amateur" first and last; his ideas were as new as pins and as prickly to handle, so the generals used their immense ability to quibble over his proposals and nullify his schemes with the age-old arts of obstruction and delay. And when his fame grew and his organization expanded in spite of everything; they saw to it that Friedenthal was given pitifully short commons.

Throughout that year of Allied victory Skorzeny kept probing for chinks in the enemy's armor; in the Middle East particularly he saw great hope: Iraq, Suez, Baku were promising openings in the chain mail.

Saboteurs were to wreck the Iraq oil stations which pumped the fuel of Britain's Mediterranean campaign from the Persian Gulf to Haifa and Tripoli, but the air squadron attached to Skorzeny's headquarters had no long-range planes. He thought—why not use American bombers which had been forced down behind the German lines? Six captured Fortresses were put in order. When all was ready they were destroyed by an Allied bombing raid. No long-range planes could be wrung out of the Air Ministry so the whole scheme came to naught.

Frogmen of Skorzeny's Danube group were taught to blow up ships across a waterway; this technique might have choked the Suez Canal for weeks or months, forcing the Allies to use the long way around the Cape to the Far East. But by the time the High Command approved, the Allied grip on the Mediterranean was too tight.

The main Soviet oil center of Baku was picked out for a visit; airborne parties, by blowing up a few points, might have stopped the flow of petrol to the Red armies. Once again, it took so long to get the scheme agreed to that by then the Balkan airfields from which Skorzeny's troops could have taken off had been lost.

One project after another on which much effort had been spent was buried with the epitaph "Too late." Skorzeny struggled on; he would clutch at any straw to slow Germany's rush to destruction. His men shared his disregard for odds; but the most desperate venture he embarked on was in partnership with a woman.

Slight, fair-haired and blue-eyed, Fräulein Hanna Reitsch was a test pilot of almost insane bravery: the only woman, indeed the only civilian, throughout the war to win the Iron Cross First Class. Before anyone knew jets were being built in Germany she took up one of the first jet planes; it was faulty and crashed. For months she was in the hospital, then for months she fought to get her nerve back. Unable even to sit on a chair for fear of falling, she had herself carried to the roof of her house in order to master her terror. One day she invited friends to luncheon at the airport. They arrived to find a new type of plane circling overhead. It came down, and out jumped Hanna. "I can fly again; I can fly!"

Meeting her at Hitler's headquarters during that summer of 1944, Skorzeny had been struck by her fanaticism: like Joshua, she would have the sun held in the sky until victory was won. They talked of Peenemünde, and the series of V weapons which was being produced at the secret rocket-research station there.* Some time before, Skorzeny had seen the trial of the V1; as he watched its tearing flight over the Baltic and later examined its simple mechanism he thought: if you could put a steersman into a naval torpedo, then why not a piloted flying bomb? Instead of falling at random, a V1 could be driven dead onto an exact target—the House of Commons in full session, if you liked—by a pilot who was willing to die. Skorzeny had a horror of missions with no hope of return but, after all, thousands of German airmen, grounded by the aircraft shortage, were going into the line as untrained infantry: any among them who volunteered to pilot a V1 would know, at least, that his life was not being thrown away for nothing. One life for a Ministry, a warship or a troop transport: it was an expedient worthy of Germany's straits.

Flying back from Peenemünde, Skorzeny called together that same evening technical experts from the Air Ministry and the aircraft firms Heinkel and Focke-Wulf. They worked all night at Friedenthal on drawings and calculations; by morning the design was ready and next day it was on the desk of the air chief, Marshal Milch. For the first time Skorzeny invoked the Leader's name, insisting brazenly that Hitler had himself approved the idea of a piloted V1 and wanted immediate results. Objections by three Air Force commissions were overcome and Milch gave the plan his blessing: they might hope to start construction in about three months' time, he thought.

It was then that Skorzeny spoke of the idea to Hanna Reitsch. Why, this was wonderful, she cried; the same idea had come to her during a trip to Peenemünde, but no one would listen to it. Fired by Hanna's excitement, Skorzeny

---

*Read *V-2* by Dr. Walter Dornberger, the general in command of Peenemünde. Another volume in the Bantam War Book Series.

went back to Friedenthal with the determination to cut Milch's three-months' timetable to three weeks. Hangars sprang up; engineers and mechanics worked night and day; in a fortnight the first V1 with a cockpit and controls was wheeled onto the airfield.

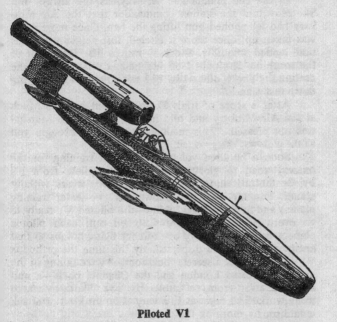

Piloted V1

Then came the trials. Instead of the usual rocket start, the V1 with its pilot was lifted into the air by a mother plane and released at three thousand five hundred feet; then, with its wake of flame, it shot off at nearly four hundred miles an hour. After a few circles over the airfield, the pilot came in to land. He crashed; technicians could not make out why.

Hanna saw the shattered V1, and next day another which met the same fate; both pilots lived but were too badly injured to explain what had gone wrong. Skorzeny was resigned to defeat when the Air Ministry put a stop to further trials. But Hanna would not have it. "Ignore the ban," she said, "and I'll take the next one up myself."

Skorzeny was scandalized. As a last plea he urged that if anything happened to her he himself would lose his head.

"What!" cried Hanna. "And they told me you were a soldier with the courage to disobey."

In the end Hanna got her way, as she always did. Skorzeny told the station commander that the Air Ministry had telephoned him lifting the ban. Once more a V1 was taken up; once more it circled, lost height—and this time landed smoothly. Skorzeny ran to lift Hanna out of the machine. She pulled off her helmet. "I knew it," she declared. "Those other two did not know how to bring down fast planes."

After a score of trials Skorzeny went back to Milch at the Air Ministry and told him the truth. The Marshal was not pleased. "This madness might have brought you to the gallows," he growled.

Soon a hundred volunteers were in training for the oneway road to glory. Thirty were ex-pilots from his Friedenthal battalion, the rest Air Force flyers without planes. Test models were followed by two-seater training planes, and at last the real thing—the piloted V1 ready to go over. New tactics were sketched out; each piloted plane would fly in a covy of ordinary flying bombs so that enemy fire would be dispersed. By this time the orthodox V1 was no longer a secret; "buzzbombs" were falling in the hundreds around London and the Channel ports—a nuisance, but far from an intolerable one. Skorzeny dared to hope that in a few weeks a very different kind of attack would start.

But he had reckoned without the bureaucrats: gradually the fuel supply was screwed down, and training slowed with it. In vain did Karl Radl send over to Berlin his salvoes of forms and departmental minutes, in vain Skorzeny spent hours on the long-distance telephone or pacing the corridors of the Wilhelmstrasse. Promises were all they got. By the autumn, training came to a stop, never to be resumed. The mother of parliaments still stands.

Constantly Skorzeny seemed to be caught between the two extremes—generals who believed nothing and Party leaders who believed anything. Shortly after his piloted flying bomb had been abandoned—and the Air Force volunteers had "stowed away" in one or another of the

Friedenthal commando units—he mentioned during a visit to Hitler's headquarters the prospect of launching V1's from U-boats at sea.

Himmler jumped up in sudden excitement. "That's the way we can bombard New York," he exclaimed. "Skorzeny, you must push on with research at top speed. Here is a God-sent chance to punish America for bombing Germany!"

Skorzeny protested that the V1 was far from accurate, even from land bases. Launched from a rolling submarine . . . But Himmler was scarcely listening. He had gone over to an immense map of the Atlantic and stood before it, entranced with his new vision. Skorzeny looked around for an ally: Schellenberg was in the room; the young careerist who had advised him always to greet the ideas of his superiors with rapture was nodding delighted approval, even though Himmler's back was turned. Having survived the terrors of the July 20 plot, Schellenberg had stepped into the shoes of the disgraced Admiral Canaris; there was no help for Skorzeny there. But he tried once more to disabuse Himmler. Bombing of such an aimless kind would infuriate the United States, he objected, without doing real damage. Now if they had agents ashore to steer in the V1's with an electronic device which the scientists were perfecting—but Himmler was lost in his map of the world. "It is America's turn to have some bombs," he repeated; "they will never stand up to them." As he turned back to Skorzeny his pale eyes behind the pince-nez glistened with unwonted emotion. "Let me know how it goes," he said. "Keep me informed."

While Germany was being sucked down, weeks had to be devoted to harebrained schemes for wonder weapons which could not be used. Often Skorzeny wanted to throw in his hand; then some horrifying emergency on one front or another would claim his energies. After all else had failed, the generals and politicians thought of Friedenthal; for when it came to getting them out of a pickle, Skorzeny was their man.

In September 1944, Germany was shaken by the great airborne landing over the mouths of the Rhine. It was a bold bid, and might have shortened the war by months had it fully succeeded; Skorzeny was thankful that the Allies had not gone instead for Berlin. Even the High Command had been transferred to the capital, where all the strands of headquarters and commands were now knotted together.

The Allies tried for the lesser prizes of clearing Antwerp as a supply port and outflanking the Siegfried Line at Arnhem. They were beaten by bad weather, but the First Airborne, even after withdrawing from Arnhem, clung to a bridgehead across the lower Rhine and were still there when the British Guards Division took Nymegen. Within this salient of a few score square miles were the twin road and railway bridges of Nymegen, which had been called "the gateway to the Fatherland."

Hitler sounded the alarm: for ten days the salient was the most savagely contested corner of the earth. German division after division, at least a dozen attacks by infantry and armor, were beaten off. Göring's remaining dive bombers went up; nearly six hundred planes tried to smash the bridges and failed. With every hour the British grip tightened.

Skorzeny's frogmen went to this battlefront in Holland. The Allied line swung over the Waal and curved back to recross the river fifteen miles on; at the center of this arc, protected by thousands of troops and ringed with guns, lay the two bridges which carried the spearhead of the thrust into Germany.

German headquarters lacked even a good chart of the river; Skorzeny had to draw on the memory of an old Rhine steamer skipper for details. Then Captain Hummel, a frogman who had sunk nearly forty thousand tons of Allied shipping single-handed, went out on a sortie. In rubber suit with camouflage net over his face, Hummel swam downstream through the enemy. It was night, but presently tracer shells showed him the outline of the road bridge; he clung to a slimy arch, alone and defenseless, working out his plans, while the enemy tanks and guns rumbled over his head. Then he moved through the water for another half-mile until a pylon of the railway bridge loomed up: a monolith, quite thirty feet across from the upstream side of the bridge to the other, and twelve feet thick. Silently he swam on until he gained German-held territory again beyond the salient.

Already Skorzeny's men had brought some half-ton U-boat torpedo mines to the upstream edge of the salient; under darkness the mines were trundled down to the river. It was a lively journey: one or two shells burst nearby, wounding some of the helpers. In the water the cigar-shaped mines were linked in couples—each couple would span a bridge pylon—and fourteen frogmen, led by Hummel, set off to guide them with the current.

German Frogman

The bridges were reached, the mines secured; valves opened, time fuses set to go off when they touched the river bed—here the utmost damage, by violent displacement of water, would be done. Then the swimmers slipped away downstream. They heard the explosions—and at once the river was aflame, with the British on both flanks firing at everything that moved. Dawn was creeping up and bullets splashed all around. Two men were wounded; their comrades held them up but, when they got ashore, found they were dead. Four others were brought back unharmed by Captain Hummel. The rest were forced out of the water and taken prisoner.

Not for some time after did Skorzeny learn the result of that night's work, although a slackening of pressure against the German front could at once be felt. The railway bridge was destroyed; seventy yards were blown away altogether. The road bridge was badly damaged and the British had to build a Bailey bridge on pontoons. For a day or two the British in the salient were cut off. Skorzeny does not doubt that if his frogmen had been called on earlier both bridges could have been completely wrecked; the "gateway to the Fatherland" would have been barred. As it was, for the cost of two lives, Skorzeny's frogmen succeeded after divisions of troops with tanks and an armada of planes had failed.

Arnhem and Nymegen gave the Allies pause; the thrust to the heart of Germany would have to be delayed. Already the cementing of the southeastern front had freed German forces for a venture which was in Hitler's mind even before the Hungarian crisis arose. This was the hour Hitler had been awaiting. It gave him the chance of a supreme gamble and part of his plan was so outrageous that only one man could fill the bill.

"Send for Skorzeny," he said.

X

We can still lose this war!

GENERAL PATTON,
during the Battle of the Bulge
December, 1944

At the height of Hitler's last offensive in the West, which came to be known as the Battle of the Bulge, four men in a jeep tore up to a filling station behind General Hodges' First Army front in the Ardennes forests: "Petrol, please!" the driver shouted.

That was a mistake. American soldiers do not ask for petrol but for "gas"; nor, in a hurry, do they say "please."

"Where are you from?" somebody asked. The driver did not wait. He put in his clutch and drove off down the icy road—into a convoy of trucks. The jeep overturned. When the occupants were pulled out it was found that under their G.I. jackets they wore the field gray of the German Army.

Soon a shaking prisoner, told to speak up or be shot, blurted out that his jeep was only one of many; German troops disguised as Allies were filtering through all along the front. Thousands more were to cross the lines—with American uniforms, vehicles, tanks and guns. The purpose of the operation was to converge on Allied headquarters in Paris and kill or kidnap General Eisenhower. Colonel Otto Skorzeny was their leader.

Skorzeny—the man who made off with Mussolini! From that hour, as reports flashed in from one point or another on a hundred miles of raging battlefront, similar

captures threw Allied Supreme Headquarters into consternation. Always the same story when the prisoners
broke down—objective: to get Eisenhower; leader: Skorzeny.

Now the fact is that Skorzeny never tried to lay hands
on Eisenhower—it was not in his orders: he was playing
a very different game. His real mission, and its bizarre
consequences, had a more significant lesson for the future
than another Skorzeny kidnaping attempt could have offered.

The affair began as usual, with a trip to Hitler's
headquarters. It was moving day: the Wolf's Lair was in
danger of becoming a "front headquarters" in fact as well
as name; so the High Command was being shifted before
it could come under the Red Army's guns. In spite of this
upset Skorzeny was received by an effusive Hitler who rewarded his success in Hungary with promotion and the
German Cross in Gold. Then, when they were alone, the
Leader drew him aside with a conspiratorial gesture.

"I have something to tell you," he began dramatically.
"The world thinks Germany is finished, with only the day
and hour of the funeral to be appointed. I am going to
show how mistaken they are. The corpse will rise and hurl
itself in fury at the West. Then we shall see!"

He took Skorzeny over to a wall map. It showed
how Germany's armies had been driven back to where
they stood in 1940 before starting the *blitzkrieg* which
shattered France and threw the British off the Continent
in three summer weeks. Now the last thing anyone would
foresee, Hitler contended, was a second attack on the
same sector: that was where he meant, in the coming
winter, to strike a sledgehammer blow that would split
the Allied front in the Ardennes.

He put a finger on the Belgian supply port of Antwerp: the target, to be reached in a week from D-day.
The enemy in North Belgium and Holland would be cut
off—Montgomery's British and Canadian armies as well
as most of the American First Army—and would all be
driven into the sea. The rest of the American armies
south of Antwerp would be strung out for nearly five hundred miles from the North Sea to Switzerland. With their
northern wing chopped off, they would have more stomach
for recrimination than for fighting.

Such was the plan of attack which Hitler unfolded to

Skorzeny on October 20. Later, military writers were to call it the "battle of impossibilities": the place, the time, even the idea, of a German counteroffensive were unthinkable to experts on both sides. German generals in the West hoped for no more than a holding action while Hitler, or his successors, negotiated surrender. Eisenhower and Montgomery agreed there was no fear of Hitler's fighting power being revived.

Any suggestion that the quarry might leap at the throat of its hunters was ruled out. General Omar Bradley, whose Twelfth Army Group was to take the brunt of the offensive, later defended this view in military logic. "When anyone attacks, either he is out to destroy the hostile forces or he is going for a terrain objective. Neither objective could be attained in the Ardennes."* What the Allies could not guess was that Hitler had abandoned military logic and was now in the stratosphere of political intuition.

He told Skorzeny that he meant to exploit Allied uneasiness over the advances which were bringing the Russians so deeply into Western Europe. Many British and American leaders would welcome any means of stopping this landslide, but they could do nothing in the face of their peoples' admiration for their "heroic Soviet allies." A violent shock might bring the masses to reason; confronted with a second Dunkirk, they would be ready to cry quits. Then, under cover of a truce with the West, Germany could turn and throw her whole weight against Russia.

Hitler explained that he had been waiting for this opportunity ever since the landings in Normandy. The Allies' supply lines were stretched, their equipment was worn from continuous fighting, their armies were both overstrained and overconfident. On the other hand, Hitler expected thousands of new tanks, guns and jet planes from the factories; his roads to the front were short; new divisions were freed for action in the West by the plugging of the southeast front.

When he came to the part Skorzeny should play, Hitler was aquiver: it would be as complete a surprise as the horse of Troy; and on its success the fortunes of the whole operation might turn.

The first obstacle facing the German armies after

---

*A Soldier's Story. New York: Henry Holt and Company, 1951.

cracking the Allied crust would be the Meuse River, he said. Somehow they must pursue the fleeing enemy across it without respite. The one way to do that was to seize the Meuse bridges before they could be blown up. That task he would entrust to Skorzeny—and also the means to do it. He must raise an armored brigade in the image of the enemy; wearing their uniforms and driving their vehicles. Such a brigade could mingle with the routed Allies and hold the bridges for the German armies to cross over. Smaller groups of disguised troops would scout ahead for the brigade and do everything they could to demoralize the enemy.

Skorzeny's first thought was that every man who joined such a venture would face a firing squad on capture. Hitler reminded him that British commandos had often used German uniform, and quite lately some Americans had slipped through at Aachen by the same ruse. "We will give these people a dose of their own medicine," he said.

A dose? An armored brigade in Allied uniform might be called the whole pharmacopoeia. And as if to make the mixture more abhorrent to Skorzeny, Hitler forbade him categorically to cross the lines with his troops: "That will not be necessary; and we cannot afford to lose you at this stage."

Skorzeny was silently deciding that to slip over to his men *after* they had crossed would not infringe the letter of this injunction, when the Leader added almost casually, "You have until the first of December to make ready." Skorzeny at once pointed out that in so short a time he could only hope for a rough-and-ready job of improvisation. Hitler heard him out, then replied, "All that is true, but in five or six weeks' time we must attack. I know that you will do your best."

Given all the good will in the world, five or six months would have been little enough for so extraordinary a task, but soon Skorzeny saw that he would have to fight tooth and nail for any help at all. Hardly any of the Army chiefs outside Hitler's personal staff had yet been informed of what was coming. The one commander who did know all and whose support was most essential, was Field-Marshal von Rundstedt—and he was bitterly against the whole idea.

Not long before, von Rundstedt had been sacked

after a stand-up row with Hitler; now he returned to take charge of the Ardennes attack. But anyone who jumps to the conclusion that von Rundstedt believed in the offensive misunderstands the nature of this military basilisk; privately he called Hitler's plan "stupid and nonsensical"; he had no faith in it at all. Why, then, did he agree to lead it?

"As commander-in-chief in the West," this haughtiest of generals later complained, "I found the pressure of Hitler behind me was always far worse than the pressure of the Allies in front. I had only enough independence to change the guard at my gate."

Von Rundstedt's pride was further bruised when Hitler gave Skorzeny a direct briefing; it became clear that the new brigade would have to get itself born in spite of him.

And then the High Command itself committed one of the sublime blunders of the war. Field-Marshal Keitel signed a circular to all units in Germany:

> VERY SECRET: *To Divisional and Army Commands only*
>
> Officers and men who speak English are wanted for a special mission. Volunteers selected will join a new unit under the command of Lieut.-Colonel Skorzeny, to whose headquarters at Friedenthal application should be made.

Skorzeny passed his copy to Karl Radl to add to his anthology of High Command *incredibilia;* then he sat down and wrote asking that his mission should be canceled. Since the secret had been advertised it would be foolish to go on.

The Armed S.S. liaison officer at the High Command was General Fegelein, who in 1942 had married the sister of Eva Braun. Fegelein was shocked at Skorzeny's lack of realism. Surely he must know that his part in the offensive could not be put off unless they went to the Leader about it. And how could they confess such a mistake to Hitler? The mission would proceed as planned.

It happened that no harm was done; like so many bungles it was neutralized by one on the other side. General Bradley said later that the order did indeed reach Allied Intelligence; but no one took much notice of it.

Skorzeny had little time to brood. The volunteers came streaming in to Friedenthal from every part of Germany. Their spirit was magnificent; they were hot for adventure, ready for anything—except a language test. Then most of them began to scratch their heads or else replied "Yes" or "No" at a venture. A few hundred insisted they had been fluent at school—the language would come back to them. About a hundred and fifty had an academic knowledge of English; some thirty or forty had been abroad and spoke it quite well.

Skorzeny made the High Command realize that to create an effective, English-speaking brigade out of these volunteers in the short time he had left was no more than a pipe dream. He demanded, and got, a group of complete units—two tank battalions, a paratroop battalion, and signalers. To these he added two battalions of his own, making up a striking force which would give a good account of itself with or without disguise. He also made the High Command agree that the brigade would not be sent into battle in American uniform unless a full-scale rout of the enemy had already begun. To fulfil the second half of Hitler's order—for disguised scouts to go ahead of the brigade to bring back information and sow confusion —he built up a special commando company of the best English-speaking volunteers. All were told, on the authority of a German military lawyer, that it was a legitimate *ruse de guerre* to wear enemy uniform so long as you did not actually fight in it: Skorzeny hoped that the Americans would share this view—if they had ever heard of it.

The brightest candidates were sent off to an interpreters' school, but on their return a fresh problem arose. It had now been decided to use his brigade entirely against the American sector of the front, so all the men must pass as Americans. A few volunteers were sent into prison cages to "wise up" on the idiom: the real prisoners usually "got wised up" first, and at least one impostor was badly beaten at one of these finishing schools. In the end Skorzeny had to advise most of the men to rush past the enemy with teeth clenched, as though shell-shocked.

But even a deaf-mute column must somewhere come to rest and be exposed to close observation. G.I. behavior was taught to the men, but the bark of the Prussian drill sergeant still echoed in their ears. Whenever Skorzeny came on a group they would stiffen to attention. "Relax," he would beg—and the stamp of boots to an "at ease" position would ring across the square. To stroll by, hands in pockets; to chew gum, and park it; to flick a cigarette out of a "pack"; all the effortless arts—even that of failing to see, and hence salute one's officers off duty—had to be expounded. To these puzzled proselytes, the democratic way of life was "something else again."

In a special training camp near Nuremberg, Skorzeny sorted out his men, nearly three thousand five hundred of them, and made section leaders; then he waited for the American equipment. General Jodl had promised there would be plenty for all—"just ask for what you want." Experienced in whittling down his needs, Skorzeny decided to sacrifice all extras, even to field kitchens, in favor of fire power. He put in a request for twenty Sherman tanks, thirty armored cars, vehicles for three battalions of motorized infantry, guns for antitank companies and an antiaircraft company.

But Jodl had been optimistic when he said there was booty for all needs. Continuous retreat is not the way to capture arms and equipment.

Of the twenty Sherman tanks Skorzeny wanted he got two—with apologies from the Inspector of Armored Vehicles who had no more to send. German Panther tanks had to make up the lack. Their outlines were altered with sheets of tin—and the farther you stood away from them, said Radl consolingly, the better they looked: with great good luck they might be mistaken for Shermans a mile away in the dusk.

Six American armored cars arrived. Protests brought four more, but they were British: how could their appearance in an American sector be explained? Discussion ended when all four broke down on trial—obviously they had been left for junk. Again, German cars had to be camouflaged with khaki paint and white stars on the hoods.

Jeeps: every other officer Skorzeny met seemed to have captured a jeep for his private use. But on the day Jodl's order called them in, every jeep in Germany vanished. So much, scoffed Radl, for requisitioning: he sent out foragers, who found fifteen jeeps hidden in barns and warehouses. A few German Fords were painted khaki, and Czech and French cars were added.

The guns arrived: only half as many as they wanted,

but still more than they hoped for. Ammunition came too, several railway wagons of American shells, most of which exploded next day thanks to inexpert unloading by newly arrived men. In the end only the special commando company could be fitted out with American weapons. To every protest the High Command now had a single answer: "Why worry? There will be plenty for the taking when the Americans begin to run."

The first load of uniforms had to be sent back: they were British. Then came a variety of American greatcoats; since the troops opposite were in field jackets, these were useless too. Field jackets at last appeared—covered with prisoner-of-war triangles which had to be got off. "Never mind," they told Skorzeny, "you can pick up all you want after the breakthrough." He could discover no American uniform of his size, and in the face of Hitler's order not to cross the lines he dared not ask for one. So the brigade commander had to wear a khaki sweater.

Then the rumors started. You cannot put thousands of men behind palisades, forbid them to go out, censor their letters, submit them to a strange training scheme and prolong the mystification week after week without producing a forcing ground for stories of all kinds. Rumors—there was no killing them; they drew fresh life from each denial. At first Skorzeny was worried; then, as the guesses became wilder, he decided to confirm the most extravagant, so to speak, with a wink.

For a while most of the volunteers believed their mission was to strike across France and relieve the Germans cut off in Brest and Lorient: someone or other had even seen the plans for this. Then, one morning, a talkative young officer sought out Skorzeny: he knew Paris intimately, and so could be of much help in the coming operation. "Why," said Skorzeny, "what do you suppose we mean to do?" The young man looked around to see if they were alone. "We're going to dash through the American Army and capture Eisenhower's headquarters!"

Skorzeny was startled; he tried to look concerned as well; "Where did you hear that?" he exclaimed. "Don't mention it to anyone . . . When the time comes, I will call on you."

Next day the camp seethed with the news of the coming swoop on Paris, where Eisenhower's H.Q. were presumed to be. The story fell in pat with Skorzeny's reputation; it also suited the code name of the operation: "Greif." "Greif" is a mythical bird, but it can also mean "grasp": hence the young officer's inspiration. Soon everyone knew that disguised columns would race to the century-old Café de la Paix—no obscurer rendezvous would do—and there join forces under the shadow of the green-domed Opera House to "grasp" Eisenhower from his office chair. Skorzeny did nothing to discourage the report: it might help to confuse the enemy if it got about.

Presently he had graver preoccupations. During the priming of the Ardennes offensive he attended three High Command meetings; with the Wolf's Lair in East Prussia abandoned to the Russians, Hitler had moved his staff—and his last hopes of victory—to the Chancellery in Berlin. The gloomy howl of air-raid sirens matched the depression that sank into Skorzeny as, at each meeting, the promised totals of men and matériel for the main offensive dwindled.

When Hitler first confided in him he had talked of six thousand guns smashing the Allied front line, of a thousand tanks to spearhead the way to Antwerp, of the three thousand jet planes which Göring was building to challenge the Allied mastery of the sky. Now it became obvious that nothing like these totals could be hoped for: thanks to incessant bombing new armaments were not coming off the production lines on time and the wherewithal could not be gleaned from other fronts: every commander, especially in the East, clung to what he had—nothing, nothing could be spared.

Twice D-day was put off while the High Command scraped up what they could. The final meeting at Hitler's Chancellery was macabre. There sat von Rundstedt, sunk in aggrieved silence, nominal leader of a cause in which he did not even profess belief, while the experts conjured up phrases to fill the gaps in matériel. The flying bomb—"a wonderful weapon, its aim is much improved"—must make up for the lack of artillery and bombers. All other deficiencies would be met "when we have broken through" —including four-fifths of their fuel needs.

The last total which Skorzeny heard, mentioned almost casually, was that of jet planes ready to take off. Instead of the promised three thousand, Germany would have three hundred and fifty.

Me 262

The day came. Surprise, complete, knocked the breath out of the Americans at dawn on December 16. Bombing of their forward airfields, followed by fog, held the Allied air forces down. Snow and ice clogged their reserves.

Skorzeny's advance scouts, who had been given the best jeeps, and the most convincing uniforms and identity papers, went ahead with the spearheads of the Sixth S.S. Panzer Army; they were to cross the lines after splitting up into several groups.

The rest of the brigade waited at their jumping-off posts; when the tanks broke through they would rush ahead to join up with the rout. Above all they were not to open fire, Skorzeny warned them; their job was simply to occupy the Meuse bridges as American soldiers so that the rest of the army could take them in its stride.

Everything fulfilled Hitler's hopes—except that the Americans did not turn and run. Though von Rundstedt sheared his way fifty miles toward Namur, though the front was torn in two, the German advance stopped while the arms depots, the oil dumps—all the spoil the High Command had banked on—still lay beyond reach. While the defenders tried to gather their wits, easy-living lines-of-communication troops, cooks, signalers, supply-corps sergeants, were thrown into the breach. Then came the battle of Bastogne, the road junction which was held against all comers until General Patton's tank column pounded to the rescue.

Operation "Greif" should have been started soon after zero hour; when, twenty-four hours later, there was still no breakthrough for his brigade to exploit, Skorzeny wanted to call it off. "Give us another twenty-four hours," the Sixth Army pleaded. Meanwhile he had sent two more of his "American" groups to reconnoiter the Meuse bridges, so that if the rout began no time would be lost in seizing them. Another twenty-four hours went by, and the enemy still did not break. Heavy reserves were coming up behind the Americans: they had rallied from the surprise—there would be no breakthrough now. So Skorzeny told his brigade to cast aside their camouflage and soon they were all caught up in the swirl of battle.

Behind the German lines the traffic was in chaos, as Skorzeny found when he tried to reach another sector for a council of war. Someone at headquarters had forgotten to cancel orders for the second phase of the advance, although the first phase had been frustrated. Driving past convoys stranded for lack of fuel, tankers went forward to fill up at "captured" Allied depots—depots which remained miles behind the American lines.

Skorzeny left his car on a jammed main road and trudged through the slush to the top of the hill. There he found a gigantic trailer stuck; it had been trundling V1 parts up to a proposed new launching base which still had to be captured. He ordered the hundreds of idle transport crews out of their lorries; together they heaved the encumbrance over the edge of the road and cleared the way —until the next V1 trailer came along. A few days later, when a misdirected flying bomb fell within a hundred yards of him, Skorzeny again cursed the High Command optimists: "A wonderful weapon—it's aim is much improved!" Luckily, the missile failed even to explode.

By now the Americans were hitting back; Skorzeny put in his brigade to save the northern shoulder of the German salient, where von Rundstedt's spearheads might be severed at their base. Day after day he went from one shaky point to another, leading his troops in fighting of a grimly orthodox kind. On December 21 one of his officers blundered across the lines into Malmédy and found it thinly held; Skorzeny saw a chance to take the town. Though the brigade had no artillery left and only ten tanks, he sent in a two-pronged attack. Then up came the Americans in force. The Germans were beaten off with heavy losses: last of all to return was von Foelkersam, who was slightly wounded. Before the day was over Skorzeny also was wounded, in the head. Patched up at once, he got back to his troops in time to welcome a long-promised battery of heavy guns; now they would get some of their own back—and perhaps Malmédy too. The gunner officer was sorry: he had only sixteen rounds for each gun with no hope of any more.

That was Christmas Day.

On December 28 they were relieved; already clearing skies had unleashed the Allied air force, and all the way back from the front the dwindling German columns, black against the snow, were strafed by bombers. Soon the Ardennes offensive became a great retreat; altogether they lost almost a quarter of a million men in casualties and prisoners. The rest of von Rundstedt's armies were swept back into Germany.

But what had happened to Skorzeny's "Americans"? In bits and pieces, as some of them came back, and later on when he could talk to all those who recrossed the lines, Skorzeny put together a picture of the little war they had conducted.

The first group of disguised volunteers had driven over the Belgian front until they reached a crossroads near the Meuse: they were at Huy, midway between Liège and Namur, caught up in a swirl of jeeps and trucks. The German leader tried out his accent by asking the Americans what reinforcements they expected. After some hours an armored regiment thundered up toward the front.

"You can't go that way," the German shouted. "You'll have to make a detour"—and he gave them one which would land them up the other side of Belgium. Off they went—"and thanks for telling us." The German said, "You're welcome."

A second group ran head-on into a company of Americans, dug in with wire and machine guns, who misread their alarm at the confrontation. "What are you running from?" the Germans were asked. Their officer, in top sergeant's uniform, took his cue. "Scram, fellows," he called out. "They've broken through all around us!" The defenders left in haste.

Moving about almost as freely as if they were invisible, Skorzeny's groups turned signposts around to misdirect reserves, severed telephone and cable lines, looped red ribbons to trees to indicate that this or that road to the front was barred by mines. If "for want of a nail the battle was lost," one can imagine what such deliberate but unsuspected malevolence can do.*

But far more devastating than any material damage was the moral chaos caused by Operation "Greif." When the first disguised troops were pulled out of their capsized jeep and made to confess, waves of shock ran through the front and rear of the defenders. A brigade of Germans in American uniform! An attack on General Eisenhower's headquarters! Otto Skorzeny in command of a specially trained murder gang! It was incredible—yet here, in these wretched prisoners, was the proof. The rockbound certainties of army life collapsed, the laws of probability were swept away.

The stories which the prisoners had brought from Skorzeny's training camp struck root in the alluvium left in the wake of Operation "Greif," and flourished into monstrous growth. A week later Radio Calais was claiming that some two hundred and fifty men in American uniform had been rounded up—and Skorzeny knew that very few of them were Germans. Years afterwards he was to meet some of the victims of mistaken zeal. One American captain, because he was seen wearing a pair of German boots picked up at the front, spent a week in jail. Two others, visiting staff officers who rarely tasted canned food, incurred suspicion at a frontline mess by remarking on the excellence of the lunch; they ate their next meal under close arrest.

The prisoners' stories now linked up with Keitel's appeal for English-speaking volunteers which the Americans had filed away; stricken with remorse, U.S. Intelligence more than made up for past insouciance.

---

*The author's thanks are due to Supreme Allied Headquarters for reminding him of the doggerel; it was framed on the wall of their Supply Headquarters in London.

The warning went out: "Otto Skorzeny, specialist in the art of kidnaping and assassinating high personages," was on his way to Supreme Headquarters with some two hundred armed men in American uniform, all sworn to get General Eisenhower. Similar columns were looking for Montgomery, Bradley and other Allied leaders. They spoke English, and had American papers and 'vehicles; their one oversight was that they carried no "dog tags"— the metal identity discs worn next to the skin. Such a detail, of course, could be checked only by challenging impostors who were reputed to throw phials of acid in the eyes of people who came too close. Furthermore, it was said that "maybe some gangsters do have dog tags, at that."

Soon half the army was waiting for Skorzeny. The air was full of hostile specters, in and behind the lines. Anyone might be an enemy. Those trucks beside the road could be an ambush; that quiet stranger in the bar—was he a saboteur? Such fancies did nothing to steady the defenders as they strove to recover from the Ardennes punch.

To General Bradley, in his Army Corps headquarters at Luxemburg, it was the last drop in a cup brimming with vexation. Soon he was commenting on the spectacle of "half a million G.I.'s . . . playing cat and mouse with each other every time they met." He could not even drive to hardpressed First Army headquarters; General Hodges' staff begged him to wait for a plane until the fog cleared—"because the rear areas were being panicked by disguised Germans."

High-ranking officers rushing from one conference to another found roadblocks all the way; badges of rank now meant nothing, and even passwords were distrusted. In this extremity folklore shored up the crumbling routine of the Army: suspects—and everyone was suspect— had to take part in a quiz game to establish their American birthright.

When at last General Bradley took the road in his three-star limousine, it was to find that "neither rank, nor credentials, nor protests" spared him the common inquisition. At every crossroads he had to prove his nationality: "the first time by identifying Springfield as the capital of Massachusetts (my questioner held out for Chicago); the second time by locating the football guard between the center and tackle on a line scrimmage; the third time by naming the current spouse of a blonde called Betty Grable."*

Montgomery was taking over part of the ruptured American front; his liaison officers, speeding through ice and snow, found tommy guns thrust over their frosted windows. "Who is Pruneface?" a hoarse voice would demand. "Where does Li'l Abner live? Who works with Jiggs?" British officers unfamiliar with the Declaration of Independence or the title of a whistled sample from tin-pan alley, were put under arrest; for was it not said that some of the dissembling Germans had performed a quick-change into British uniform; even that one of them was riding around as Field-Marshal Montgomery? No chance could be taken—and none was. Such was the burlesque offered by the impresarios of Security and enacted on a stage that was in flames.

Nor were Paris and Supreme Headquarters without Christmas enlivenment. It was at the Café de la Paix, on its famous corner by the Opéra, that the Skorzeny columns were supposed to meet. Security set an ambush with guns and tanks—but how could one distinguish between such colorful impersonators and real American troops, on leave or in transit, to whom the café terrace was a honey pot? An eight P.M. curfew was enforced; Security hoped that Skorzeny's men would come careering into an empty capital; then they could be pounced on. Of course, if Skorzeny took the risk of coming in by day—or, a horrifying thought—if his troops were already there . . . So hundreds of disgruntled Americans were challenged on the boulevards; to reach the Café de la Paix before curfew they had to run the gauntlet through cordons of M.P.'s.

Civilian cars, also, had to be checked, and ironical French comments endured by patrols whose ears were already smarting from the abuse of G.I. drivers in a hurry; and as rumor added new weapons—plastic explosives, grenades fired from a pistol—to Skorzeny's reputed arsenal of terror, the inquiries became unceremonious.

And now General Eisenhower had a foretaste of the seclusion he was to suffer in the White House: report said

*A Soldier's Story. New York: Henry Holt and Company, 1951.

Kampfpistole

that a "suicide squad" of at least three score Germans was heading for his home. "The story," he recalls, "was brought to me by a very agitated colonel who was certain that he had complete and positive proof of the existence of such a plot. He outlined it in great detail and his conclusions were supported by other members of the Security Staff."*

For months the Supreme Commander had motored about France and Belgium with only an officer or an orderly as escort. He had also been living a free and easy life in a villa (formerly occupied by von Rundstedt) at St. Germain, half an hour's drive from Paris.

Security were aghast at their past laxity; the general must at once move into the "compound" of Supreme Headquarters behind the cordons and patrols of Versailles with reserves nearby. In vain did Eisenhower argue that the Germans must have enough to do without sending troops far and wide looking for Allied commanders who could all, presumably, be replaced. Security did not share the Supreme Commander's views on his replaceability. Eisenhower had to pack and shift into the Trianon build-

*Crusade in Europe. New York: Doubleday and Company, Inc., 1948.

ing at Versailles—if only "so that soldiers should be used on the battleline and not in trailing me around."

Supreme Headquarters' own little D-day was described in the diary of Eisenhower's secretary and aide, Lieut. Kay Summersby.

To say this report [of Skorzeny's imminent arrival] upset SHAEF [Supreme Headquarters] is pure understatement.

Security officers immediately turned headquarters compound into a virtual fortress. Barbed wire appeared. Several tanks moved in. The normal guard was doubled, trebled, quadrupled. The pass system became a strict matter of life and death, instead of the old formality. The sound of a car exhaust was enough to halt work in every office, to start a flurry of telephone calls to our office, to inquire if the boss was all right. The atmosphere was worse than that of a combat headquarters up at the front, where everyone knew how to take such a situation in their stride.

The intended victim was the only officer at SHAEF unperturbed by the report. General Eisenhower had the war, the Bulge, to worry about; he couldn't be bothered by this one fantastic story.

The staff insisted he move in from the von Rundstedt house, which was comparatively isolated from the Trianon. They pointed to the lonely, wooded stretches along the road; they emphasized the Germans knew every inch of that territory from their Occupation days. They said the General's security was impossible under such circumstances.

Finally—only after his closest associates begged, as personal friends rather than staff officers, him to leave the von Rundstedt house—he reluctantly moved into the compound.

"But only so you'll forget about the damned business and get back to the war," he growled.

Security even asked General Eisenhower not to walk outside the office, for fear a sniper might have slipped through the toe-to-toe guard.

We were prisoners, in every sense of the word.

This new, personal tension, coupled with the flood of bad news and rumors from the Ardennes, left most of headquarters frankly apprehensive and depressed. Ike, the one solely responsible for the success or failure of our counterattack and therefore the only one entitled to the luxury of depression, had to smother his own feelings and act as the eternal optimist.

Next day the diary reported:

Another night of uneasiness. E. is just pinned to his office all day; at night he goes upstairs and sleeps . . . I stay across the way from the office. Everyone's confined to the compound. What a life. . . .

I lay awake for hours envisioning death and worse at the hands of S.S. agents. Sleep was impossible—with the tramp, tramp, tramp of heavy-booted guards patrolling our tin roof.

On December 22 the diary read:

On our personal front Intelligence passed along a report the sabotage-assassins had made their way into Paris proper. It was said they would rendezvous at the Café de la Paix.

This warning failed to bother the General. He came out of his office cell grumbling, "Hell's fire, I'm going for a walk. If anyone wants to shoot me, he can go right ahead. I've got to get out!"*

The stolen walk was in the courtyard of the buildings with guards all around.

Next day Eisenhower was allowed a visit from his naval aide, Capt. Harry C. Butcher. Butcher had got back

---

*Excerpts reprinted with permission of the publishers from *Eisenhower Was My Boss* by Lieut. Kay Summersby. Copyright, 1948, by Kay Summersby. Published by Prentice-Hall, Inc., Englewood Cliffs, New Jersey, 07632.

only the night before to Paris, darkened and under curfew, after stopping at roadblocks all the way from the front. Hearing of his chief's isolation he drove out to see him, and his impressions of the prisoner of Versailles were recorded in a diary to which, like Lieut. Summersby, he confided "both high- and low-level views of the Ardennes attack."

> Saw Ike today. He . . . is thoroughly but hopelessly irritated by the restrictions on his moves. There are all sorts of guards, some with machine guns, around the house, and he has to go to and from the office, led, and sometimes followed, by an armed guard in a jeep. He seemed pleased to have someone to talk with like me, seemingly from the outer world.*

This outer world was what Security meant to keep at bay. Shepherded to Versailles "for two or three days," Eisenhower found himself detained throughout Christmas week on one pretext and another, for Security were playing a double game. Unknown to the general, they were using a human decoy to trap Skorzeny: one Lieut.-Colonel Baldwin B. Smith, who was said to have the "Eisenhower look." Daily the colonel drove in the Supreme Commander's car between his house at St. Germain and Versailles, saluting with that quick flash for which "Ike" was known—and waiting for a bullet or a pistol-fired grenade.

It may be asked how Skorzeny's men were supposed to penetrate the network in which Security had now enclosed their chief; a popular theory was that they would slip on M.P.s' brassards and escort Skorzeny—now in *German* uniform—to Versailles for interrogation. Did they have dog tags? The question lost relevance since military police themselves were suspect.

On December 27 Eisenhower broke loose. He left to take the train for Brussels like a schoolboy off to town —and found the Gare du Nord seething with troops and police.

My Three Years with Eisenhower, New York: Simon and Schuster, Inc., 1946.

I sharply queried the Security officers about this use of men, but they assured me that they had merely assembled in the station individuals who were normally on duty in that vicinity.

However, after we were well started on our journey I found that a squad of soldiers was accompanying me. At every stop—and these were frequent because of difficulties with ice and snowbanks—these men would jump out of the train and take up an alert position to protect us.*

Arrived at Brussels for his top-secret conference with Montgomery, Eisenhower ran straight into another flurry of precautions because a cavalcade of British staff cars headed by a red-tabbed Skorzeny was said to be driving through Belgium. Security did not breathe freely until they got their truant home.

Months after the Ardennes battle, M.P.'s still carried Skorzeny's picture to compare with powerfully built strangers of the killer type, while all the French police had a notice to say that this was a most dangerous man; he must be hunted down with prudence. Until the end of the war, perhaps to avoid alarming the public, Supreme Headquarters kept the story from the Press; then, with the Armistice, newspapers burst out with accounts of how "handpicked assassins, led by the giant kidnaper, had been sent to murder Eisenhower." Skorzeny's arrest brought anticlimax; instead of thousands of English-speaking desperadoes, ranging far and wide, the total who went over the lines was finally agreed at—twenty-eight. Skorzeny himself questioned every soldier who got back; he is sure there were no more.

So there it is: a handful of half-trained, ill-equipped adventurers, seldom knowing where they were or what next they should do, were able to throw an enemy into turmoil and isolate its commander-in-chief. It was a success of almost alarming magnitude compared with the means employed—and Skorzeny was almost the last to hear of it.

On New Year's Eve he was receiving from Hitler the

---

*Crusade in Europe. New York: Doubleday and Company, Inc., 1948.

Mention clasp of the German Army for staving off front-line attacks in the Malmédy area during the crisis of December 18–28—the very week during which Eisenhower was held at Versailles for fear of him.

The summons to G.H.Q. (temporarily set up in a Rhineland forest for the Battle of the Bulge) saved Skorzeny's right eye; at the sight of his bandages Hitler sent him to his "court surgeon" and he spent several hours on the operating table. It was in the sick bay that an acquaintance, Dr. Rudolf Brandt, told Skorzeny how the Leader was now relying on drugs and injections to keep himself going. And the war going too, it seemed, for when Skorzeny got back to Hitler's room it was to hear him talking cheerfully of another big gamble in the Southeast; although it was clear that he had played his last card, and lost. Others at headquarters referred vaguely to more wonder weapons just around the corner which might turn the tide.

Declining an invitation to the generals' mess—extended with rare condescension by Marshal Keitel—Skorzeny left to rejoin his brigade; he heard the chime of midnight bells as he passed through the wreckage of Cologne.

What might the New Year bring? This was a question no German dared ask on the first day of 1945, but it came up when Skorzeny reached his headquarters. Von Foelkersam was waiting for him, with a request that would not be denied. The brigade was being disbanded; up at Friedenthal there could be little scope in the future for delicately balanced missions.

He asked for the command of the Eastern Task Force.

XI

We know what our enemies would do to the German people if they could. They would enslave many millions and starve the rest. Our existence is at stake: the existence of our children and our children's children; everything that makes life worth living.

Hitler's declaration at the turn of the year.

Acceptance of the Morgenthau Plan (whereby Roosevelt and Churchill agreed at Quebec in the autumn of 1944 on the permanent division of Germany and her destruction as a modern industrial state after the war) was surely a monstrous and unmitigated mistake of statecraft. . . . It is impossible to escape the conclusion that many thousands of German soldiers decided that it was better to face death in battle than undergo the slower death by starvation which was the alternative the Morgenthau Plan seemed to offer.

PROFESSOR WILLIAM HARDY McNEILL,
America, Britain and Russia

Adrian von Foelkersam was the idealist in uniform that Skorzeny could never be: apologetic for others' failings; harsh toward his own; fretful only when he felt he might do more. He combined an inner intensity with the hawk-like spirit of those Baltic vikings from whom his line had sprung: by habit he was gay, on principle uncaring, yet sometimes he would sit alone; then Skorzeny would be reminded of their first meeting.

An irascible young man, he had thought, when an unknown subaltern was ushered in during the early days at Friedenthal. Then the name and the decoration on the stranger's tunic brought to his mind a piece of quite insensate daring during the German advance into Russia: even then, the Knight's Cross was not easily earned. The visitor, still scowling, stammered out his embassy. There were eleven of them, he said, ten brother officers and himself from the Brandenburg Division who wanted brisker work. What hope of joining these new commandos? When Skorzeny promised to see what he could do, the youngster's face cleared wonderfully.

It was over the transfer of this little group of officers that Skorzeny underwent that first and last interview with his Intelligence Chief, Admiral Canaris. Beaten by this master of evasion, he and Radl changed their tactics and eventually smuggled in the eleven runagates by the back stairs. An age had passed since then: it seemed to both of them that Adrian had been always there—a third musketeer without whom no new venture was coinceivable.

But that was just the point, said von Foelkersam in support of his petition; there were no new ventures in sight, and none was likely. The High Command would have no use for fancy troops and wildcat schemes in the short life left to Germany. To put it brutally, his present job as Skorzeny's chief of staff was a blind alley: high time he got back to regular soldiering, and since Friedenthal was seeking a new commander for their Task Force East—why not let him have the post?

Skorzeny was not deceived. Armies on both sides in the West had been left groggy by the Ardennes tussle, but in the East the Soviets had opened an offensive that was tumbling the defenses before Berlin: his friend wanted the one battalion under Skorzeny's command most likely to be sent on the next stopgap mission. But no one could hold von Foelkersam when there was something unpleasant to be done. He set off to the front as one on whom the gods had showered their choicest favors.

On January 18, Task Force East was at Hohensalza, with orders to hold the city to the last man. For centuries this junction of routes between Poland and Prussia had been disputed—now the Red Army were sweeping around it: what could a thousand men do in that human sea of enemies? Before the Russians closed on Hohensalza Skorzeny rushed in a few lorry-loads of munitions.

Three days later von Foelkersam radioed, "Position untenable." The problem was beneath the notice of the High Command; here, there and everywhere sacrificial stands were being demanded of isolated units and battle groups. Skorzeny felt it right to override an order which had become purposeless. He radioed "Break out tonight," hoping that some, at least, of the men might get through the Russian ring. A last radio message reported von Foelkersam had been badly wounded. Of all that picked battalion, there returned to Friedenthal two officers and three men. Von Foelkersam was not among them.

These last months of war took on a nightmare aspect for Skorzeny. Men whom he had trained in his single-minded fashion, men who had grown as close as brothers, had to be squandered on hopeless missions in a cause already lost. Nor was the task made easier for him because they went open-eyed and willingly to this unnecessary end.

[The author once heard Skorzeny refer to some of his special troops: "beautiful men," he called them, in the glowing assurance that he would be understood. These were the élite who always stepped forward: soldiers whose devotion transcended his own, since they could seldom be told where they were going. He had first been captivated by this spirit during the Mussolini search. Week after week his volunteers had waited in their camp: up to the very day of the Gran Sasso attack none of them except Karl Radl had any idea what lay before them—and even then were told only that few could hope to live through what was ahead. One mission after another confirmed his view that anyone can lead—since he knows where he is going —but it takes courage to follow a leap into the dark. Skorzeny insisted that this point be clear; and now the author's promise is redeemed.]

Perhaps the mission which troubled Skorzeny most deeply during this high season of contumacy was the attempt to salvage a "lost legion" from the depths of Russia. For months it clouded all his days and made his nights a torment; wherever his work took him he was pursued by it; his dislike for the harmless, necessary bureaucracy still turns to fury at the memory.

A telegram summoned him to Jodl's presence: he found Hitler's Chief of Operations with two officers in the red-striped trousers of the Staff, and at once divined from their solemnity that he was to be offered what Radl used to call "a specially important mission—one which it is specially important for the High Command to wash its hands of."

The guess proved right. An unwelcome problem had arisen from the stubbornness of a regimental commander, who had gathered up the pieces of a dozen broken units after the collapse of the central front in Russia. Twenty-five divisions had surrendered on the central front that summer in unimaginable catastrophe; whole regiments had thrown down their arms; yet this Lieut.-Colonel Scherhorn and his hybrid army remained in the field when the Red armies had swirled on. German agents had radioed repeated reports of fighting. It seemed that Scherhorn still had some two thousand men under his command near Minsk, in the forests of White Russia, but the latest message said he could not hold out much longer. What could be done?

Skorzeny thought it out. Scherhorn had been cut off in June: now it was September. With three months gone and nothing done, it was too late for any action except the most precipitate—hence his telegram from Jodl. The whole affair was plainly an embarrassment to the High Command, who always believed that the best way to deal with embarrassments was to ignore them. One advanced, after all, or one retreated; well-geared machinery had always existed for both evolutions, but the generals had no technique for dealing with lost legions out of teleprinter range. Jodl anxiously asked whether Skorzeny would take over the responsibility. He could not refuse. For men like Colonel Scherhorn, and the troops who had stuck it out with him, no trouble was too much.

Flying back to Friedenthal, Skorzeny wondered at his own foolhardiness in taking on such a task when Germany herself faced the deluge. And yet, he thought, while such exemplary lunatics as Scherhorn struck out against the tide there would always be others ready to plunge in too. And if, by any thousandth chance, Scherhorn were to be saved, the rescue would lift spirits on every front and in every home in Germany.

An unlikely crew lined up at Friedenthal a few days

later: heads roughly cropped, chins thick with stubble, they carried Soviet automatic pistols to go with their sack-like winter uniforms. Their papers, worn and greasy, tallied with the Russian names and units which each man rattled off. Only a clumsiness in the way that some of them thumbed black tobacco into scraps of newspaper and drew on these homemade cigarettes might have betrayed them.

Eight of the volunteers were Germans who, coming from the Baltic provinces, spoke Russian well. Twelve or fourteen more were Russians who had changed sides. The party was split up into four groups, each with a radioman; one by one the groups would be dropped over the area, now hundreds of miles behind the Russian lines, where Colonel Scherhorn had been reported.

Group A took off at dusk. Five hours later their radio crackled out: "Poor landing. Enemy have seen us. Machine guns firing." Then silence.

Gorup B went next. No signal this time, even to report their landing, until the fifth night. Then the decoding clerk called Skorzeny with a shout. Group B was safe—and they had found the lost army! Here was Colonel Scherhorn himself to radio his thanks.

Group C jumped next night to link up—like Group A, they vanished without trace. Group D followed. Failing to find Scherhorn, they worked their way home on foot. Again and again they were accepted as Russian soldiers; best of all was the night when their leader walked into a Red officers' mess and stayed to feast on roast goose and looted wine.

Skorzeny's elation at hearing from the lost legion was short-lived. He had banked on getting them out by air lift after they had cleared runways in the forest; but Scherhorn's men were hungry and shivering in the rags of summer uniform; many were stricken with wounds or disease: they were too exhausted for heavy work. A doctor jumped to help and broke both legs. A second doctor landed safely and got a field hospital going, its equipment being delivered by air. Then an airfield expert parachuted: by the time they had cleared runways in a few weeks the longer nights would lend cover for the rescue planes to land.

Planning was one thing, supply another. The lost legion wanted concentrated food, clothing, ammunition,

stores—large stocks of everything hard to find—and the
planes to carry them. After quarreling with every Army
branch in reach, Skorzeny got most of Scherhorn's needs:
as they rained down, the lost army was built into a fighting
force again.

But the throb of aircraft flying over every night at-
tracted unwelcome attention to Scherhorn. Fresh attacks
by Soviet troops drew off his strength and used up his supplies: how could airstrips be built? Then at Friedenthal
they had an inspiration. Some two hundred miles north of
Minsk there stretched a region of lakes. If Scherhorn
could fight his way there during the next few weeks, planes
might lift his men straight off the ice—there would be no
need for building runways.

A wave of hope excited the planners at Friedenthal.
Scherhorn hailed the new scheme with delight—and a request for new cargoes of stores to put them on the road.
Again the old bugbear: droves of Berlin officials had to be
routed out and activated. More food was wanted, weapons, heavy clothing, a hundred things for every one of the
two thousand. It was mid-November before Scherhorn's
exodus began: blizzards were closing in. The few lorries
they had were filled with wounded; all the rest plodded
slowly in columns which wound their way across the white
monotony of Russia: ten miles the first day—this was a
burst of energy, for on the second day Scherhorn signaled only six. After that they seldom covered more than
three or four miles each day. Sometimes fighting pinned
them down: this meant Skorzeny must plead for more supplies to replace those expended. Most of his stocks fell
wide and were lost.

Time rushed on. Emerging from the Battle of the
Ardennes Skorzeny found his fuel for the supply flights
reduced. He protested—it was cut again. The powers were
implacable. Though huge dumps were being abandoned
in the German retreat through Poland he had to fight for
every drum of fuel. Radl, too, did his best, swearing that
when the enemy broke into Berlin they would find an
Everest of stores stamped "Never to be used."

Still the Russians rolled west, with Berlin tensed now
for the onslaught. Skorzeny's freight planes had to fall
back to airfields deep in Germany; each flight was longer,
each cargo smaller.

January came; still the Scherhorn columns crawled

across the dimly lit spaces, beating off attacks. In spite of
his overwhelming exertions on the Oder battlefront, Skorzeny kept badgering Berlin for help to Scherhorn while
he radioed him messages of false confidence—what else
was there to do? Then came word that Scherhorn had
joined up with the first group of parachutists who had
been lost—and at last, on February 27, after fourteen
weeks of travail, Skorzeny got the heart-lifting report he
had awaited for so long: the advance party were on the
lakes!

At Friedenthal they were down to one supply trip by
one plane a week—and now the fuel line was cut; they
were destitute. There would be no more fuel: there *was*
no more—Berlin's reply was final.

Another radio from Scherhorn: "Where are the
planes? Send to fetch us. Hurry. We are running out of
food."

The fragments of the lost legion met their unrecorded
end. The leader of Group B, who found Scherhorn and
led him to the lakes, was promoted, and his Knight's
Cross, one of the last to be awarded, was dropped to him
from the air. Thanks were signaled—but by whom?

This story, with its strange, quixotic gleam, is one of
many which lit up for Skorzeny the opportunities behind
the Russian lines. Equally, it pointed the penalty of failure.
Nothing has been heard of Scherhorn's survivors: whether
they starved and froze into the snow, where the Russians,
the war being over, left them; or whether they were over-
whelmed by the enemy, we do not know. There is a report
that their leader was freed, broken in health, from a prison
camp long after the war, but the rest are among the host
of Germans cut off in Russia who have still to be ac-
counted for.

Men of the type who parachuted down to organize
the lost legion had a special gusto in their work: danger
seemed to lure them on. Such secret missions were usually
led by a German officer; one such, a youth of extraordinary daring, was Lieutenant (later Captain) Walter Girg,
who passed and repassed the Soviet lines so often as to
lose count. Radl used to say that Walter played his own
version of Russian roulette, with five bullets in the revolver
instead of the conventional one.

Girg took luck for granted and it never failed him.

With his mild blue eyes, blond curls and lisping Austrian speech, only the unassailable fact that he had won two Iron Crosses and was not yet twenty-three induced Skorzeny to accept him as a volunteer. That was in 1944, late enough for heroics, but the newcomer at once became the *enfant terrible* of Friedenthal. "Moscow or bust" was plain common sense to Girg; Skorzeny had to take him severely in hand to stop him from overshooting the mark on almost every mission. Again and again he fell into preposterous scrapes and came out smiling. If someone was wanted to test the indulgence of Providence under extreme provocation, Girg was the man.

His most famous success was in delaying the Red Army in Rumania while the Carpathian defenses were taken up by the Germans; he was cited for helping to extricate a whole army corps from disaster. That was in August 1944, when the Balkan front had fallen in. No one knew what was going on. The Russians seemed to be everywhere.

Skorzeny then received this message from the High Command: "Form two special platoons for immediate operation to start from Temezvar airport, Rumania. The object is to bar the Carpathian mountain passes, reconnoiter behind the enemy, wreck his communications and help German civilians to safety."

A tall order, and to be fulfilled at a moment's notice. Skorzeny got together special troops, demolition experts, a dozen Russian-speaking commandos—and Walter Girg: just before take-off he sent over a scouting plane which returned with the news that Temezvar airport was in Russian hands. So they landed instead at an emergency field in Rumania and struck into the unknown: forty men against the invincible Red armies, trusting to their luck and to the Rumanian uniforms they wore. As a last touch, red armbands were added to denote the change of allegiance since Rumania's armistice with Russia.

Girg had his party split into four. Each squad started by blocking the passes in its area—the Russian advance was thus slowed for several days. Then they concentrated on rescuing the old-established German colonies in Rumania; several hundreds were led out to safety. But it was left to Girg himself to pluck the rewards of supreme effrontery. His party ran into a Russian column—on their way, the comrades shouted, to occupy Kronstadt which the Rumanian Government had handed over to their new Soviet masters. Chanting: "Long live the Red Army: soon be the victory!" Girg's men led the march into Kronstadt with flowers, picked on the wayside, stuck in their rifles. Alight with wine and song, after much fraternal uproar in the town, they went on their way.

Later some of Girg's men came across a German antiaircraft regiment, abandoned in the rout of armies, waiting to surrender. The unit had the latest rapid-firing guns; the men, in perfect trim, might have left their depot an hour before. The two thousand gunners had not fired a shot—indeed, they had yet to see a Russian. Hundreds of them were shamed into joining in a breakthrough, and nearly all got home. Many such units yielded helplessly to the "Russian neurosis."

On his way back, after foraging over hundreds of miles to locate the Russian units, Girg, with four of his men, was trapped. Two were clubbed to death with rifle butts; Girg was being led out, stripped to the skin, for execution, when he broke away. The Russians chased him, shooting wildly. He fell wounded into a swamp and there sank out of sight. Next morning a naked man appeared at a German outpost, asking for the commander. Once more Girg had spun the revolver's cylinder to an empty chamber.

Before the debacle in Germany, Girg led a tank dash through the Russians in the north; again he had a mixed crowd of fifteen Germans and twenty-five Russians, all in the uniforms of the "Red" Rumanians. Using Danzig as a sally port after East Prussia had been cut off, he broke through to the beleaguered garrison at Kolberg, along the Baltic coast. Skorzeny got a radio message from the garrison's commander who could not believe that Girg was really a German officer, still less that he had brought a group of tanks a hundred miles through the Russian lines. So he had arrested the whole party as spies and proposed to shoot them forthwith unless Skorzeny could vouch for their story. Skorzeny radioed to Kolberg just in time.

This Russian siege of Kolberg presented one of warfare's giddiest tergiversations. French soldiers enlisted in the S.S. Charlemagne Division fought to hold open a corridor through which German refugees were fleeing to the west. German Reds, prisoners of war enrolled in the Seydlitz Division, were battling to cut their compatriots' escape route.

Girg reached home only three men short, after a tour of four hundred miles in Soviet-held territory. His radio operator, drowned when the ice broke as they were crossing the frozen Vistula, was buried in a cemetery with military honors and Soviet troops standing by. On their return Skorzeny handed out wrist watches to Girg's Russians and was rewarded by their exuberant delight.

For his part, Girg admired the German civilians left behind by the ebbing German tide. Although terrified of the Red Army, they never denied him help: the women, especially, would take any risk if he showed them the Knight's Cross, won in Rumania, which he always wore under his scarf.

As the Russian flood widened and rushed onwards the scope for work behind the lines was greatly enlarged. A last effort was put into helter-skelter rescue missions of one kind or another; and not only on land, but down that artery of Central and Southeastern Europe, the Danube.

Flowing through half a dozen countries, the Danube wound in and out of the fighting line. Skorzeny had a task force of sailors, intelligence experts and strong swimmers mobilized, as soon as the Russians reached the river, for a mimic naval war known as Operation "Trout." Soviet tankers were attacked with mines and explosive boats; frogmen blew up craft and bridges; in a few months some thirty thousand tons of shipping was sunk. And it was down the Danube that Skorzeny tried to send help to Budapest.

The months gained in the Balkans were running out. The Russians had crossed the Carpathians and broken into Budapest, where the Germans and their Hungarian allies still fought on. Skorzeny followed the battle news earnestly. He deplored this street-by-street destruction of one of Europe's fairest cities, and at the same time he was concerned for his friend and former senior officer in Russia, General Rumohr, who now commanded the armored division caught inside the city.

Hitler's prestige was engaged in Budapest: he did all he could, even to sending down three more of his best tank divisions, to raise the siege. The Russian grip was too tight. The garrison seemed doomed—but at least the end could be staved off if they could have medical supplies and ammunition.

Skorzeny suggested the river route. One of the fastest freighters in Vienna was loaded with five hundred tons of stores and manned by a special crew, all Danube officers, who welcomed the chance of teaching the Russians a trick or two about "their" river. The journey took them twice through the Russian lines; then a sorry radio message reached Skorzeny—their ship had run upon a sandbank. But the crew did not give up. One officer got to Budapest in a small boat; there he stole a motor launch, and with it cargoes were repeatedly run through. A scouting party later found the freighter still on its sandbank: but before they got there the radioman signed off with a message that the crew were all going down into Budapest to join the defenders.

The Battle of Budapest raged on for a full month. Then the garrison were ordered to break out. Of tens of thousands, a hundred and seventy reached safety. General Rumohr was wounded and Skorzeny heard later on that his friend had shot himself rather than fall into Russian hands.

XII

> *The last great battle has begun. Enormous masses of troops, tanks and aircraft are being hurled against us in the East. The Russians are out for the final decisions.*
>
> Berlin Radio,
> January 12, 1945

> *The salvos of triumph continue to boom nightly from Moscow and with abundant reason, for never in the history of war has so tremendous a military operation been undertaken in winter as that which is now sweeping on from victory to victory.*
>
> *The Times,* London,
> January 25, 1945

For nearly two years Skorzeny had scarcely been a "soldier," as the word is normally understood: he had been a buccaneer, a military highwayman—a spectacular trapeze artist upon whose lone brilliance Hitler had counted to pull the show together.

And suddenly, in the last weeks of the war, when Germany was in extremity and the Russians were on their last lap to Berlin, Skorzeny was once more the man they turned to—but this time to do an ordinary soldier's job: the kind of thing he had not thought about since those days when he was a lieutenant in Russia. A lieutenant? Overnight he became a major-general—in all but rank and pay.

He was sitting in his Friedenthal office one evening at

the end of January 1945 rewriting a report which some beribboned bureaucrat had called for—his first version had been returned as "too truthful." The telephone rang. It was Heinrich Himmler: now that Hitler classed most of his generals as dunces or traitors, Germany's head policeman had been turned into a generalissimo on the Eastern front and given command of "Army Group Vistula"—which was no longer an army group and nowhere near the Vistula. Indeed, its new commander sat in an office near Berlin, and the front, if there were one, was but a couple of hours' drive away.

Himmler ordered Skorzeny to march "at once," with every soldier he could scrape up, to the river Oder, to a town called Schwedt which lay on the road toward Stettin, and there, from a bridgehead east of the river, he was to halt the Russian advance. Not merely was he to form a bastion which would save Berlin: he must establish a base from which the great counteroffensive Himmler had promised could be launched. From there two army corps would drive the Russians back: two army corps which did not yet exist.

It was five in the afternoon. From then on the telephone from Himmler's H.Q. was never quiet: "Have you started yet?"—"Why haven't you started yet?"—"We have already reported to Hitler that you have started"—and so on. Skorzeny got away at five next morning, with a parachute battalion under his command and four companies of his special troops—one of them a babel of Dutchmen, Belgians, Danes, Norwegians and even Swedes. He marched into the blue. No reports about Schwedt existed; nobody at Himmler's H.Q. or anywhere else knew where the Russians were.

On the road he learned by chance that the Russians as yet were some miles south of Schwedt near the Oder; he found the old town—its normal population about fifty thousand—sleepily inert with the flag still flying from the pile of the castle by the river. The long bridge over canal and river looked down on ice thick enough to bear an army. He sent patrols across it, to drive forward and seek out the Russian positions. Then he had time to think.

Around him and behind, all hope seemed to have gone. On the roads—retreat, rout, panic: the sad stream of refugees, the straggling remains of a defeated army. Ahead: a triumphant enemy surging on through a "de-

fense" that was broken and numb. In his rear: capricious
and hysterical leaders whose plans were fantasy; a com-
missariat whose stores and armories were empty.

From this slough of moral and material penury he
had to stop the Russians. There was only one thing to do:
he must himself turn fantasy into a weapon: create, on his
side of the front, through sheer will and example, a resis-
tant force by recruiting and inspiring every man and
woman who came his way able to use rifle or shovel; and
on the enemy side, produce an illusion of strength by immediately taking the offensive, by attacking all the time
here, there and everywhere and chopping off the heads
of the Russian columns as they appeared.

Improvise, invent: hoodwink yourself and everybody
else. As for the rear: lull the leaders with promises, and
refrain from looking over your shoulder.

He had, in fact, to pit his own personality, drive and
imagination against the twin enemies of chaos here and a
powerful, victorious enemy over there.

First, what forces had he to build upon? Besides the
troops which he had brought with him, he found in
Schwedt—

One reserve battalion, so called, of five hundred ill
or aging men;

About a hundred and fifty N.C.O.'s and officer cadets
who happened to be in Schwedt on a course;

A handful of pioneer men able to handle a rifle, perhaps, but not to march;

The sick and wounded and stranded, left behind when
weeks ago all fit men had been swept away to other fronts.

But an unheeded source of fighting manpower quickly
became apparent to him: the procession of stragglers
which wormed into the town from the east. Skorzeny's first
step, after pricking out a perimeter for his bridgehead—
an arc of tactical posts within about four miles of the
town—was to gather up these stragglers as they trooped
in and put them to train under the efficient N.C.O.'s he
had found there.

His second step was to enlist not only the labor of
the civilians, but also their enthusiasm. He did not say to
the mayor and Party officials: "Get the people out with
pick and shovel"; he said: "Go out yourself with pick and
shovel, and the people will go with you." By the second
day the population believed—because Skorzeny had told

them and shown them—that they could save Germany, that upon them the safety of their friends and relations in the rear depended, that they were the rock against which the Russian wave would break.

To Himmler in Berlin the Oder had seemed on the map a natural barrier before the capital. Skorzeny found it was no obstacle at all: ice-breakers and dynamite were needed before the river could make a tank obstacle; and before the marshland between canal and river could be flooded.

Very soon he felt that his bridgehead, with its outer perimeter of strongposts covering every approach and its inner ring of defenses dug by his labor force, was strong enough to delay the invaders for at least a few days: until he had collected and trained a sizeable garrison and could back it with something like the right kind of weapons.

He kept all his best officers and N.C.O.'s in the town —a few had to be detached to deal with refugees and the evacuation of women and children—to train his new and hourly growing "army"; within three days two complete battalions had been formed, fit to man part of the inner ring.

Meanwhile, aggressive patrols were day and night sallying thirty or forty miles deep into Russian-held country, taking Russian advance guards by the throat and bringing back hourly reports of enemy movement. At the same time, inside the bridgehead and coiled, as it were, like a strong spring, a picked striking force was held ready to attack any Russian column which advanced so far and thus to prevent a break-in from becoming a break-through.

Orders of an irrelevant and—to the man on the spot —absurd kind kept arriving from Army Group. These Skorzeny could at some risk ignore; but he could not ignore his shortage of weapons, particularly artillery, and the neglect of H.Q. to answer his requests for supplies. Told that no antitank guns were available, he would not leave it at that—if Berlin could not give him any, he would find some for himself. And he did: from a factory thirty miles to the south which Berlin had written off because it was within range of the Russian guns he collected an invaluable number of 75-mm. guns—the only kind which could knock out the T34 and Stalin tanks. And at a dump near Frankfurt-on-the-Oder his men got as many of the special MG 42 machine guns as they wanted.

Skorzeny made up his lack of field artillery by collecting some antiaircraft guns which he mounted on lorries. Two Home Guard battalions had been added to his

MG 42

force. One came from Hamburg: dockers and stevedores who, tough Communists until about 1936, were now to fight like lions against the Russians. The other had been raised for the defense of Königsberg, some eight miles to the southeast; Skorzeny now felt strong enough to hold this town as an advanced strongpost. Here his paratroops and the two Home Guard contingents would take the first Russian shock before falling back through the bridgehead's outer ring.

Hermann Göring rang up: "How is it going?" From the first he had taken a benevolent interest in the bridgehead, and frequently telephoned. "I could do with some more troops," Skorzeny answered. Next day a brand-new battalion of the Hermann Göring Division arrived, commanded by an eager and much-decorated young officer. They were fine troops—except that, being airmen, they had no notion of an infantryman's job. So, to the dismay of their commander, Skorzeny split them into groups

which he scattered among his own units—and infantrymen
they became in no time.

One day, driving around his bridgehead, Skorzeny
came upon a troop of cavalry, smart and well-mounted
on well-cared-for horses—like something out of a romantic film. The subaltern in command trotted up to him and
saluted. "Can you use us, sir?" "You bet I can," he answered—delighted, but wondering what on earth might
turn up next.

As the days became a week, his motley army had
reached division strength: fifteen thousand men or so,
speaking almost every tongue in Europe—he had Russians
and Rumanians now, as well as the Westerners he had
brought up with him from Friedenthal. "My European
Division," he called it.

Time had been won; but the Russian attack must
come soon. One morning he sent out a small patrol to look
at Bad Schonfliess, a small watering place beyond Königsberg: they came under fire, and lost two. That afternoon Skorzeny went out himself. Toward dusk he and his
men left their vehicles on the outskirts of Bad Schonfliess
and crept to the fringe of deserted houses. Three civilians
lay in the road; one was a woman.

A solitary civilian appeared—but still no sign of Russians. The enemy had arrived two days earlier, the
man said—they were at the railway station at the other end of
the town: troops and munitions were arriving all the time.
Skorzeny's patrol worked their way through the dark
town: there were the Russian tanks, fifty of them, outside
the station. No time to waste—back through the silent
streets. He waited long enough to tell the townspeople to
go back to Königsberg, only five miles away. But two days
of Russian occupation seemed to have deadened their will.
The patrol drove back to Schwedt with a few German
children who had lost their parents; no one else would
leave the doomed town.

The Russians struck. Forty tanks and several battalions drove into Königsberg. Fighting house by house,
Skorzeny's men destroyed ten tanks in their retreat—a
fighting retreat which proved that even the freshly raised
Home Guards would hold.

After a night of battle Skorzeny returned to Schwedt
to be greeted by the commander of the Königsberg Home
Guard—his soldiers were still in the thick of the fight.

"I've been waiting all night, Colonel, to report that all's lost in Königsberg," the fellow cried; and Skorzeny promptly put him under arrest.

He was the Nazi Party boss in Königsberg who, as such, automatically commanded the Home Guard. Palpably he had deserted in the face of the enemy: Skorzeny had him court-martialed and hanged him in the public square.

This reached the ears of Martin Bormann, Hitler's Party deputy, who from his Berlin office sent a furious message claiming that senior Party members could be tried only by a Party tribunal.

Skorzeny told Bormann's emissary: "We tried your man not as a Party official but as a soldier—but are not cowardice and desertion punishable in Party leaders too?"

Skorzeny did not care a fig for the Party if it interfered with his military duty or intentions. He showed this a second time during this same battle. An order, again from Bormann in Berlin, said he was at all costs to seize or destroy a couple of vehicles stranded fifteen miles behind the Russian lines—they contained vital "State papers." Skorzeny inquired further: these were no State papers—they were Party papers from Bormann's own office, documents which Bormann for personal reasons did not want to reach Russian hands.

So he replied that he would not waste men on such a mission: the order could not be obeyed.

Ten days after the bridgehead was formed came a welcome addition to his force: Lieutenant Schwerdt, who had been with him for the rescue of Mussolini, and a first-rate company of commandos—among them ten of his own veterans who had also dropped with him at the Gran Sasso.

Königsberg was abandoned; the bridgehead was withstanding a crack Russian Army corps headed by a great weight of tanks and supported by Sovietized Rumanians. The enemy was held on the perimeter: but numbers of advanced posts had been given up.

It was then that Skorzeny nearly got himself court-martialed for flouting Himmler himself. A village had been abandoned on Skorzeny's orders; Himmler signaled: "Is the company commander concerned being court-martialed or has he already been shot?" Skorzeny replied that he had taken no action; nor would he. Then he drove to the front where a Russian breakthrough had to be stopped.

Another message: Skorzeny would report to Himmler's H.Q. at four that afternoon. He put it in his pocket—and, after driving back the enemy, reported to his army group commander four hours late. Himmler was raging: court-martial, reduction to the ranks, mutiny—he stormed threats and accusations at Skorzeny.

Skorzeny told him that, firstly, he himself had ordered that the village should be abandoned, and that secondly, ever since he had been at Schwedt he had received a stream of nonsensical orders but never an ounce of supplies.

This seemed to shake Himmler into reasonableness. "Tell me about your bridgehead," he said to Skorzeny—and asked him to dinner. By the time the meal was over, Himmler had given him an assault-gun battery and promised all possible help.

The battle for the bridgehead raged; villages changed hands; there were withdrawals. But Skorzeny knew that he could hold. He felt so secure there that he told himself he would "grow old and gray" in Schwedt; and he was at least prolonging the life of Berlin and giving thousands of refugees time to reach shelter in the West.

A signal at his advanced H.Q.: Göring was in Schwedt, waiting to see him. Actually—a big shot had come to his bridgehead: the first visitor he had had the whole time! Göring in plain field-gray: without medals, his belly somewhat shrunken, no bluster or blather this time. He arrived during a severe battle.

The grand Panjandrum wanted to go into the bridgehead: so he should, but not, his entourage nervously hoped, where there was much risk. Göring was jolly to all, doling out cigarettes and brandy. He went with Skorzeny almost up to the front line. Then he left, his duty accomplished, and his curiosity appeased.

The battle continued, but the bridgehead held. Skorzeny had done his job—the job of an orthodox, textbook divisional commander.

Then he remembered—he had never found time to fill up the lengthy forms which would have brought him the appropriate rank of major-general. The B.B.C. did it for him: just before his recall to Berlin. "The well known S.S. chief Skorzeny," the broadcast from London went, "who carried out Mussolini's rescue, has been promoted major-general and charged with the defense of Berlin. He has thus become the most powerful man in the German capital. . . . He has already started to liquidate all unreliable elements in the Berlin population."

Skorzeny was tickled by the bulletin; it reminded him of the night before his Gran Sasso rescue when the B.B.C. had transported Mussolini from Italy to North Africa on the radio waves to nonplus his would-be liberators. It seemed an eternity ago, and here they were, still at it. Now Skorzeny was to be used as a bogeyman in some game of "political warfare." He was hugely amused; no sixth sense warned him how this cloud on the horizon no bigger than a man's hand presaged a storm which would burst over his head.

He left Schwedt at the end of February on orders from General Jodl, who had been directed to give him a still more important and secret task. A few days later his successor in command was ordered to evacuate the bulk of his troops. Their stand had served its purpose.

XIII

Where there is much light there is also much shadow.

GOETHE, Goetz von Berlichingen

With his recall from Schwedt, the life Skorzeny knew was almost over. After the rigors of the Oder bridgehead it was back to work at Friedenthal; desk work which he found more and more unreal as his special forces were thrown into breaches made in the defense by enemies who might be stayed but not in the long run stopped.

One last stupendous mission was entrusted to him,

but first there came about the dissolution of most of the front-line battalions under his command: von Foelkersam had been right; no one would have time for "fancy troops" in the last spasm of Germany's life. The generals were left in possession of the stricken field.

Some days later they had second thoughts: when the American First Army, by luck and drive, had reached Remagen and seized intact the great Ludendorf bridge.

"Send for Skorzeny," came the cry from G.H.Q.

Already the Americans had driven a bridgehead six miles deep across the Rhine: "The traditional defensive barrier to the heart of Germany was pierced," writes General Eisenhower. "This was one of my happy moments of the war. The final defeat of the enemy . . . was suddenly, now, in our minds, just around the corner."*

As at Nymegen six months before, the High Command did everything they could with bombers, tank columns, and long-range guns to recapture or destroy the bridge; then Skorzeny was told to send his frogmen in. For the first time he refused to obey an order unconditionally. Each man of the group he brought up from his Danube training center must make up his own mind, when the hopelessness of the task had been explained to him, whether he would take it on or not.

The water, he told them, was only a few degrees above freezing; the whole area was fully manned and gunned by the enemy. Searchlights were playing over the approaches to the bridge—the Americans expected just such an attack. There was practically no chance of coming back alive and still less of the enterprise succeeding. Now would they volunteer?

They did. A few survivors were hauled out by their American captors. The bridge remained.

All that was left to Skorzeny was to rage at the dull idiocy of the orthodox; given a delicate weapon whose edge was tempered for surprise, they had once again used it in a tardy frontal attack. He saw his band of swimmers go to their fate in the icy, bloodied waters of the Rhine; then he drove to Berlin: for once the muddlers would share his shame.

While Skorzeny was waiting in the bomb-blasted

---

*Crusade in Europe. New York: Doubleday and Company, Inc., 1948.

Chancellery to report to the High Command he was greeted, on Hitler's behalf, by a young woman. She was fair-haired, pleasant-looking—a suburban figure among the marble wreckage. She told Skorzeny she had heard so much of him. "You must come to tea soon and tell us about some of the things you have done," she said. A month later her marriage to Hitler was retrieved from banality by death. She was Eva Braun.

Hitler was now living his last tortured days and nights in a bomb-proof suite alongside the Chancellery. Once, coming out for a conference, he saw Skorzeny and stretched out hands that trembled. This man who was holding Germany on the road to self-destruction by his single will was bent, shaky and old.

"Skorzeny," he said. "I have not yet thanked you for your stand on the Oder. Day after day it was the one bright spot in my reports. I have awarded you the Oak Leaves to the Knight's Cross; and I mean to hand them to you myself. Then you can give me a full account. For the future, I have other work for you. . . ."

He shuffled on. Skorzeny did not see him again.

The Chancellery was still peopled with illusions: it was a stage scene in a heap of ruins. Guards of honor presented arms; generals squabbled about Orders of the Day and bits of ribbon.

Everyone who was anyone gathered in the shadows of Hitler's world: even Hanna Reitsch—she was lying ill in a shelter when Skorzeny found her. "I can still fly," she whispered. "I can replace an airman. I shall soon be in the thick of it again."

Hanna had her way, as usual. Soon after, when Russian guns and troops ringed the capital, she landed an airplane in a cratered avenue. Hitler had asked her to fetch General Ritter von Greim, whom he had appointed to replace Göring as commander-in-chief of an extinct Air Force. Greim was wounded on this wild flight; but four days later he was packed off again with orders to arrest Himmler, accused of contacting the Allies. Again, Hanna Reitsch was in the cockpit, skimming the roofs and tree-tops of the capital to avoid the shellbursts.

Twenty-four days were left for Hitler when Skorzeny bade farewell to Berlin, but no issue except victory could be mentioned. Nations which have never lost a war, peoples who have never known invasion, could not under-

stand why German soldiers went on fighting; Skorzeny
himself hardly knew what drove him on as he tried to
reassemble the remnants of his task forces to prepare their
last stand against a world in arms.

For such was the final mission that was given him.
Centered on the Eagle's Nest, Hitler's aerie on the Austro-
German border, twenty or thirty divisions of troops were
to be welded into a hoop of steel around the Leader. Behind their snowy mountain wall, in caverns, tunnels and
ravines they had armories and stocks of food; they would
hold out, if need be, for years. Skorzeny was ordered to go
ahead of the main garrison and create the nucleus of a
"Corps for the defending of the Alps."

He drove from doomed Berlin to take up the Wagnerian assignment. But first he visited Vienna in the hope
of finding some of his own units which were stranded on
the crumbling southeast front; and drawn there, too, by a
desire to see again his home.

He drove at dusk into a darkened city. Not a lamp
was lit; the empty streets were thick with smoke from
smoldering buildings. Now and then a shadow crept along
the broken walls; there was distant gunfire. Along the
littered Danube quays he sought the house where his
brother had lived—its ruins blocked the street. His mother's house was wrecked; one of her neighbors crept out to
tell him that she had left Vienna a few days before.

A great silent hulk of a capital: barricades, with no
troops to man them; abandoned German tanks; a deathlike
silence, cracked only by sudden rifle shots, quite near.
Once or twice he must have driven across the lines, even
though there was no "front." At an apparently deserted
barricade he stopped his car to look around. Two figures
emerged from the shadows: policemen. They introduced
themselves: "We are the garrison—the Russians are just
over there." Vienna had lost everything except her humor.

Skorzeny found his old office. No light, no telephone,
no gas. But his partner and girl secretary were still there;
they made tea over an oil stove, and talked by candlelight.
As the Russian tanks sounded still nearer, some of his old
workmen appeared: "I hope you get away, sir. And think
of us."

It was time to go—yet he must first see his own
house in Peter Jordan Street. The gardens were ghostly, as

they might have seemed in his childhood. He went from room to room; everything as he remembered it—the rugs his wife had loved, the silver they had bought together, the familiar pictures. The clocks had stopped at different times. He left all as it was, for the Russians to move in.

Now for the command post—what would be happening at the Castle? Along the road into Vienna there had been signs of precipitate retreat, even of panic. But deep in the Castle dungeons such notions were not entertained. Against a setting of baronial luxury, Baldur von Schirach, district leader of Vienna and former paladin of Hitler Youth, sat beneath gilded chandeliers alive with dozens of candles, gazing at a chart.

"I suppose you know," Skorzeny ventured, "that the Russians can march in just when they want—indeed, they're doing so now."

"Ridiculous!" Von Schirach was huddled over his map. "My two S.S. divisions will attack from the north; I shall close my pincers from the west. Thus shall we liberate Vienna as Prince Stahremberg liberated her from the Turks in 1683." Skorzeny left him: playing his ghostly game, maneuvering his phantom armies. "Here I shall fight and die," were von Schirach's parting words.

On Skorzeny's way north he signaled to Hitler's H.Q.: "In my opinion Vienna will be lost today"—it was not his domain, but he had been told to report matters of importance direct. He got no reply.

Then on to the Alpine redoubt from whose icy walls Hitler would defy the world. Radl joined him at their new headquarters near Radstadt; soon after came a courier from beleaguered Berlin: his Oak Leaves to the Knight's Cross!

Next, a surprising embassy from Dr. Walther Funk, who had stepped into Dr. Schacht's shoes as President of the Reichsbank and Minister of Economics. He sent two of his officials to ask whether he might put the State Treasure—and his own person—under Skorzeny's protection. The answer was a short one: among the things Skorzeny needed for the task before him were neither a civilian Minister nor a fortune in gold and jewels.

The castles of the Alpine redoubt were Hitler's airiest imposture. Skorzeny and Radl searched the region and found it innocent of war. A few horse-drawn carts were climbing the roads with provisions: machines were lying

about, waiting to be installed—they had been brough
from the factories which were supposed to be transferred
to make it a self-contained stronghold. But the underground armories were empty; the storerooms were bare.
It was the last dream to vanish with the awakening: there
was nothing to fight with; and nothing they could do.

April 30: Hitler was dead. So much for the Alpine
Redoubt . . . So much for Germany. Looking across the
empty mountains, Skorzeny heard six days afterwards that
the war was over. An air-force officer offered to fly him
with some friends to Spain. Skorzeny refused; he must see
to the surrender of his men; the last orders had to be
given.

With Radl and a few others, he went to a mountain
hut and set about trying to get into touch with the nearest
Allied headquarters. Mountain people said, to his astonishment, that American troops in the area were searching the
countryside for him, and in the course of the hunt arrest-
ing dozens of disarmed German officers and soldiers. It was
only now that he began to suspect the warped aspect of
the renown he enjoyed with the Allies; he learned that for
months "wanted" posters with his photograph had been
displayed in France. So he sent three letters saying he
wanted to give himself up; how and where should he surrender? No reply came from the Americans; it appeared
that they regarded his approaches as a ruse.

Waiting for something to happen, in the sudden re-
pose that "peace" brought, the group around Skorzeny
began to talk of the future, of the consequences of peace.
In the snow and sunshine it was like an unexpected holiday: a few days without cares, and each seemed endless.

They discussed the ideas which the end of war
brought to many minds. And they seemed to arrive at
agreement: that the time for narrow national states had
passed. Europe, they decided, was the smallest stage on
which all, friend or foe of yesterday, could meet. The
European idea must grow naturally out of the chaos.

But if in the rare, cleansing air of the mountains such
sentiments could unfold, the spirit of trustfulness was not
yet abroad below. Luxemburg Radio, the new mouthpiece
of the conquerors, began appealing to one and all, "good"
Germans as well as Allies, to help lay by the heels the
leader of a murderous conspiracy—Otto Skorzeny. News-

papers took up the hue and cry: "The most diabolically clever man in Germany is still free. He is being hunted everywhere by the top brains of Allied Intelligence."

A sardonic turn of events; away from all the bulletins and headlines, the subject of them was doing his best to give himself up. At last, Skorzeny, Radl and two more officers, descended to the plains. It was ten days after Germany's surrender. Armed and smartly uniformed, they sought out the nearest American command post, there to give up their weapons and take their places in a prisoner-of-war camp with their men.

It was not to be so easy. For once Skorzeny had forgotten the numbing effect of surprise. The last thing which the Allies expected was that Otto Skorzeny, prototype of cunning and treachery, who was to be looked for behind any disguise and brought to bay only after desperate resistance, would walk up to them and say, "Here I am."

They found an American depot. The sergeant at the desk shook his head: to him Skorzeny's name happened to mean nothing; and he was too busy to book in prisoners. But he could provide a jeep to take them to Salzburg; there, if they liked, they could talk about surrender at Divisional H.Q.

Such was Skorzeny's introduction to the informality of Germany's new masters. The driver of the jeep, a Texan, had heard the name all right. "Skorzeny, is it?" He pulled up at a tavern and they bought a bottle of wine: "If you're Skorzeny you'd better take a drink. Tonight you'll hang."

In Salzburg, however, the Texan left them alone, still armed, outside an American-occupied hotel; that was the last they saw of him.

At last a U.S. major sent them elsewhere, still armed, to pick up "orders"—but the orders, when obtained, had to be signed in yet another town.

And then it must have dawned on someone that here, right among them, stood the man who was being hunted all over Western Europe: six feet four inches of him and a pistol in his holster. Skorzeny was ushered into the dining room of a villa and asked to sit down for a chat with a brace of American officers. In a trice the three doors and all the windows were flung wide from outside: machine guns covered him from every direction.

The Americans were no longer casual. Quickly he
was disarmed, searched to the skin and bundled with
Radl and another German officer into jeeps—one German
to each jeep. Fore and aft of the convoy an armored car
its guns trained on the jeeps. A military policeman held
his automatic pressed to Skorzeny's heart.

Thus they were driven back to Salzburg during the
night. They stopped before a house with all its windows
ablaze. A swarm of guards fell upon them and bound their
arms behind their backs; and Skorzeny was led alone to
the first floor. The scene was set: two American officers
with an interpreter formed a kind of tribunal; opposite, in
a row of chairs, the audience. On either side of Skorzeny
stood two armed policemen, watching his every movement.

The spectators, he discovered, were war correspondents and cameramen in uniform. He was blinded by ex-
ploding flash bulbs.

"Skorzeny certainly looks the part," wrote a New
York woman reporter that night, with a verbal shudder.
"He is striking in a tough way; a huge powerful
figure. The Beast of Belsen is something out of a nursery
in comparison." She added for her readers: "He has blue
eyes."

"It was thought best," a message published in a London newspaper ran, "to keep Skorzeny with his hands
manacled behind his back. When he was given a cigarette,
it was lit and he had to have the ash shaken off for him.
A glass of water was held to his lips."

Chicago read next day that the interview ended "with
a clicking of pistols as the M.P.'s prepared for what might
happen next." And the *Daily News* reporter wound up:
"I'll say this. He was a true Nazi throughout. He walked
out with his head high—and with a flock of American
soldiers wishing he would make just one dash for freedom."

Now for the questions—and an irritating delay. The
prisoner said he would not answer while he was manacled;
he also complained that his wrist watch had gone. This
was the one inscribed for him by Mussolini—and for
months to come Skorzeny was kept busy saving it from
souvenir-hungry G.I.'s.

The watch was restored, the handcuffs—after telephoned appeals to "Security"—were removed; Skorzeny
walked to the window, chancing a bullet in his back, and

shouted to Radl who had been held with his companion down below: "Are you two still manacled?"

Radl replied, "Yes," whereupon Skorzeny said their hands must also be freed before he would speak. Again he got his way, aided by the manifest anxiety of the reporters to get down to business.

And now the cause of the "Wanted" posters, radio appeals, the congregation of the Press at Salzburg, was revealed to him by the first question: "Why did you try to murder General Eisenhower?"

Skorzeny said: "I didn't," and inquired how the suggestion had arisen.

The reporters had come a long way to get the "inside story"; they were in no humor for prevarication, and here was the First Murderer saying that he knew nothing of the plot; nor could he be shaken on it. A cool customer, was the impression they gave next day to the world's Press —and, of course, not for a moment to be believed. *The New York Times* man could hardly be blamed for begging the whole question in a bland sentence: "Handsome despite the scar that stretched from ear to chin, Skorzeny smilingly disclaimed credit for leading the mission to murder members of the Supreme Command."

Asked to prove, in the teeth of the statements from Security, that he had never harbored any such intentions, Skorzeny replied with an infuriating show of reasonableness: "If I had ever been ordered to attack Allied G.H.Q., I should have made a plan to do so. If I had made a plan, I would have carried it out. And no one would have been left in doubt of what I was trying to do."

To Skorzeny this seemed simple logic; his disillusioned audience thought otherwise. Even the *Christian Science Monitor*'s correspondent cabled home that the prisoner had "an aggressive personality to go with his physical equipment—and," he added tartly, "a mind adapted to subversive activity."

Skorzeny and Radl spent that night together. They sat on a bench with their hands tied behind them and under the eyes of guards who kept their fingers on the triggers of their guns. Next day they were driven north to Augsburg with four other prisoners. Three were German generals. The fourth was Dr. Ley, Hitler's Labor Minister, who faced the future in sky-blue pajamas, a huge cloak, carpet slippers and a round Tyrolean hat.

Next day Skorzeny was questioned by Colonel Henry Gordon Sheen, Eisenhower's very able chief of Counter Intelligence, who had hurried down from Versailles at the news of the "capture." They spent six hours together. Sheen was upset, at first, by the prisoner's insistence that he had not even crossed the lines in the Ardennes, for several witnesses had "positively" seen him. But in the end he was convinced—and told Skorzeny so—that the Americans had been led on a wild-goose chase; faces at Supreme Headquarters would be red. Just before leaving, though, Sheen put a last, sudden question:

"What were you doing in Berlin at the end of April?" Nonplussed, Skorzeny said he was not there.

"Come now," Sheen urged, bringing all his techniques as an interrogator into play, "you know perfectly well that you yourself flew Hitler out of Berlin on April 30. Where did you take him?"

Skorzeny could only say that he had not been in Berlin since the tenth of April—and went on to prove his alibi. Sheen believed him in the end; but the story that Skorzeny whisked Hitler out before Berlin fell became as durable as the legend of Eisenhower's escape from his clutches. He was to be asked the sudden question posed by Sheen not scores, but hundreds, of times—by G.I.'s and generals, by journalists and judges, by Englishmen, Frenchmen, Russians and anyone else who got the chance to ask it. It pops out to this day: "Where did you leave Hitler, really?"

Skorzeny can think of no better answer than the argument he offered Colonel Sheen: "I'm sure Hitler is dead. And anyway, if I *had* taken him somewhere to safety, why, in heaven's name, would I have come back to surrender?"

Sheen saw the sense in that, but many other faces have betrayed a quizzical doubt which Skorzeny reads like this: "I wonder! After dropping Hitler somewhere, couldn't this fellow have returned to Germany just to throw the Allies off the scent?"

The fact is, of course, that Skorzeny had become a figure in modern mythology; he was capable of anything, from infanticide to disappearing in a cloud of brimstone through the floor. A week after Colonel Sheen's visit to Augsburg, General Walter Bedell Smith, Supreme Headquarters Chief of Staff, thought he would kill the myth.

He went to the Scribe Hotel in Paris, where Allied correspondents nested, and took the penitent's stand with a "top-level retraction." There was not, he said; there never had been, an Eisenhower murder plot. The security staff had confused various reports. It was a snafu.

War correspondents are used to snafus, a cynical abbreviation which may be interpreted as "situation normal, all fouled up"; but this was a most aggravating one. What of the official "releases" on the plan to attack Allied leaders? reporters asked. All withdrawn, the general said. Pained questions were put by journalists who had accepted the statement on Skorzeny's mission behind the lines and added "color" of their own—how would they explain this upset to their editors? And then, they had got corroboration in the Security stampede. Was it not true, for instance, that a "double" of Eisenhower's had used his car while he was imprisoned at Versailles? General Bedell Smith blinked at the reminder; having to justify this impersonation when his Chief came to hear of it can have been no pleasant task.

The Press went off disgusted: denials were a bore; there *must* be something in a story so circumstantial—and Skorzeny's custodians thought so too. He went from one grilling to another; from a second prison to a third and a fourth and a fifth. In the sixth he shared a hut with Field-Marshal Kesselring; then there was a seventh and an eighth. And each time the questions would start all over again.

May 19: Wiesbaden prison: locked in a hut with Dr. Kaltenbrunner, one of the chiefs of the Secret Service: it was obvious to both that hidden microphones were to record their chatter about State secrets. The couple talked interminably of university days; and also they discovered the scraping of boots on the floor was a means of further exacerbating the ears of listeners.

Life, for one of Skorzeny's disposition, still had its amusing moments—or could be made to: one when he took charge of an interrogation and became, so to speak, his own film director.

"Two very smart American guards," he recalls, "took me to a room where sound-film cameras were mounted. A captain and an interpreter were sitting at a table. Then the fun started: just as if a real entertainment film were being shot—except that the star was the only participant not being paid for his performance. After an hour and a half things were still not going right, so I suggested we should rehearse each scene first—go through the questions and answers beforehand. We did: the final shooting was a great success." And he adds, with enjoyment, "I have heard of no other prisoner who had a sound film made of his own interrogation, and directed it himself."

The round went on—interviews with a British secret service chief and a Frenchman. "Waited on" by a Filipino G.I. who must have been reading *Stars and Stripes* with its colorful descriptions of the "giant kidnaper"—he would drop Skorzeny's food tray on the threshold and vanish like a flash of his own native lightning.

A red code-mark on the card outside his cell meant: THIS MAN IS DANGEROUS.

June 21: "Get Skorzeny ready"—three American generals were waiting in the office to see him. But the wooden hut he lived in was an oven in the summer heat: he was in pajamas. "Go as you are," advised a friendly sergeant, "and let them see what it's like." Geniality from the generals. Whisky. Apologies—promises of a change. He is moved with ceremony to the local prison: bombed out, and verminous.

The ultimate luxury: admitted by an amiable guard to a small door in the corridor labeled "Americans Only." The ultimate misery: another warder, not so amiable, removed his straw palliasse for the night.

More questionings of the military sort—straightforward, increasingly polite. On August 11 at Oberursel Karl Radl is allowed to share his cell: release to an ordinary prisoner-of-war camp must surely be near. "Get Skorzeny ready": handcuffs again; then—Nuremberg.

September 10: A real V.I.P. trip, this one, in an airplane. Fellow-guests include Grand-Admiral Dönitz; General Guderian, sometime Chief of Staff; Minister Ley of the sky-blue pajamas—and, surely, Youth Leader Baldur von Schirach, whose last words to Skorzeny in Vienna had been: "Here I shall fight and die." Star actors in the unprecedented, unrehearsed drama of the War Crimes Trials which was about to be produced before a world audience.

At the gates of Nuremberg prison it was noticed that Dönitz and Skorzeny still wore their shoulder badges; so each in turn ripped off the other's last vestige of rank.

Across the passage Göring nodded cheerfully through

the trap of his cell door. Gaunt Rudolf Hess, always hand-cuffed to his escort, was seen at exercise in the prison yard.

Two suicides—Dr. Ley's was one—induced a rule that prisoners must sleep, if sleep they could, under a blinding light and with their faces toward the door.

Interrogation again: by a man worth talking to, General "Wild Bill" Donovan, of the Office of Strategic Services, Skorzeny's nearest equivalent in the U.S. Army.

After ten weeks at Nuremberg, transfer to the "open" witnesses' wing, shared with more than fifty celebrities. It was a shock to find that many seemed eager to save their skins by testifying against intimate colleagues. One who kept his dignity was Marshal Kesselring. He went out of his way to stage a reconciliation between Skorzeny and Admiral Horthy, whom the Americans had rescued from the Bavarian castle in which Skorzeny had immured him. Now the ex-Regent had a V.I.P. cell at Nuremberg as a witness with special privileges—one of them a supply of cigarettes. Skorzeny listened politely to his apologia: Horthy had always been a friend of Germany and had not wished to betray an ally. He listened and he smoked.

Weeks of monotony; then one day the chance to ob-tain a long-forgotten luxury fell into his hands. Linen sheets, a stack of them! He snatched up three as he passed on his way to his cell. One went everywhere with him, softening the travail of his nights for the rest of his cap-tivity; one he gave to poor old Marshall Blomberg—who was to die shortly after in the prison hospital; the third to General Glaise-Horstenau—like Admiral Horthy, he had been A.D.C. to the Emperor Francis Joseph—who committed suicide some months later.

But though Skorzeny was behind bars, his legend stalked outside. One day the prison dreariness was en-livened by a military stand-to: troops were multiplied; armor-plated strongposts were sited to enfilade the cor-ridors; machine guns were posted all around, antitank traps hastily erected outside. The chuckling prison chaplain explained the excitement on a visit to Skorzeny's cell. A visiting general had told the chaplain in the Mess that remnants of the German Army outside were plotting to storm the Nuremberg prison and Palace of Justice—their leader was the notorious Colonel Skorzeny. When the chaplain insisted that Skorzeny was safely locked up inside the prison, the general said this could not be so—if anybody inside was calling himself Skorzeny he must be an imposter!

This scare had some foundation: long afterwards Skorzeny heard that a few of his own men had indeed concocted a wild scheme to get him out of jail.

May 1946: a move to Dachau; back to Nuremberg. . . . With Marshal Kesselring to some other camp, then to Darmstadt and back to Dachau. Dysentery, an eight-day hunger strike, hospital; an operation—his gallbladder out at last. Trigger-happy G.I. guards played poker by his bed all night, while the radio blared without stopping. The inevitable accident: a bullet through the ceiling!

"Guarded like a cobra," *Stars and Stripes* announced, reporting Skorzeny's "repeated escapes" from prison while he lay helpless on his back.

There was one comfort. With a few other "Skorzeny boys," Karl Radl had got a job in the prison kitchen gardens at Dachau. His convalescence was helped along by delicacies they smuggled in to him.

"Get Skorzeny ready." His best memory of those endless journeys was of one exciting day when, failing to reach jail in time, he and his guards stayed until next morning in a village. For the first time for months he found himself dining off china—with a knife and fork in addition to the regulation spoon. And he slept in a bed, while down below his escort celebrated.

It would have been easy to get away that night. He stayed to see it out and to prove that he had nothing to hide; besides, with legal freedom beckoning, why should he run away? He often remembered that chance to make a break—and sometimes wished he had been less nice in putting it aside.

XIV

To forgive our enemies their virtues—that is a greater miracle.

VOLTAIRE

"Get Skorzeny ready." Toward the end of July, 1947, the familiar cry took him into the commandant's office at Dachau—and before a blaze of flash bulbs.

The chatter of reporters and photographers died down as he was marched in. With pleasure he saw that the Press had changed their warlike panoply for ordinary clothes; everyone looked friendlier. Release at last?

His hopes were high. Eight weeks earlier a War Crimes expert had come to Dachau to advise finally whether there was a case for trial. The decision seemed to turn on Operation "Greif"; in ten long sessions Skorzeny took his visitor through every stage of it and answered all his questions. His inquisitor was satisfied. "You have convinced me," he said, "that you did nothing which calls for punishment."

As time ran on without further word Skorzeny told himself that the War Crimes machinery was overburdened—more than a thousand of these cases were brought before the courts—and that with the law delays were almost mandatory. Already more than two years had gone by since the snap of handcuffs shattered his naïve belief that his surrender would be accepted like that of any other officer who had merely done his duty. His spell in jail—a string of jails—had been as long as the whole of his "commando" career. He had had time to learn some of the causes of Allied rancor: all he wanted now was to forget the wasted years, the treadmill of interrogations, the repetitious journeys, the body searches before and after Göring's suicide in Nuremberg.

He looked around the commandant's office. Inside the ring of expectant newspaper people were a group of officials and, he observed, a very pretty secretary. Then eight more prisoners of war were led into the room; officers from various German services, he assumed they were all to be let out with him. A tall, spruce figure in American uniform advanced: it was Colonel Rosenfeld, who having led a high Security post during the Battle of the Bulge, was one of those who had closely questioned Skorzeny after his arrest.

Rosenfeld began to read from a document. His easy drawl was followed by a phrase-by-phrase translation into German. Skorzeny heard something about fighting in American uniform—it sounded like anything but a preamble to release.

The two voices droned on: a charge of stealing Red Cross parcels—he hardly took it in. What he had quite clearly followed, yet made nothing of, was an accusation that, with the other officers there charged, he had "conspired to ill-treat, torture and kill at least a hundred American prisoners of war."

Who were these other German officers? He scanned their strained faces; all but two he could not remember ever having seen before—how, then, could he have conspired with them?

Rosenfeld came to a stop. Shocked and bewildered, Skorzeny had to wait while another barrage of flash bulbs was let off. Then armed guards hustled the prisoners into the courtyard, where he was at once the center of a babble of horrified questions. How had this murder charge come about? Where had the massacre of Americans taken place —and when? Skorzeny assured them that in all his interrogations no one had asked about such a crime. It was new to the others, too.

That day which had promised so brightly ended behind the bars again. The nine prisoners were locked up three to a cell—which at least allowed them to put their heads together to concoct measures of defense. His companions seemed to be a random bunch of army, navy and air force officers. All wore the pallor of prison years. Like Skorzeny, they had seen the jail doors open for their release—and then clang shut again: some were nearing the end of resistance to the moral pressures of defeat. Twenty-six months had gone by since the Armistice, and thirty since the Battle of the Bulge; they had supposed that nothing new could be brought up against them. But here was a charge of dreadful gravity.

There was no habit of comradeship between these strangers to unite them in misfortune. Three of them might even have been expected to plant seeds of discord among the rest. The first had sworn an incriminating affidavit in the hospital: later he was to go back on it. Another, whose nerve had snapped, proved in the end to be useless to either side. The third was a young naval lieutenant whose English mother had taught him to hate everything German. After some weeks he went to Skorzeny and confessed his impulse to work off this resentment on his fellow prisoners; now that they had come to know each other he would be a loyal comrade.

Skorzeny did all he could to raise the spirits of his dejected companions and bind them together for what lay ahead. But with the arrival of the chief lawyer appointed for their defense, hopes of a fair trial seemed to fade. Colonel Robert Durst was an American military lawyer and a cavalry officer of the hard school. Tight-lipped, with sharp eyes and an uncompromising chin, Durst stumped from one cell to another cross-questioning the defendants: the series of grillings which Skorzeny now suffered was the stiffest he had known. Durst showed no trace of sympathy for his German clients: their own lawyer seemed to be trying to force confessions. But on the fourth of his daily visits he broke into a broad smile and shook hands for the first time. "I am sure of your innocence on every charge," he declared. "Now I know you have nothing to hide I will fight for you as if you were my brothers."

Durst kept his word. He campaigned with foresight and daring against a tough, unrelenting Prosecution. No less devoted to saving the necks of their late enemies in the field were his juniors, Lieut.-Col. Donald McClure and Major L. I. Horowitz. It was Colonel McClure who was later on to tell the court that, having known the prisoners for weeks, he would feel proud to have such men in a unit under his command.

But before the three American officers could get

down to work on the defense, six German barristers came
forward to help—and without hope of fees, since the defendants were destitute. One of them, an Austrian lawyer
called Dr. Peyrer-Angerman, even got himself arrested so
as to be driven to Dachau with a new batch of prisoners,
there being no other means at that time for a civilian to
cross the re-erected Austro-German frontier.

This galaxy of talent produced a crisis of its own.
Colonel Durst said that unless they were to be at legal
sixes and sevens he would have to lay down the main lines
of the defense himself: it would also be best if Skorzeny
alone gave evidence on behalf of all the prisoners. Some
of the German barristers objected to putting German lives
wholly into the hands of an American officer. Skorzeny
trusted Durst, but felt his proposal that one prisoner
should speak for all was an odd elaboration of the de-
mocracy they had heard so much about. Finally, a vote
was taken on Skorzeny's suggestion and the other prisoners
agreed to give Durst and Skorzeny full powers. Three of
the German lawyers walked out, leaving an attenuated
team, but a united one.

Durst took another bold risk when the names of the
tribunal were given out; this time with less happy results.
Objecting to the nomination of the president, he was overruled.

During these weeks before the trial the defendants
were lodged with thieves and pickpockets and guarded by
newly recruited Poles. The Polish guards had no love for
Germany—less still for America. They assured Skorzeny
that if by any chance he escaped the Yankee hangman it
would only be to face a Soviet executioner, for the Red
Army were going to swallow the rest of Germany very
soon. In 1947 Europe could certainly have been overrun
in a week or so, but the Poles were off the party line in
supposing the Russians wanted to "get" Skorzeny—except
for their own use.

One night, a fellow prisoner was ushered, with respect, into Skorzeny's cell. He introduced himself: a Polish
officer awaiting sentence as a Soviet spy. Enjoying the
freedom of the prison because his guards were Communists, he could leave whenever he liked, he said, and take
Skorzeny with him: a glowing future awaited Mussolini's
rescuer behind the Iron Curtain. Skorzeny laughed; he
thought the officer was boasting. But three days later the

Pole did in fact make off for the East, with the help of his guards.

His next visitors were three American officers who had much more difficulty in smuggling themselves into his cell. Giving their names and units, they offered to help in getting Skorzeny off by giving evidence that Allied troops had more than once killed Germans who surrendered. Skorzeny declined their offer: even if two wrongs could make a right, he had not killed any disarmed Americans, nor had his troops.

Later, Skorzeny was to compare the sporting gallantry of these former enemies with the weakness of some so-called friends. One was a German general, met months before in the witness wing at Nuremberg, who volunteered that during the war he had helped to list Allied breaches of international law. Though Skorzeny had no time for such legal ingenuities, Durst thought the general might usefully give evidence about British commando raids. But the general did not wish to risk the disfavor of Germany's new masters. He could remember absolutely nothing, he sighed, either of the conversation with Skorzeny or of the supposed list.

Meanwhile, interest in the trial was rising outside the prisons walls. Skorzeny heard that bets were being laid right and left on the verdict. His guards kept him posted on the odds, which started at ten to one on his being hanged. Counsel and officials were reported to be handsomely backing their opinions, and the gambling fever infected American troops as far away as Munich.

Skorzeny tried to enter into the spirit when the date was fixed for the trial. It would start on August 18—the anniversary of his plane dive into Sardinian waters during the search for Mussolini: that day four years ago he had escaped death by a hundred-to-one chance; surely he could beat lesser odds in a court of law.

August 18, and all was ready. To gratify their military judges with a tidy and regular appearance, the men had exchanged their varied uniforms for American prisoner-of-war garb stamped with the foot-high letters *PW*. The final touch of uniformity was lent by identity numbers which were hung around their necks. Skorzeny, dangling an oversize Number One, felt like a prize animal as he headed the parade out of the side door of the prison.

Across fifty yards of courtyard, from the "trial cells" to which they had been moved a few days earlier, the prisoners were marched by armed guards to a converted wooden barracks hall which was swarming with military police. Guards stood behind them, hand on holster; the white helmets of military police were dotted about the court and they were reinforced by ordinary troops who seemed ready for anything. Skorzeny hoped that these flattering precautions would not have the effect of impressing the tribunal with the desperate character of the accused.

Used to solitude and narrow cells, he found himself under the gaze of hundreds as the men were escorted to what looked like a row of wooden cinema seats alongside the defense counsel. The public benches were crammed with American officers and German civilians: *fräuleins* more buxom than at the end of the war, businessmen with brief cases, long-haired youths who had never worn a uniform. The Press were there in force.

Nine beribboned U.S. colonels took their places on a platform under the Stars and Stripes: the tribunal. And as they settled down all eyes were turned on a single figure across the room: Colonel Rosenfeld, now Chief Prosecutor. He stood beside the wall map—the Battle of the Bulge again—and laid down the pattern for his coming attack in the broad terms of the indictment. This done, he called the first Prosecution witness: Karl Radl.

For a stunned moment Skorzeny thought he had misheard. But up to the witness chair on its foot-high dais in the center of the hall there walked his comrade in arms, his closest friend, to give evidence against him.

Radl's round face was scarlet. In a choked voice he confirmed that he was at Friedenthal headquarters when the volunteers for the "American Brigade" came in, and that he knew of Operation "Greif." A few more questions and Radl left the chair: he had been summoned only to confirm a document which was not even in dispute—that misbegotten appeal for English-speaking troops which Marshall Keitel had put out.

Colonel Durst rose to expostulate. Radl had been needlessly obliged to speak for the Prosecution—was this intended to make friends of Skorzeny's think that his adjutant had turned against him?

Another of Skorzeny's officers, Captain Werner Hunke, refused to open his mouth. For years the luckless

Hunke had had to put up with being called by Radl "our old China hand," on account of his being posted by mistake to Friedenthal as a Far East expert. True enough, Hunke had been born in China, but his parents brought him home when he was a few months old and he had never left Europe since. Now he gave the discomfited Radl a lesson in the art of saying nothing.

The prisoners might have had worse luck with a supply captain who was sent to Friedenthal in the last months of the war and there rapidly antagonized most of his brother officers. Skorzeny had always defended him as a man of ability, and used to say that without his work during the Oder battle they could not have held the bridgehead so long. Now he was the one man from Friedenthal to turn "state's evidence." Unwilling to meet the eyes of his comrades in the court, he stammered out a statement that galvanized the Press box and sent reporters racing to the telephone. Here was a sensation indeed: Skorzeny had distributed bullets with a red ring around them —poisoned ammunition—to kill Americans in the Battle of the Bulge.

On this note the court rose for the day, leaving Durst to ask what Skorzeny knew about the charge. The answer was a strange one. He could not deny that there had been poisoned ammunition at Friedenthal. He could not deny that he had given it out.

One day in Russia, Skorzeny recalled, as the excited spectators trooped out, the Germans had pounced on two Soviet agents who were creeping into a German headquarters near Smolensk. They admitted they had been sent to kill a general, and their pistols were found to be loaded with unusual ammunition. Laboratory tests disclosed that each bullet contained a virulent new poison. An animal shot in the leg with one died inside a minute.

German experts copied the bullets and sent two sample boxes of twenty-five to Friedenthal. Skorzeny used to hand one to any volunteer who was afraid of being forced to give away secrets if captured on a dangerous mission. "Put this bullet for yourself in the last chamber of your revolver," he used to say. "It will give you confidence, even if you never have to use it." Skorzeny also kept one in his own revolver because he did not want to fall alive into enemy hands during the war.

These bullets, he now told Durst, must be what the

witness was thinking of—unless the man had mixed up two different things. By morning, they would know.

Back in his cell, Skorzeny got to work to procure the evidence he needed. He had won over a guard or two and now he smuggled out a message to Karl Radl in the ordinary prisoner-of-war camp outside the jail. Radl passed it on to friends in the town by way of the camp grapevine. The answer came with Skorzeny's breakfast—a bullet in a piece of bread.

When the court met, Durst cross-examined the witness. Now pale and trembling, the supply officer confessed that he had also given evidence against German comrades at Nuremberg—and that it had been proved false. Then Durst held out the bullet Skorzeny had given him on his palm.

"Is that your poisoned ammunition?" he demanded.

The tribunal craned forward to see the exhibit, which was later brought around for their inspection. It was an ordinary-looking bullet, but with a red ring around it; and the witness said yes, that was the type which Skorzeny had issued to his commandos for the Ardennes battle. Then Durst forced him to admit that it was simply a water-proofed form of normal ammunition and that the poisoned pellets were altogether different.

If this description of the trial were limited to what Skorzeny remembers there would be many gaps—periods during which his mind flashed to some past incident or rummaged for a mislaid fact. In a pad held on his knee he scribbled ideas and arguments; hundreds of pages a day were torn off for translation by the English-speaking naval lieutenant, who then handed them to Durst. At night Skorzeny worked in his cell, seven feet by four, shared with a footpad who wondered at such industry. It was a double-bunked room, without a light, but through a hole in the corridor wall there came the faint beam of an electric bulb. Questions, comments, reminders—twenty or thirty sheets of close work; he had accepted the duty of prisoners' leader and must overlook no point that might help them. When it was done, the pages had to be taken to another cell for translation and then brought back ready to be passed to Durst when the court met next day.

At last Rosenfeld reached the main charges. On that of fighting in enemy uniform "in contravention to an *annexe* of the Hague Convention of 1907" he had two wit-

nesses. An American lieutenant told of capturing Germa.
wearing U.S. windjackets. Then came the affidavit signed
by the sick prisoner in the hospital. While in U.S. uniform,
it said, he had fired on an American sergeant and missed.

The defense challenged this version of a momentary
incident in the hurly-burly of the Ardennes. Even if the
absent prisoner had fired, could he be said to be "fighting"
if his opponent was untouched?

This promising controversy was cut short by a message from the hospital: after seeing a defense counsel the
prisoner had withdrawn his affidavit.

On the count of stealing Red Cross parcels—American uniforms, according to the Prosecution, were the
object of the theft—a U.S. officer testified that his parcels
were held up during the Battle of the Bulge when he was a
prisoner-of-war. He had dropped three pounds in weight.
Skorzeny, who had lost fifty since his arrest, wondered
when Rosenfeld was coming to the point.

Day after day the prisoners had waited and worried
for some clue to the killing of "more than one hundred
American prisoners," but when Rosenfeld reached this
charge, he announced it would be withdrawn. The Prosecution rested its case.

Durst demanded his clients' immediate release. But
for the empty charge of killing prisoners, he claimed, the
men might not be in court.

The tribunal decided that the trial should go on: the
fate of the accused would now hang on the question of
fighting in American uniform.

Then came a four-day break, which Durst used to
prepare Skorzeny for the witness stand. Public interest
had ebbed: arguments that swung back and forth on judi-
cial points had worn down the patience of the gallery, and
when the court resumed two-thirds of the benches were
empty. The Press had gone—never suspecting that the
real "sensation" lay just ahead.

Durst told the tribunal his first aim would be to clear
the air of prejudice. The Prosecution had tried to discredit
Skorzeny as a blackguard and a brute. He would show
there was nothing treacherous in his conduct and, what
was more remarkable, that he had always tried to spare
lives—his enemies' as well as those of his own men.

In answer to Durst's questions, Skorzeny gave examples of his efforts to avoid bloodshed. He quoted also the order he had given his commandos before rescuing Mussolini: "The first shot to be fired will be fired by me—regardless of any action of the enemy and regardless of whether the enemy fires first." In the outcome, no shot had been fired at all.

Then, Operation "Greif." With wall map and pointer, Skorzeny delivered a lecture on his part in the Battle of the Bulge—he could have done it in his sleep by now. All went smoothly until Durst asked about the famous plot to kill or capture General Eisenhower. This question the president ruled out of order: instead of being brought down in open court, the Eisenhower *canard* escaped again to flap its way around the world.

Now for the central problem: the rights and wrongs of wearing other people's uniforms. It was a tricky subject, as Durst had told Skorzeny in his cell. He thought there would be broad agreement with the German opinion which formed the legal basis of Operation "Greif": that you can go up to the enemy in disguise so long as you throw it off when fighting starts. How such theatrical quick-changes were to be performed on the battlefield did not concern the Law: there was room enough for argument over problems such as how closely the enemy might be approached under false colors, how far disguise could be carried and what is meant by "fighting." One court might interpret the rules with hairsplitting exactness; another might be liberal.

There was a wide area of doubt, and over this dubious territory Durst now began to lead Skorzeny in the hope of finding firm ground on the other side. His first cautious move was to ask whether his witness had considered the rules of war "so as to conduct Operation 'Greif' within those rules."

Skorzeny said he had. "I gave the emphatic order that my men should not fight in uniform. Disguise should be worn only until they reached their destinations."

The next questions revealed the course Durst meant to take. He would make his way along the stepping-stones of precedent—but of Allied precedent, which alone could take the weight of the defense. For if it turned out that the victors had gone before them on this route, either the "rules of war" were obsolete or the Allies were guilty of the same crimes.

So Skorzeny found himself answering that he was not the first to use enemy uniform; in fact, the Germans came across the notion in Intelligence reports on Allied operations. He recalled that British officers had been captured wearing enemy uniform in Hungary, and were not shot. In both Italy and Yugoslavia German depots were often raided by partisans to get uniforms which they then wore in battle. The Polish patriot General Bohr used German uniform to start his Warsaw rising in 1944. Russians, to his knowledge, had frequently adopted this ruse. The Japanese had done the same thing. And so had the Americans.

Looking around the attentive court, Skorzeny repeated what Hitler had told him of Americans in German uniform at Aachen. There were other such instances. At Saarlautern, for example, Americans bluffed their way in a German tank over the bridge which led to Frankfurt. But it was the Aachen deception which had given Hitler the idea for this very Operation "Greif." And in every instance he had mentioned the men were armed and, where necessary, had made use of their arms.

For two days on the witness stand Skorzeny stood with Durst as his companion in the center of the legal morass. Assertions were made which offered firm footing —but proof was not easily had when the Germans had lost all their records. However, said Durst to the judges, they could see that the use or abuse of another's uniform was commoner than was supposed: certainly than was officially admitted. How did it square with the much-discussed rules of war?

He invoked the experience of this tribunal of senior officers to testify that international law could not consist only in the series of overlapping treaties, codes and conventions formally agreed by nations in the bygone past. Commonsense changes in the usages and customs of the belligerents made up an unwritten law which was practiced by all.

In accusing Skorzeny of using American uniform, the Prosecution had invoked an *annexe* to the Hague Convention of 1907—but that article, already forty years old, had been outdated by two world wars of a kind the legislators had not dreamed of.

With high forensic skill Durst conjured up a vision of the written law always trying to overtake new weapons, new techniques, even new dimensions such as air warfare, and never quite succeeding. It was an exposition to delight the legal mind, but Durst knew that in a military court an ounce of practice outweighs a ton of theory. And so, with an air of finality which puzzled his onlookers, he produced another witness: "Wing-Commander Forrest Yeo-Thomas."*

A short, sturdy figure in the faded blue of the R.A.F. walked to the witness chair, sat down, and looked quizzically about him. Wondering what on earth a British officer might have to say for the defense, Skorzeny noticed that he wore some exceptional ribbons; among them French decorations for gallantry and the George Cross.

Durst, who loved surprises, had sprung one more, and although it was not until long afterwards that Skorzeny learned Yeo-Thomas's singular record, it soon became evident that here before his eyes was one of the most formidable and bizarre personalities that even the British Secret Service could enlist.

During the war Yeo-Thomas's *nom de guerre*—the White Rabbit—became famous to the French underground. One of the inner ring of Secret Service chiefs directing French patriots from London, he used this code name in radio messages to the Resistance. But stirring up trouble in which he took no active part was not to Yeo-Thomas's taste: he decided to strike out on his own. First he parachuted into German-occupied France to find out what his friends needed. Then he went back to London, leaving them a promise to return shortly—and not empty-handed.

Arms and equipment for an underground rabble who would make life unpleasant for the Germans? Highly romantic, the experts said, but quite impracticable. Goaded by this skepticism, Yeo-Thomas stormed Downing Street singlehanded; in a hard-hitting interview he won Churchill over to his faith that, no matter how slim our own resources, it would pay to arm the French. That agreed, he dropped back into France to get Frenchmen of all politics united in a plan of insurrection when the Allies landed.

---

*Read *The White Rabbit*, Yeo-Thomas's own story of his war with the German Gestapo. Another volume in the Bantam War Book Series.

Wing-Commander Forrest Yeo-Thomas

Yeo-Thomas was betrayed into the hands of the Gestapo. But the White Rabbit was too tough to talk and too determined to hold. Condemned to death, he escaped after D-day from Buchenwald, leaving there a corpse in his place, and walked back over Germany until he burst across no-man's-land into the Allied lines to carry on his war. After the Armistice he went back to Germany for uncompleted business: at the Buchenwald War Crimes trial the evidence of this Allied Secret Service chief got twenty-two of the guards and doctors hanged.

Hardly the man, one might have thought, to help in saving another group of Germans charged with war crimes; but Durst had studied the evidence at Buchenwald and decided that some of the White Rabbit's ways, as he scuttled about under the noses of the Germans during the war, were very much to the point.

Yeo-Thomas's appearance gave the trial a fresh turn and a wildly improbable climax; yet few outside the thinly filled court ever heard of it. The Press had drifted back to their offices in London, Paris or Frankfurt; glutted with war trials, their newspapers had put Skorzeny out of mind until they had the verdict. As for the Prosecution, they were baffled by this apparition: palpably this British officer had no cause to love his late enemies, yet two years after being demobilized he had put on uniform again and crossed Europe to give evidence for them. Why?

This question was soon answered—and with a devastating candor. Yeo-Thomas told the court he had never met Skorzeny or any of his companions, but he wanted to say that in his opinion there was nothing wrong in the "crimes" they were accused of—whether they had committed them or not. From all he had heard, the prisoners had behaved like gentlemen.

It being plain that this witness was a man of few words, all unequivocal, Durst invited him forthwith to cross the doubtful zone of international law. Had Allied forces, he innocently inquired, ever used disguise and the appropriation of enemy identity as an instrument of war?

Yeo-Thomas advanced without hesitation. Of course they had, he said. Enemy insignia, arms and equipment— everything. Durst asked him to quote an instance from his own activities, and after a moment's reflection Yeo-Thomas told how he had planned the rescue of a Resistance comrade who was arrested by the Germans while Yeo-Thomas was on a visit to London. To do so he had first to parachute back into France.

"My comrade," he said, "was in prison at Rennes, in Brittany. I reconnoitered the jail and bribed one of the guards to find out when rounds were made and the general procedure.

"Then I put some of my men who spoke German into German uniform and secured copies of German papers required to take a prisoner out of jail. We stole a German car and I also had a van rigged up to resemble a prison van.

"The plan was to ring for the gatekeeper and show him false papers. We would drive in with the German car and then bring the van in and stall it so that they could not close the gate.

"The men in German uniform, one of them disguised as an officer, were to go into the guardroom. If the prisoner were not delivered to us on sight of the papers, if there were any hesitation, we would dispose of the guards quickly and silently. To make sure there would be no alarm I had planned to cut the telephone."

As Yeo-Thomas paused, Durst led him to the denouement.

Did you obtain German uniforms for this purpose?—Yes.

How were they obtained?—The details I could not tell you. I gave instructions to obtain uniforms by hook or by crook.

Did you also contemplate the use of German insignia?—We contemplated everything that could be used to ensure the success of the operation.

Insignia of rank or other German insignia?—Absolutely.

Did you also plan to go armed?—Certainly: we had to dispose of the guards.

Precisely what do you mean by that?—If necessary, kill them. We couldn't take prisoners.

Were these plans for the use of German uniforms put into effect?—Yes.

On the eve of the raid at Rennes, Yeo-Thomas himself was arrested, so Durst turned back to the matter of "usage." Was it the custom of the British Secret Service, he asked, to use German uniforms for a ruse?

Yeo-Thomas answered in this form: "We were given

assignments to do and we were told 'Go ahead and do them. We don't want to know how you do them; but if you are caught that is your pigeon; we shall disown you.' "

Now for "fighting" in enemy uniform. Durst trod delicately: he did not yet know his man.

"When using German uniforms," he inquired, "did the operators of the Secret Service go armed?"

"Yes," said Yeo-Thomas.

"To prevent danger of discovery," asked Durst gently, "what would the practice be?"

Yeo-Thomas glanced around the court: from the tribunal of soldiers which had to pronounce on these profound and intricate problems of behavior, to the breathless gallery and across the Colonel Rosenfeld, with his law books and his wall map of a fading battlefield—and then this man whom the resources of the modern torture chamber could not break brought down in ruins the whole edifice of reasoning and precedent, conventions and annexes, with five words.

"Bump off the other guy," he said.

Durst hid a smile, and Skorzeny knew the case was over. There remained the question of pilfering Red Cross parcels to obtain uniforms—again no time or place was stated in this count—and Durst took the opportunity of asking how the British acquired German uniforms and identity papers.

"Well," said Yeo-Thomas ruminatively, "we had means. We used to steal them from German headquarters in France. Quite a number of the French Secret Service used to kill an occasional German officer or man and take his papers . . . and there are many other ways I could not tell you about."

Durst asked: "Were papers ever taken from prisoners of war?"

The answer came: "Most decidedly. It was the duty of a prisoner not to have any papers if he was taken. If he had them, it was just too bad."

So there it was. Yeo-Thomas had illustrated the "changing usages of war." When he had testified against the staff of Buchenwald it was in order to punish their brutality against helpless civilians: for his own part, he was a soldier, and must look after himself. He asked no quarter of his enemies and offered none. His appearance on the legal scene had put international law itself on trial in that wooden barracks hall at Dachau.

Because Yeo-Thomas came out roundly with the fact that the Allies had also done things of which Skorzeny was accused, the court had either to acquit the prisoners or declare that there was one law for those who won, another for the side which lost. To soldiers wondering whether in the future they were expected to go into action with a copy of codified international law against which all orders could be checked, it gave a glimpse of daylight. You can break the written law if the enemy breaks it too—but to be doubly sure you had better emerge on the winning side. Such are the rules of war. "Bump off the other guy." Kill or be killed. If you come out of it—a medal maybe and no questions asked. If you don't—"too bad."

As the wing-commander stepped from the dais, Skorzeny gave a quiet order; together the prisoners stood to attention and bowed. Then they sat down again.

Skorzeny was not allowed to see his new ally before he left Dachau that day, but he sent him a note of thanks. He got this reply: "You did a damned good war job. I'm sure you will get off. In any case I have a flat in Paris if you should need somewhere to lie up." Yeo-Thomas added his business address in the Rue Royale—Molyneux, the dressmaker: for it was from that perfumed *atelier*, of which he was a director, that the White Rabbit went running home to be in England when danger threatened her in 1939.

The verdict was not in doubt: the accused were acquitted on all counts. But then opened a strangely drawn-out epilogue on which the curtain refused to fall.

The first *envoi* was Colonel Rosenfeld's. He congratulated the prisoners: they must understand that he had merely carried out his orders as a soldier. "Just like us!" Skorzeny retorted. The colonel had an afterthought which he imparted to the Press: "I still think this Skorzeny is the most dangerous man in Europe."

No freedom—yet. From the "open camp," to which he was carried shoulder-high by his fellow prisoners and where comrades pressed gifts on him—a cake, sausage, an apple—"to celebrate" he was sent back to the cells: a camp party for the Mussolini rescue anniversary, on September 12, had to be held that night without him.

What had happened? Denmark and Czechoslovakia each wanted Skorzeny: it seemed there were terrible crimes to answer for. A fortnight of bewilderment and then: it was all a mistake—neither nation had asked for his extradition. But headlines had again revived the legend of the ruthless killer. So back to the "open camp." Now, at last, he knew real friendliness; from the commandant down nobody could do enough for him. His prison clothes were in rags: an American sergeant got some German Army cloth and had a suit made for him. "Everyone I meet," he wrote to his family, "makes me feel again that I am a soldier among soldiers, even though I am still sharing the lot of prisoners of war."

He and Radl were asked to help the U.S. Army Historical Division to prepare an account of the Mussolini operation. They consented, and went jolting down the road in a wired-over truck, back to the old interrogation camp at Oberursel—and back into felons' cells again.

This time they struck for better quarters, and got them. The camp had adopted an odd security rule: all Germans must use code names. Radl was "Baker" and Skorzeny "Abel"—which did not deter the G.I.'s from shouting for "Skorzeny" whenever he was wanted. Two old friends arrived: "X-ray" and "Zebra." The mad hatter's party was joined by "Axis Sally"—an American who had earned her pseudonym on Goebbels' radio: later she was sent to prison for ten years. Her snow-white hair bobbed over the exercise books as she gave Skorzeny lessons in English.

Christmas came, but no release; instead, he had a fortnight on parole. Hanna Reitsch was living in Oberursel; Skorzeny called on her before hurrying to Munich to see his family. It was a winter of famine; the city was a gutted ruin full of homeless beings. "If I could look openly into these poor devils' faces," he says today, "it is only because I, too, had lost everything in the war."

A punctual return to Oberursel, to hear that he had been shadowed while away: the Americans still thought Hitler was alive and Skorzeny might lead them to his hiding place.

January passed, a bitter month. February: their work

for the American War Histories was complete. And then —an American Commission, hot on Hitler's trail. A German aircraftman had said he had seen Hitler a few days after his reported death landing with Skorzeny from an airplane. Doctors interrupted the questioning to announce that the aircraftman was not right in the head.

Now it was almost over. One more wildcat story about Hitler which impelled the Americans to take Skorzeny back to Nuremberg for examination, and the Allies had finished with him. So—he was moved from a U.S. prison camp to a German one.

Long before, he and Radl had volunteered for the mysterious process of "de-nazification"; now another waiting period set in. To fill up time they helped to clear the bombed ruins of the nearest town; any afternoon in Darmstadt you could have seen the late chief of Germany's special troops marching to work with pick and shovel, or riding along the tram tracks on Darmstadt's "rubble express." A few recognized him; students who brought a precious cigarette or two, housewives with ersatz coffee.

Four or five more months went by like this. His case was postponed seven times. New documents had come up, new charges were in the air. Officials shrugged: "We don't understand what it's all about. It's nothing to do with us." Skorzeny wrote to Yeo-Thomas for advice. The White Rabbit replied: "Escape!"

It was nearly a year since his acquittal. More than once he could have absconded; he stayed because he stubbornly wanted to clear his name of any taint. Now he had had enough. He went around the camp, telling all his jailers that he would remain no longer.

On July 27, 1948, Skorzeny got out. Without wire clippers, rope ladders, bribes or tunneling. He stowed away.

A transport pool car was due to leave the camp. No guards in sight. A word with the German driver and he squeezed himself into the luggage compartment. Three or four other prisoners shielded the scene of struggle while Radl, convulsed with laughter, forced the door shut on Skorzeny's ample bulk. The car drove through the gate. Around the corner the driver released an apoplectic fugitive who then subsided into the seat alongside him.

Friends outside the wire had arranged for a suitcase to be waiting at a railway halt ten miles from Darmstadt.

He changed in a wood, then took the train to Stuttgart. Next day he was at Berchtesgaden, in the high mountains that were to have been Hitler's last redoubt.

How would his flight be taken? A broad hint soon came that the German authorities were glad to be relieved of the decision on Skorzeny's future. They had nothing against him, but the release of "the most dangerous man in Europe" might upset the apple cart of Allied bounty to Western Germany. He should stay out of sight until the fuss was over so that they might not be forced to rearrest him.

Skorzeny refused to live in hiding: disguise, then— that was the answer! A phial of peroxide sufficed to confuse the curious: snapshots taken at that time show a fair-haired giant hugging his daughter who had been brought to Berchtesgaden on a visit. He spent some months in sunbathing, climbing, tree-felling, and was content. His tribulations had made deeper inroads into his strength and emotional reserves than he had been willing to admit.

By early spring in 1949 he was ready for a wider world; and his escape had been forgotten. Near Munich, with his wife, he rediscovered good fellowship alongside, among many others, the American town major. That summer he drove openly about Germany, seeking out a wartime comrade here and there, and finding too often a widow and a family without a head.

October, 1949: they went to French friends at St. Germain-en-Laye; Paris, untouched by war, was within all too easy reach. A camera shutter snapped: the picture of Skorzeny walking up the Champs-Élysées was seized on by *Humanité* to rouse Red riot in the capital. Reporters rushed out to look for him; he was gone. On a farm near Lyons he passed the winter and regained some of his old verve. Then up to Megève, in nearby Savoy, for skiing; there he read how one Otto Skorzeny was constantly dashing, in the "neo-Nazi cause," between Cairo, New York, Buenos Aires and Rome. He found humor in the Press and much solace in the friendliness of all the French he knew: those "historic animosities" between nations were strangely absent in the people he met, even when they knew who he was.

Another spring found Skorzeny himself again—and ravenous for work. But his return to Germany was an unseasonable reminder of the martial virtues at a time when it was all-important for the Bonn Government to turn a new face, pacific, decorous, upon the world. On requesting a work permit Skorzeny was reminded that he came from Austria—and had not Austria been liberated from the German fatherland since the war? Why, then, all he need do was travel to Vienna and throw himself into the arms of the Allies as a liberated Austrian! For a man who believed that "at certain turning-points, there is only one way to go," this was no signpost. He was the soldier of a defeated country which had tried to fight the Allies to a standstill: such he must remain.

Spain offered domicile, with a Nansen passport issued to the stateless. And the move fitted in with Skorzeny's last military plan.

War had flared up again in the summer of 1950, threatening to sweep from Korea across the world. The Western Allies were in the first days of their rearmament; they could not stop a Russian advance short of the Pyrenees. Skorzeny thought the Spanish Army—brave, disciplined and inured to guerrilla hardships—might slow down the rush if trained to modern ways. Knowing how a little yeast could leaven the military loaf, Skorzeny thought he might raise four or five crack divisions around which could be built the first "European Army" for special tasks in the defense of the West.

Germany was full of ex-soldiers who could find no place in civil life: the Allies, too, held many prisoners of war: let the best among these volunteer for the new corps. If finally driven out of Spain the troops could be used to defend Spanish North Africa from Russian attack across the Gibraltar Straits. Nor were Skorzeny's intentions all defensive—many a shock can be inflicted on an invader in Spain by a leader who keeps his wits about him.

Those few German generals whose prestige survived defeat welcomed Skorzeny's plan; the Pentagon was interested, and the Spanish authorities, too. Then politics and protocol clogged the machinery of agreement. After years of ostracism by the West, the Spaniards insisted that the first official approach should come from Washington: the Americans said it must come from Spain. Meanwhile, the danger of general war receded: in the spring of 1951 Skorzeny abandoned the plan and turned with relief to mend his own affairs.

With a desk, a filing cabinet and a little borrowed capital, he had already founded an engineering agency in two rooms overlooking the Gran Via, Madrid's main street. Work, work, work: a formula so rare in Castilian business life could scarcely fall short of success.

Spain needed everything an engineer could make or get, and suddenly Skorzeny found he had what the business world so prizes—connections. In the witness wing at Nuremberg, where he was kept for months during the War Crimes proceedings against German commercial trusts, he met as fellow jailbirds many leading industrialists, scientists and economists: their hours of discussion there taught him much about the business world. So it was that in 1952 he was able to arrange the biggest postwar deal between Spain and Germany for five million dollars' worth of railway stock and machine tools. Hardly a week goes by now without one or another of his colleagues from the witness wing arriving in Madrid to look him up.

In the midst of his new preoccupations came a bulletin from Bonn: Skorzeny had been "de-nazified" in his absence by the court of Hessen. His record was found to be unspotted—after seven years. Already the Allied Control office in Madrid which investigated ex-enemy aliens had approved Skorzeny's request for travel documents. So he could go abroad, drumming up business.

Last summer, meeting Skorzeny again on his return from a circuit of Africa, the author was struck by the highly placed people who had welcomed this unusual salesman: British, French, Spanish, Belgian, Portuguese officials in all the territories he had visited. The legend, then, was still alive, and the interest that opens doors. A predictable postscript: having called on Egypt's rulers, he was confidently rumored to be sending frogmen against British ships in the Canal.

A name for lawlessness, however undeserved, is not easily shaken off. When later on the deposed Sultan of Morocco was whisked from Corsica by his French guards to an island in the Indian Ocean, Paris reported that the move was intended to foil the Arab League, who had offered Skorzeny £500,000 to carry the Sultan off to his friends in Cairo. Asked to comment, Skorzeny could only express mock surprise—if the French Government were really so anxious, why had they not made him a still better offer to insure the Sultan's safety—by doing nothing? "After all, I'm a *retired* kidnaper," he says.

The world's a stage; those who win fame are expected to repeat their rôles interminably. But while report harks back to his past, the man himself finds the new world of affairs far more engrossing. In Spain, today, he has all sorts of enterprises under way, his favorite being a project for harnessing the wind to drive new industries with a gush of power, free and inexhaustible. The first machines, prototypes with three propellers each, are being assembled and he dreams of setting one on every other hilltop. A fancy worthy of Cervantes? Skorzeny grins: "If you are thinking of Don Quixote, remember that I want to build windmills, not knock them down. I am constructive!"

As ever, the truth about Otto Skorzeny lies in a contradiction of the obvious. Just as, when you get to know him, that "gangster" scar speaks for a youth of study and self-discipline, so, too, his windmills are not the picturesque anachronisms that spring to mind. They are extremely practical and realistic, the latest thing in steel.

XV

In war it is not men, but the man who counts.
NAPOLEON

If the secret weapon is Man, the missile it fires is surprise —but not what most staff officers mean by that word. And so, unlike some unconventional commanders who threw away the book of rules, Skorzeny took care to learn the routine off by heart, if only to foresee what his opponents, being "real" soldiers, would do. His success indicated that shock attack can also overcome general staffs and politicians who live in the past. A soldier, an army, a nation even, may be stunned for long enough to gain one's ends. If you can strike in places and by methods they have not dreamed of, you may have it your own way.

How this simple doctrine can be applied in a world become so vastly complicated stimulates rather than dismays Skorzeny. Size and complexity delay reactions. Now that warfare has become laden with hundreds of divisions and mountains of machinery, there is scope for a flexible form of attack in which weight of arms may be a hindrance.

What can be expected from surprise achieved with the use of small specially trained forces?

Imagine ourselves back in 1940, just after Dunkirk. Churchill declares that Britain will fight on, "if necessary alone," but flies to France and makes a final effort to retain his last ally. He fails. France falls into Hitler's hands.

Recall the scene. Pétain and Weygand, French army chiefs, are bullying their Cabinet into seeking a separate peace with Hitler. They refuse to continue the war or even to surrender their forces in France while allowing a French Government to carry on resistance from overseas. They insist that the entire State surrenders. All the pleadings of Churchill and their own Premier, Reynaud, are in vain. Instead of making a fighting retreat to North Africa, the two generals force an Armistice and usurp the Government.

Should the British have allowed France to break away? Skorzeny's disposal of the two Horthys who wanted to surrender Hungary to Germany's enemies suggests an immediate alternative—the fatal counselors of the French Cabinet should have been bundled into an R.A.F. plane and flown into captivity.

Then the indomitable Reynaud would have had his way and kept North Africa still an Allied base, with the French battle fleet intact. Even if Germany had burst through Spain to reach Gibraltar, the Mediterranean situation must have been transformed.

His sea lines cut by the Anglo-French fleets, Mussolini's first defeat in Egypt would have brought about the early destruction of his desert armies. Rommel could not have come to the rescue with the Afrika Korps. No need for the laborious invasion of Morocco and Algeria; all this region as well as the Tunisian springboard could have stayed in Allied hands with the rest of the French Empire. Italy might have been lambasted at once from close quarters. To attack Gibraltar Hitler would have had to withdraw aircraft needed in the Battle of Britain and extend his lines through Spain—a peninsula notoriously inhospitable toward foreign conquerors. Even if some of the rosier tints be taken from this picture, it is still in exhilarating contrast with Britain's "darkest hour" after Pétain and Weygand took over.

These speculations arise from a proposal which seemingly occurred to no one at that time. To kidnap allied personalities, though their behavior puts everything in jeopardy, may still appear too unorthodox. Yet count the cost of allowing Reynaud's opponents to get their way.

A month after bowing France out of her alliance, the British were shelling the French fleet at Oran in case it fell into Hitler's hands. Objecting to this "murder," Admiral Sir James Somerville had his protest overruled because it was believed that Britain's life hung in the balance. What would the slaughter of thirteen hundred French sailors in a bombardment unheralded by a declaration of war sound like in court if victors, as well as vanquished, faced war-crimes tribunals?—and Oran was only one tragedy which might never have occurred if two old Frenchmen had been carried off.

Skorzeny, who himself planned to dispose of Marshal Pétain when he began to obstruct the Germans some three years later, believes that such questions will in the future be settled by the best means available. And if a firm hold be kept on wayward associates, what chivalry will be extended to the enemy? Any tradition that protects political and military leaders is obsolete; indeed, Skorzeny still wonders why the Allies never tried to eliminate the one man whose removal might have stopped the war: it was obvious, from the consternation into which Mussolini's abduction threw Hitler's security chiefs, that they lacked confidence in their ability to defend him. Nor would Skorzeny have hesitated if he had really been ordered to kidnap Eisenhower: he regards every commander-in-chief as fair game, and attainable. The Russians share this viewpoint—Communists have never insisted on their victims wearing uniform. Next time no politician or head of state will sleep too soundly, wherever he be put.

Another conflict may well start with a series of assassinations and disappearances, and this prediction is not so farfetched as it may sound. An enemy who chose his time would find the White House open; Secret Service men are ready to guard the President against the lunatic 'or political crank, but they cannot count on stopping a professional attack based on close study of Washington's habits. Often I have walked into Washington's Pentagon Building, with its thousands of generals, admirals and staff officers, and lost my way among its floors and galleries. Downing Street seems easy prey; there are many ways in which the precautions around Britain's chief Ministers could be evaded: casual-seeming, homely ruses. Quite by chance, three friends of mine drove through the front gates of a British atomic establishment without producing permits. Such chances can be made.

More than once in the last war, plans for kidnaping and assassinating German leaders—on one occasion by blowing up a theater full of top-ranking Nazis—were rejected by the Allied authorities. Such restraint will not be practiced another time, especially if the Soviet bloc is involved. We shall not cheer airmen on their way to smash a city while shrinking from the death of an enemy leader. Horrible shocks can be inflicted by a few determined men on the directing brain—and that is bound to be a prime aim of the modern belligerent.

Now let us glance at the North Africa and Italy campaign to find scope for those lightning strokes which, in Skorzeny's words, might overturn a slower-moving adversary. Caution and delay seem to have robbed the Allies of at least two major opportunities.

Tunis, the springboard to Sicily, was struck from the final list of landing places in North Africa because the planners expected French resistance to be stronger than it was. Huge convoys put armies ashore far to the west, and when the French defenders changed sides there were only weak Allied forces in Tunisia. Marching four hundred miles from Algiers with the vanguard of the First Army, Lieut.-General Anderson arrived just too late—the Germans had poured in nearly twenty thousand troops with a speed that put the Allies to shame, for some had come from Bavaria and Austria. Thus, with his rear guarded through the long retreat from El Alamein to Tunisia and his supplies made tolerably sure, Rommel was able to hold the Allied pincers apart for six months more.

I have heard Skorzeny say that a thousand Frenchmen could take Paris overnight if they worked to a surprise plan for seizing Ministries—and Ministers. The Allies had French friends in Tunis. Could they not, the signal being given, have opened the gates to a special force earmarked for just such a moment? Day after day the springboard to Sicily had been left unguarded: the Allies arrived in strength only to find the approaches barred and locked.

Next, Italy. Mussolini was overthrown on July 26, but it took three full weeks, while German troops swarmed into the country, to smuggle an Italian envoy through occupied France and Spain to meet with Allied agents. Meanwhile, nothing was done and the first word this emissary heard was that nothing could be discussed but unconditional surrender. Then it needed a fortnight for the man to get back to Rome, and another three days for the armistice to be signed. By then Hitler had eighteen divisions in Italy; so that for the King and Badoglio it looked less a question of unconditional surrender than whether they would have anything remaining to surrender at all.

We know now why the windfall offered by Mussolini's arrest was neglected, why the Italians were left, in Churchill's words, to "stew in their own juice." The Allies could not risk the upset of their invasion plan, timed months before for mid-September, and they could think of no other immediate means of profiting from Mussolini's fall. In the end the invasion was brought forward a week, but altogether forty days were lost. Only on the eve of the landings was Eisenhower's aide, General Taylor, sent secretly to arrange with Badoglio for an airborne drop on Rome. Too late: Rome was being overrun, the Royal Family were packed for flight, the airfields near the capital had been lost a few hours earlier. Again the Germans had made up for a late start and got there first.

"We never wavered," writes Eisenhower in defending the Allied course in the Mediterranean. "The doctrine of opportunism . . . is a dangerous one to pursue in strategy." That principle is of course impeccable—since over-all policy cannot chase every will-o'-the-wisp which may appear—but it fails to explain the lack of some resourceful effort, *outside the invasion framework,* to seize Italy when Mussolini fell. Within hours of the long-deferred landings the Allies had lost Mussolini, too—and the news that the Italian dictator had been abducted from his rock by a light glider force offered a contrast that no one could overlook. "*That* is the way to jump in," everyone felt. "*That* is the way to grasp a chance."

The July 20 conspiracy was a classic treason plot; let us see what chances went begging when, with Berlin in disorder, no one knew whether Hitler was alive or dead.

Like most people, Skorzeny expected intervention by the Allies. When action was delayed he still assumed it would come—the enemy *must* have allowed in their planning for the possibility of such a thing. But hours went by, and days, without an Allied move of any sort. The conspiracy was stamped out and the war continued, much as before.

For months after the July 20 bomb went off the world was asking why the Allies did nothing. Every guess was made except the right one: that from start to end they knew everything about the conspiracy; knew all, and did not lift a finger.

July 20 will go down into history as a supreme example of opportunity thrown away. From his briefly held pinnacle at the War Ministry Skorzeny could hardly believe what he saw—that those abroad who stood to gain most from this dislocation did not mean to follow their chance through.

Today, the story and the explanation are clear. We can draw for testimony on Hitler's People's Court; we can call on evidence taken before the Nuremberg tribunal; and we have—in Mr. Allen Welsh Dulles, brother of America's Secretary of State—a uniquely placed witness of the way it all developed.

The roots of this conspiracy reached down to pre-war days. Before Munich, even, six of Hitler's highest officers tried to bring him down. But every time they were nerved to strike, Britain and France let Hitler have the spoils he wanted. War came; when the German armies were driven back in Russia the plot revived.

For eighteen months before July 20 Allen Dulles,

working from Switzerland as America's chief agent, was privy to the schemes to get rid of Hitler. Risking death and worse, German couriers went back and forth to tell him every detail of what was planned. Their confidence could not be returned. Although Dulles knew what was being done he had no authority to offer the support which would have unified the conspirators and given them the fillip they needed. And then, in those hours when Hitler's existence was in doubt, when no one in Germany knew which way to turn, whose orders to obey, the Allies stood aloof and left the German opposition to its fate.

We have seen how Skorzeny feared an airborne drop on Berlin. He believed that one or two divisions could have seized the capital and held it for five days; given a nucleus of special troops and civilian agents in league with the conspirators, a much smaller force would have sufficed. Within that time the Allies could probably have carried off everyone they wanted in Berlin, from Goebbels downwards. At the best, the war might have been won outright. At the worst, a crippling shock would have been inflicted on the régime.

Even the Russians, with none of our advantages at the time, saw that this was no moment to be wasted. Lacking an airborne force in readiness, they sent the renegade German General Seydlitz to the radio to call upon his compatriots. "Turn your guns against Hitler," he cried. "Do not fail these brave men who tried to kill him." After his surrender at Stalingrad, Seydlitz had been fêted by the Russians and persuaded to set up a Free German Committee which appealed to German officers in their own language to throw off Hitler's tyranny. Hardly anything of this sort was attempted by the West, except in a hole-and-corner way, but when the bomb went off everybody waited—in hope or in fear—for a move from London. None came: not even a call to rise or a shower of leaflets. So far from widening the split across Germany, the Allies sealed it up. Once more the "unconditional surrender" demand was brought out with its implications, to the German mind, of ruin and enslavement; and so far from their being supported, the conspirators were left to their fate with a Churchillian "Let dog eat dog!" The entire opposition was cut down by Hitler so mercilessly that it could never grow again. One cannot better Dulles' summing-up: "Those who determined policy in Britain and

America seemed to be making the military task as difficult as possible by uniting all Germans to the bitter end."

There was a tragic irony in the doom the German opposition generals brought upon themselves. Revolution, it has been said, was a maneuver they never practiced in their youth, and now it was too late. They were hampered by tradition and by the military oath which bound them to their destroyer. Time after time they reached the edge of mutiny, then recoiled. Of course, if Hitler were killed —by whatever means—they would be freed from their fealty.

Long before the generals were ready to strike, Hitler's police were running their shears around the edge of the conspiracy; they had almost reached the center when it exploded. After six years' procrastination the last stage was fatally rushed by those who had survived Hitler's earlier purges. They took it all so fatalistically, these generals, letting their opponent pick them off one by one. Of seventeen field-marshals on the army list when the war started, only one held his baton at the end. Of thirty-five senior generals in 1939, three were left in active posts. All the rest had gone—sacked, hanged, shot or given poison. Even the bold Rommel: too late to aim a blow at Hitler, he had to accept the hemlock from the tyrant's messenger.

Taken out of the groove of honor and obedience, a general may be as lost as a well-drilled private soldier. And not German generals only—when we look back at the North African invasion. So far from hailing Allied deliverance, the French commanders, almost to a man, were ready to drive the Allies back into the sea; when Admiral Darlan, in Marshal Pétain's name, called a cease-fire, they obeyed. The Marshal's word was what mattered; since, he, too, had exacted an oath of personal loyalty from his officers. Quite logically, the outstanding exception among French generals, who had followed his own conscience after Dunkirk, was regarded as a treasonable deserter: de Gaulle had broken ranks.

Obedience was the general's charter, and after the war German generals pleaded at War Crimes trials that they could but follow orders. Churchill, sympathizing, sent a check to aid Manstein's defense; Field-Marshal Montgomery was quoted by counsel: "I am a soldier. I obey orders." All in vain. In condemning Manstein, Kesselring and the rest, the tribunals laid down that generals should not obey "wrongful" orders—a judgment that seemingly opens the doors to subversion in the highest ranks.

Another July 20 will be made easier by the ruling of these tribunals. From the first day of the war we shall impress upon the enemy's generals that patriotism points the way to treason, that we are their real friends, and that so far from surrender being somehow indivisible, it will be gladly accepted in whole or in part—and "unconditionally." There will be no more gibes like "Let dog eat dog"; instead, we shall constantly assure any opposition leaders of our heartfelt aid in overthrowing the tyranny. Victory, as the soldier-historian Thucydides wrote two-thousand-odd years ago, is soonest won by those who come as liberators.

It would be easy to draw from two world wars other instances of how the caution that must rule enterprises planned months or even years ahead repeatedly stifled hopes of a quick move to bring down the enemy's main structure. Reasons against prompt action were plausible and weighty—usually they centered on two objections: that all resources had already been committed for other projects and that new moves needed proper consultation with one's allies.

Specific proposals for clearing such obstacles will be advanced later on; but before coming to them it would be useful to examine British experience in this field and, in particular, one type of operations, virtually unknown, to which recent events have lent a sinister topicality.

XVI

Ex Africa semper aliquid novi.

PLINY

A surprising development of World War II was the appearance of so-called private armies, units of a few score men who banded together to carry the war into the enemy's camp. They arose spontaneously when Dunkirk bereft Britain of the means of regular warfare; indeed, it was this need to improvise which first gave license to these privateers.

With seeming casualness, they sailed in tiny parties to break the spell that had settled over conquered Europe. Sentries were strangled, roads booby-trapped, troop trains waylaid. In Norway, nine men on skis blew up a heavy-water factory and thus halted Hitler's program for building the atom bomb; from France, a brand-new radar station was levitated across the Channel. These "commandos"—as they quickly became known—worked in a happy-go-lucky partnership with agents behind the lines and with the various resistance movements, which were invigorated by their example of attack.

As time went on most private armies were embodied in the official Commando Brigade. A few survived and flourished as independent units—and chief of these was one which grew to the status of a brigade which roved behind General Rommel's lines in Africa, followed him across the Mediterranean to Italy and later crowned their work by helping to blow the locks and hinges off Hitler's defenses in France. When the war ended this remarkable formation was adapting to the Far East theater a technique which had extorted alarmed respect from our enemies in Europe.

No one has yet ventured to write a history of the Special Air Service.* It's early activities must nonplus those who search for origins in the official records, and the successes of its heyday were concealed by censorship. But here and there one comes across the traces; startling tales of adventure which seem the less credible when one meets the modest, inoffensive men who lived through them.

"Well, really, I can't tell you much," they say. Then follows an outline of some affair involving one's informant which is the more bloodcurdling for its casual recital. With an apology for being dull—"It's rather long ago, now, isn't it?"—he will suggest looking up so-and-so: a pillar of Church or State who was once connected with the S.A.S.

Because the Special Air Service typifies the way the British have of deriving inspiration from catastrophe, its success is an object-lesson for the future. In terms of evolution one might say that it arose from the failure of orthodox "commando" tactics to encompass strategic ends; in human terms it sprang from David Stirling's personality.

I have been assured that Stirling, when war came, was so unwarlike that the outbreak found him thousands of miles from home: with a blend of energy and nonchalance which is characteristic he was riding down the Rocky Mountains on horseback. Returning home to the Scots Guards, he found a way out of routine duties after Dunkirk by joining the crack commando column, "Layforce."

The unit sailed to the Middle East—the only area where British troops were in action—in January, 1941. Something out of the ordinary was planned for Layforce: now that the Italians in North Africa had been trounced, they were to carry out a combined operation against Rhodes.

Before this expedition could start, however, Hitler turned the strategic picture upside down. German armies overran the Balkans; the British were ejected from Greece

*This has been corrected. *Stirling's Desert Raiders* is upcoming in the Bantam War Book Series. Virginia Cowles tells the thrilling story of a small and violently effective private army.

and Crete; the newly arrived Afrika Korps thrust General
Wavell's men back four hundred miles through Libya to
the frontier of Egypt.

British hopes of clearing the Mediterranean were dis-
pelled by Rommel's threat to Alexandria and the Suez
Canal; Wavell could only hold the enemy at arm's length
while landing raiders to wreck airfields in his rear. Three
such combined operations were launched, but, since every
British destroyer was at that time irreplaceable, all three
had to be abandoned when the ships ran into danger.
Each time two hundred men or more from Layforce were
brought back to port without going ashore. Cairo headquarters concluded that Rommel was armed at all points
against small-scale attack; so they stopped the risky game
and disbanded Layforce.

Waiting for a ship home, Lieut. David Stirling, encouraged by Brigadier Laycock,* the commander of Layforce, decided with some friends to learn to parachute.
They borrowed an old plane one afternoon and took turns
jumping from the door. Last to leap, but first to land with
a faulty chute, was David Stirling: he whizzed past his
floating companions and made a crater in the desert.

A base hospital in the Delta allowed Stirling, still
unwilling to be posted home, to follow his predilection for
making plans rather than having them made for him.
What is called a "military appreciation" was outlined on
sheets of paper scattered on his bed. Reasoning from the
Layforce experiences, he had reached deductions pecu-
liarly his own: Middle East H.Q. estimated that the abor-
tive attacks were too small to break through Rommel's
defenses; Stirling judged them to be too big.

The hit-and-run raid is in Stirling's blood—how else
explain his family's survival through incessant wars and
Highland blood feuds?—and three centuries of Whitehall
rule has failed to quell it. His cousin, young Lord Lovat,
was to lead his own commando regiment in raids on the
Channel coast. That Rommel's airfields should be inviolate
simply because the Middle East lacked air strength to raid
them was unthinkable; Stirling had worked out exactly

---

*Before returning home to take over the appointment of Com-
mander, Special Services Brigade (the Commandos), at the age of
34, Laycock accompanied the Keys raid on Rommel's headquarters
and was one of the only two survivors.

how German airpower could be attacked on the ground, and he meant to do it himself.

His appreciation noted unfavorably Middle East Command's habit of putting in the strongest possible force at a single point. Why convey two hundred commandos in warships to a hostile shore, he argued, for the sake of storming an air base which is not to be held? The real aim was the destruction of its aircraft—and this might be achieved more thoroughly and at slight cost if somehow half a dozen saboteurs could fix timed incendiary bombs on the planes. Given two hundred men, this force could be split into little groups which would go for thirty or forty airfields at once. Succeeding at only one place out of four, they would still wreck many times more than the fifty odd planes which is all that could be hoped for by concentrated attack on a single field.

Lack of shipping no longer mattered, because vulnerable vessels need not be endangered. Small parties of saboteurs could land from fishing boats or submarines, drop from bombers or seek lifts on the reconnaissance cars of the Long Range Desert Group.

Of course, Stirling wrote, such troops must learn to probe their way through hostile areas, and in the dark. Why not, then, raise a new force for these special missions —and what more natural leader for it than the author of the scheme himself?

To this monument of presumption Stirling added an engaging flourish: by recruiting his new force now he would be ready to paralyze Rommel's five main advanced fields on the eve of the next British offensive. It was well known in Cairo that this big push was due in November, only three months ahead.

The penciled sheets were clipped together, but not mailed off. A point underlined in the appreciation was that Stirling should be directly responsible to the C.-in-C.: this, as he blandly indicated, would save the time of innumerable branches and departments. He was starting as he meant to continue: with the attack direct.

A few days pass; the scene changes from the hospital to a guard post at Middle East Headquarters. Lacking credentials, Stirling has suffered a rebuff. He hobbles around the corner; and with the aid of crutches which he then discards, hoists his six feet four over the fence and makes groggily for the building. A sentry spots him; he dodges down a corridor into the Adjutant-General's department where he invites a fretful staff officer to read his appreciation. The officer glances through the proposals and tells Stirling not to waste his time.

Some minutes later Stirling has invaded the office of the Deputy Chief of the General Staff. Lieut.-General Ritchie protests against this intrusion, but finds himself reading the paper. Reaching the last page, he praises the new scheme: it is exactly what the situation needs.

Three days later Stirling is in the presence of his Commander-in-Chief, General Sir Claude Auchinleck. He leaves as a captain; to make a start and recruit his force at once.

But the rearing of Stirling's brain child was not to be so easy as its birth. First of all the staff of Middle East Headquarters had to be conciliated or overcome. Furious at Stirling's impudence, and outraged by its reward, the obstructionists decided to ignore the foundling laid on the doorstep: it could starve. But they did not yet know what they were up against. In a remark made by Stirling in a letter to a friend after the war, one can almost catch an echo from rebellious Friedenthal, of Skorzeny and Radl discussing how to outwit the "main enemy" in Berlin: "While most of the branches could be helpful at the top," Stirling wrote, "they were astonishingly tiresome at middle and lower levels. In the Adjutant-General's branch, which was obstructive right up to the top, it was only by invoking the authority of General Ritchie that I could ever get my way."

But even an appeal to Caesar can be stultified—and then he took the law into his own hands. Smugly informed he would get no encampment for at least six months, he invited his friends out in a borrowed lorry. At nightfall they fell upon a tented village guarded by troops while its owners, a Commonwealth detachment, were out on an exercise. Three trips were made before dawn and next day Stirling's unit was installed in a lavishly equipped camp re-erected at Kabrit in the Suez Canal Zone.

Officers on whom Stirling had his eye might not be so informally acquired, but he got them. Paddy Mayne, an affably aggressive Irishman, was rescued from an infantry base where he had been having a difference with his company commander. Jock Lewis was extracted from the Welsh Guards. Bill Cumper, a master of explosives whose trail they followed all over the Middle East, was run to earth in a depot where Stirling found him dispensing sanitary fittings.

What should they call themselves? On the paper strength at G.H.Q. was an imaginary force known as the Special Air Service, its invention intended to persuade Rommel that the British had an airborne brigade in the Middle East where none was. To lend color to the imposture, dummy troops were dropped near prisoner-of-war cages and captives reported this in coded letters home. Mock gliders were also lined up where they could be photographed by visiting planes. Meeting the brigadier in charge of this deception, Stirling offered to adopt the S.A.S. banner and bear it convincingly into action. The deal was made.*

Former members of Layforce furnished the phantom S.A.S. brigade with its first flesh-and-blood detachment. "Establishment" was seven officers and sixty men, of whom twelve were N.C.O.'s, for Stirling had from the first subdivided his force into units of four men with an officer or N.C.O. to each. This splitting of the military atom was designed to release latent energies—independence, pugnacity, imagination.

Training was imbued with tremendous urgency: it was often said that Jock Lewis, who devised the program, had schemed for everything except time to sleep. Marching one hundred miles, back-roll jumping from a lorry at full tilt, close-quarter shooting, hardening the nerves with closer and bigger explosions—to men who had already gone through the commando mill Lewis offered a postgraduate course. Parades at Kabrit vied with St. Moritz

---

*Strong is the magic carried by a name: long after the origin of this title had been forgotten, Stirling was to be haunted by its association with parachutes and gliders. The S.A.S. quickly proved their mission was completely distinct from the work of regular airborne forces and that it was not even dependent on air transport, but still the name, and its associations, remained. A similar fallacy, that their sole aim was to attack airfields, arose because for a start Stirling concentrated on reducing the three-to-one enemy air superiority in the Middle East. As the Germans were rapidly to learn, the S.A.S. were not at all restricted either in their method of approach or to any special target behind the lines. But last of all to understand the S.A.S. role was the War Office in London, where the Special Air Service was eventually acknowledged—and placed under the control of Airborne Forces.

for the array of splints, bandages and plaster. A broken leg rated sick leave but a broken arm need not exempt one from marching; nor was exemption sought. Three months at "Stirling's Rest Camp," as the Kabrit center was whimsically known, and man had nothing left to fear. Soon Stirling commanded a dozen fighting teams that moved like one man as they practiced stealing through troop areas and juggled with wire cutters and time bombs in the dark.

As a dress rehearsal, the S.A.S. marched ninety miles to raid the British air base of Heliopolus. They got through the guards, and pasted all the aircraft with messages declaring that they had been destroyed. Stirling had proved G.H.Q.'s security arrangements a farce, which did not endear him to those whose charge it was.

On November 19, 1941, the long-promised British offensive was launched, and with it, the first S.A.S. operation—aimed at smashing the whole German desert fighter force with the use of sixty men. Everything was against the raiders. Obsolete aircraft, lacking direction-finding instruments, were all that could be spared to fly the S.A.S. over Rommel's lines; a thirty-mile-an-hour wind whipped the desert into a sandstorm and scattered the parachutists miles from their targets. One of the planes which went astray landed in error on the very German airfield it was scheduled to attack and its party were made prisoner. Of the sixty men who set out, twenty-two got back to Kabrit.

This should have ended the story. Few could have survived such an unrelieved fiasco—and the complacency with which the news was heard in certain Cairo offices. but a month later, to the astonishment of his critics, Stirling tried again, this time keeping the survivors of his unit on the ground and leading them through the open desert flank in the south. Days went by before G.H.Q. was shaken by an incredible report: carried to within striking range of their chosen airfields by the Long Range Desert Group, the S.A.S. had destroyed nearly a hundred German planes. When R.A.F. photographs confirmed the news, chortling in the "middle and lower levels" came to an abrupt end.

Before Rommel could fathom this menace, the unit sprang a score more attacks behind his lines—raids, coolly planned and brilliantly executed, on road convoys, depots, and above all the priority target, airfields. Within three months, the S.A.S. destroyed more aircraft than any fighter squadron of the R.A.F.

Surprise was the key; imagine such a raid. Sentries patrol the wired-in perimeter of a German air base. From the airport roof machine-gunners scan the darkness with night glasses. Hundreds of miles behind the battle-line, such precautions seem overdone—but this is a base which has already been visited by the S.A.S. and chances are no longer taken.

The silence is split by an explosion—that is the only warning. Flames shoot from a parked bomber and one after another the dark shapes of aircraft burst open like firecrackers. Sirens howl; searchlights reveal men racing in all directions—some are guards, some raiders—while more and more planes explode. In the midst of this bedlam Stirling and his men are perfectly at home; they go about their work in a chaos foreseen, calculated. As a fuel dump roars skywards the visitors depart, tossing their last bombs through a mess window or planting them among the crowded lorries near the gates.

Of all the discoveries in his new trade, the most satisfactory for Stirling was the small number of men he lost in what were reputed to be suicide raids. Confusion was his screen.

Rommel doubled and redoubled his guards. When he put a sentry on every plane, the sentry would be blown up too. At one air base near Benghazi, Italian troops were matched by a strong German detachment on the other side of the tarmac; when the S.A.S. concluded their visit the two sets of defenders were hotly firing at each other across the wreckage of their planes.

Rumors of these goings on swept the Middle East, attracting to Kabrit more and more of the quick-thinking men the S.A.S. wanted to enlist. Stirling also made use of trips to Cairo for casual proselytizing; a typical encounter is described by his kinsman Brigadier Fitzroy Maclean, M.P.

"David was a tall, dark, strongly built young man with a manner that was usually vague, but sometimes extremely alert. He asked me what my plans were. I told him. 'Why not join the Special Air Service Brigade?' he said. I asked what it was. He explained that it was not really a brigade; it was more like a platoon. It was only called a brigade to confuse the enemy. But it was a good thing to be in. He had raised it himself . . .

"He went on to elaborate his ideas on small-scale raiding. They were most illuminating. We could operate in the desert first of all; then in southern and eastern Europe. Small parties could be dropped there by parachute and then picked up on the coast by submarine. There were endless possibilities."

Maclean joined the S.A.S and one of the missions he describes was a call on Benghazi harbor, when with Stirling and Randolph Churchill—another newcomer—he bluffed his way through all the defenses of the port in a Ford station wagon painted with the Axis identification stripe. Maclean sums up:

> David, for his part, brought to these ventures the striking power and, to their planning and execution, what Lawrence has called "the irrational tenth" . . . like the kingfisher flashing across the pool: a never-failing audacity, a gift of daring improvisation, which invariably took the enemy by surprise. . . . Working on these lines, David achieved, in the months that followed, a series of successes which surpassed the wildest expectations of those who had originally supported the venture. No sooner was one operation completed than he was off on another. No sooner had the enemy become aware of his presence in one part of the desert and set about taking countermeasures than he was attacking them somewhere else, always where they least expected it. . . . In order to protect their rear the enemy were obliged to bring back more and more front-line troops. And all this was done with a handful of men, a few pounds of explosive and a few rounds of ammunition.
>
> One thing, perhaps, contributed more than anything else to the success of these operations: that David both planned them and carried them out himself, and that, in the early days at any rate, every man in the unit had been picked by him personally.

A supreme chance came early in May, 1942, when battered Malta was waiting for a convoy. Rommel's air force commanded most of the route from Alexandria and intelligence had pinpointed nine bases from which his bombers would fly. Seven were along the coast of Libya; two more straddled the Mediterranean in Crete. The Director of Military Operations in Cairo said that if Stirling could help to keep down Rommel's air force during the coming battle it might affect the course of events throughout the Mediterranean.

Stirling saw a turning point in the affairs of S.A.S. He suggested that G.H.Q. were asking rather a lot of a unit without proper status: would it not look better if the war in the Mediterranean were saved by a regiment instead of by a free-lance detachment? The general retorted that British regiments were not created every day. Anyway the S.A.S. would be broken up at the end of the war with all the other commando and parachute battalions: what could they offer that the Army lacked?

Unabashed, Stirling expounded his faith in the S.A.S. technique; it was something entirely new which would have wide use in the future. Commandos and paratroops could be made out of ordinary infantry, but only exceptional troops carefully trained could carry out the S.A.S. rôle—nor could they be controlled through the usual military hierarchy which understood nothing of this delicate new medium. The unit must always be responsible for its own planning and their directive must come from the very top.

The general protested that Stirling seemed keener on establishing his damned regiment than on the business of winning the war. "In my view, sir," said Stirling, "the two objects coincide."

Seven of the nine enemy airfields were attacked on the same night, those in Crete being reached by two parties who paddled ashore from a submarine to clamber over the mountains with knapsacks full of bombs. About seventy-five planes in all were destroyed; many more grounded. A signal of congratulations from Middle East Headquarters was addressed to "Commanding Officer, 1st S.A.S. Regiment."

With this accolade, and an expanded force more than three hundred strong, the regiment got going just at

the time when there appeared from over the Atlantic an accessory which the S.A.S. promptly seized on: the agile and far-ranging jeep. Soon the whole regiment was on wheels. Colonel Stirling "had by now given it a cap badge, blue affair with a white commando dagger and the words *Who Dares Wins* beneath it. All his men were parachute-trained . . . and with the cap badge went a pair of wings, which officers and men who had done exceptionally well on operations were allowed to wear on their chest. When he considered that he had done well enough, Stirling awarded them to himself. One day, on the steps of Shepheard's, he met General Auchinleck. 'Good heavens, Stirling,' said the General. 'What's that you have on?' 'Our operational wings, Sir,' replied Stirling, saluting smartly.

" 'Well, well,' observed the General, 'and very nice, too . . . very nice, too.'

"The insignia of the Special Air Service had received its official blessing."

In September 1943, while the armies were stalemated at El Alamein, Stirling led the most ambitious—and least successful—of his missions, a battalion-strength raid on Benghazi. He took his troops around on a seventeen-hundred-mile circuit of the desert, only to be driven back with heavy losses, in vehicles if not in men.

More in the S.A.S. style was a secret base set up deep in Rommel's rear from which armed jeeps went raiding. They switched their attacks from landing grounds to radio stations, from road convoys to bomb dumps, from the desert railway back again to airfields. Patrols often ived behind the lines for two or three months at a stretch.

After Rommel's defeat at El Alamein, Stirling ranged behind his lines of retreat, blasting his depots, harrying his convoys; for come what might, the Afrika Korps must be kept on the run past El Agheila, where the terrain narrowed. Sixteen S.A.S. sub-bases sprang up behind El Agheila to help in cutting the veins and arteries of Rommel's supply while the Eighth Army drove him back. El Agheila duly fell; Rommel retreated toward Tripoli, with the S.A.S. still behind his lines. To avoid their pestilential nightly raids the German convoys were forced onto the roads by day, when the R.A.F. took over the attack.

With the end of the African campaign in sight, Stirling was preparing to carry death and devastation into Hitler's Europe. The first regiment had grown to five hundred officers and men, including the Special Boat Section and a Greek squadron for raids across the Eastern Mediterranean; and already an S.A.S. group had flown to Algiers to raise their banner of the Flying Dagger there. Soon, under Stirling's brother, Colonel "Bill," a second regiment had been formed in French North Africa. Newcomers who inquired what those initials stood for were told: "S.A.S.? Stirling and Stirling, naturally."

And so it happened that early in 1943, while their respective main forces were still hundreds of miles apart, patrols from the two Special Air Service regiments linked the Allies across Africa.

Just as this seal was set on David Stirling's work he was trapped on a sortie hundreds of miles inside the enemy lines and became one of the best-guarded prisoners in Germany. In the Rommel Papers his adversary gives tribute to "the most adaptable commander of the desert group which caused us more damage than any other British unit of equal strength."

Stirling's war was over barely two years after his arrival in the Middle East as an unfledged subaltern aged twenty-five—and, as luck would have it, just when Otto Skorzeny began to twist the Allied tail. Some of his ruses to stupefy the enemy were very like Skorzeny's. On the night of the Malta convoy raids German guards drove a group of French prisoners up to Rommel's most impregnable desert airfield; not until next day's investigation amid the wreckage was it discovered that both Frenchmen and Germans were from the S.A.S. Stirling had enlisted a squadron of French paratroopers at Kabrit: the "guards" belonged to a troop of anti-Nazi volunteers and many of them had served in the German army before the war.

Major Paddy Blair Mayne, Stirling's successor in command and perhaps the only man who has ever destroyed more than a hundred aircraft on the ground added great luster to the S.A.S. name. Another of his lieutenants was Earl Jellicoe, who after parachuting into Rhodes to induce the Italians to surrender (he found six thousand Germans in possession and left in some haste) went on with his Special Boat Squadron to lead raiding forces which freed half of Greece. Jellicoe's arrival in Athens helped avert civil war. Another British "irregular" with something of the Skorzeny touch was Fitzroy Maclean. To quell an anti-British conspiracy in Persia he kidnaped the commander of Isfahan; a decade later, by one of history's paradoxes, this General Zahedi overthrew Premier Mossadeq and brought the British back. Maclean's next task parachuted him into Yugoslavia at the head of a military mission which was joined by Randolph Churchill. On their estimate that Tito would in the long run put the welfare of his country before loyalty to Stalin, Britain supported the Partisans. Fitzroy Maclean was a professional diplomat. So today, is Jellicoe; demobilized as a colonel at twenty-six, he entered the Foreign Service in time to take part in the first postwar mission to Moscow. Here were two of the S.A.S. leaders who understood the place of politics in war.

After the S.A.S. had linked the Allied armies, the bureaucratic battle which David Stirling won in Cairo had to be fought all over again by his brother in Algiers. Eisenhower's headquarters were almost as suspicious of the S.A.S as the Middle East had been; amid elaborate arrangements for taking Sicily, Bill Stirling's plan for sowing his 2nd S.A.S. regiment all over the island could be carried out only in token form.

For the invasion of Italy itself Bill Stirling meant to drop the whole 2nd S.A.S. between Florence, Bologna and Spezia, where the main railways to Rome were open to attack, for it was down these lines that the Germans were hurrying their troop trains to meet the Allied invasion. Delays and doubts in Algiers whittled this expedition

to a mere twenty men with knapsacks of explosives. Five
minutes after landing the party lost their leader. Command
was taken over by redhaired Anthony Greville-Bell, one
of Stirling's youngest subalterns, who found himself in
charge of what should have been a crucial thrust of the
campaign. The raiders managed to derail fourteen trains,
but distances were too great for them to keep the lines
out of action as fast as they were repaired. If the whole
regiment had been used, the railway system could have
been halted for two or three weeks.

Cheated of this superb opportunity, most of the
S.A.S. were landed in the toe of Italy, where they took
the first prisoners of the invasion before darting off into
the blue by jeep. At one time four groups were at large,
laying waste German airfields, blasting convoys or landing by sea behind the lines to attack the Adriatic railway.
It was a sign of the enemy's impotent fury that S.A.S. men
caught by the Gestapo were henceforth in danger of execution. But the S.A.S. prefers today to remember more
cheerful incidents of their Italian sojourn, such as the
French troop who commandeered a train and drove it
through hostile territory until they reached a concentra-
tion camp; the train being loaded with released prisoners,
they returned in triumph through the lines.

Toward the end of the campaign Italian guerrillas
and escaped Russian prisoners were enlisted behind the
lines into an "Allied S.A.S. Battalion" which struck at Kesselring's main supply system and bade fair to turn his
last retreat into rout. In that spring of 1945, Major Farran
made a precipitate attack on German Fifth Corps headquarters, killing the general with several of his officers and
burning down their buildings: a piece of brigandage un-
surpassed in the war.

Early in 1944, the whole corps were brought home to
reorganize for the cross-Channel invasion—and yet a third
set of authorities had to be taught the proper rôle of
strategic attack troops. Bill Stirling insisted on the S.A.S.
being dropped far in the rear of the enemy, where they
would have room to move and space to receive reinforcements by air; his adversaries, on the other hand,
wanted to use the corps close behind the front, where they
could not even be supplied. So embittered became the
arguments that Stirling relinquished his command after he

had won his point. Face being thus saved, the authorities allowed his successor, Colonel Brian Franks, D.S.O., to reap the benefit.

For D-Day the expanded S.A.S. had its own battle order:

1ST S.A.S. REGIMENT	2ND S.A.S. REGIMENT
3RD (FRENCH) REGIMENT	4TH (FRENCH) REGIMENT

1ST BELGIAN (INDEPENDENT) REGIMENT.

The S.A.S. always had a slightly exotic aspect, enrolling all and any foreigners who had the right idea. David Stirling had promised the French and Belgians that one day they would fight on their own soil again, and now the day had come.

The cross-Channel operation was of astonishing size and vigor. Most of the brigade, as Bill Stirling had insisted, parachuted deep into France or were landed by plane with their jeeps and guns at freshly captured airstrips to infiltrate the lines. Sometimes in loose liaison with the Maquis, more often alone, the S.A.S. struck at trains, ammunition dumps and fuel depots in the midst of troop areas; they ambushed lorries and shot up staff cars—well over a thousand German vehicles were destroyed.

Within a week of D-day no road or railway from Brittany to Switzerland was safe. Strategic reserve troops from the Pas de Calais who were needed in Normandy had to hurry instead to areas like Dijon and Rheims, where S.A.S. squadrons were motoring about in British uniform. Reversing custom, the S.A.S. often traveled by daylight, when Allied bombers drove most enemy traffic off the roads. Night was the time for ambush.

After Patton's breakthrough at Avranches, S.A.S. troops behind the lines were often mistaken for the spearhead of the main armies. Beaulieu radar station, for instance, was blown up by a German garrison who made off under the fire of a small group of S.A.S. because they thought that Montgomery's tanks were close behind. All over France the Germans were harassed by rumors of imminent attack. Thus the S.A.S. came into its own, happily at work in a whirlwind of doubt and fear, killing five thousand or so Germans before they gave up counting. For months they lived amid the enemy in one of the most thickly populated countries of Europe, getting into tight corners and usually out of them again—a Robin Hood existence which lacked for nothing, for even cigarettes and letters from home were delivered by the R.A.F.

After the Battle for Germany, the S.A.S. sailed to Norway to disarm a quarter of a million Germans. That was their last task, and the last news most of their friends had of the brigade and of their methods of playing a game which they were the likelier to win since no other team understood the rules.

BANTAM WAR BOOKS

Now there is a great new series of carefully selected books that together cover the full dramatic sweep of World War II heroism—viewed from all sides and representing all branches of armed service, whether on land, sea or in the air. All of the books are true stories of brave men and women. Most volumes are eyewitness accounts by those who fought in the conflict. Many of the books are already famous bestsellers.

Each book in this series contains a powerful fold-out full-color painting typifying the subject of the books; many have been specially commissioned. There are also specially commissioned identification illustrations of aircraft, weapons, vehicles, and other equipment, which accompany the text for greater understanding, plus specially commissioned maps and charts to explain unusual terrain, fighter plane tactics, and step-by-step progress of battles. Also included are carefully compiled indexes and bibliographies as an aid to further reading.

Here are the latest releases, all Bantam Books available wherever paperbacks are sold.

AS EAGLES SCREAMED by Donald Burgett

THE BIG SHOW by Pierre Clostermann

U-BOAT KILLER by Donald Macintyre

THE WHITE RABBIT by Bruce Marshall

THE ROAD PAST MANDALAY by John Masters

HORRIDO! by Raymond F. Toliver & Trevor J. Constable

COCKLESHELL HEROES by C. E. Lucas-Phillips

HELMET FOR MY PILLOW by Robert Leckie

THE COASTWATCHERS by Cmd. Eric A. Feldt

ESCORT COMMANDER by Terence Robertson

I FLEW FOR THE FÜHRER by Heinz Knoke

ENEMY COAST AHEAD by Guy Gibson

THE HUNDRED DAYS OF LT. MAC-HORTON by Ian MacHorton with Henry Maule

QUEEN OF THE FLAT-TOPS by Stanley Johnston

V-2 by Walter Dornberger

BANTAM WAR BOOKS

These action-packed books recount the most important events of World War II. They take you into battle and present portraits of brave men and true stories of gallantry in action. All books have special maps, diagrams, and illustrations.

☐	12657	AS EAGLES SCREAMED Burgett	$2.2
☐	12658	THE BIG SHOW Clostermann	$2.2
☐	13014	BRAZEN CHARIOTS Crisp	$2.2!
☐	12666	THE COASTWATCHERS Feldt	$2.2!
☐	*12664	COCKLESHELL HEROES Lucas-Phillips	$2.2!
☐	12141	COMPANY COMMANDER MacDonald	$1.95
☐	12578	THE DIVINE WIND Pineau & Inoguchi	$2.2!
☐	*12669	ENEMY COAST AHEAD Gibson	$2.2!
☐	*12667	ESCORT COMMANDER Robertson	$2.2!
☐	*11709	THE FIRST AND THE LAST Galland	$1.95
☐	*11642	FLY FOR YOUR LIFE Forrester	$1.95
☐	12665	HELMET FOR MY PILLOW Leckie	$2.2!
☐	12663	HORRIDO! Toliver & Constable	$2.2!
☐	12670	THE HUNDRED DAYS OF LT. MACHORTON Machorton	$2.25
☐	*12668	I FLEW FOR THE FÜHRER Knoke	$2.25
☐	12290	IRON COFFINS Werner	$2.25
☐	12671	QUEEN OF THE FLAT-TOPS Johnston	$2.25
☐	*11822	REACH FOR THE SKY Brickhill	$1.95
☐	12662	THE ROAD PAST MANDALAY Masters	$2.25
☐	12523	SAMURAI Sakai with Caidin & Saito	$2.25
☐	12659	U-BOAT KILLER Macintyre	$2.25
☐	12660	V-2 Dornberger	$2.25
☐	*12661	THE WHITE RABBIT Marshall	$2.25
☐	*12150	WE DIE ALONE Howarth	$1.95

*Cannot be sold to Canadian Residents.

Buy them at your local bookstore or use this handy coupon: